Praise for *MWF Seeking BFF* by Rachel Bertsche

"Genuine, funny and thoroughly inspiring, *MWF Seeking BFF* is a tribute to female friendships and a must-read for anyone who has ever found herself sunk into her couch and scrolling through the phone list feeling like there's no one to call for a last-minute drink or Sunday brunch."
—RACHEL MACHACEK, author of *The Science of Single*

"*MWF Seeking BFF* is funny, charming, and so relatable. Throughout Rachel's journey to develop more meaningful, enduring relationships with other women, I found myself wishing she had my number."
—ROBYN OKRANT, author of *Living Oprah*

"I guess you could say Rachel had me at *'Hello'*—I found myself totally invested in her honest, earnest, oftentimes hilarious quest for meaningful female friendship. Whether you're actively seeking a 'BFF' yourself or simply recognize the value in making quality connections with other women, *MWF Seeking BFF* underscores the profound rewards we women stand to reap when we simply open up, reach out to one another, and go for it. A smart, fun, and inspiring page-turner that will surely resonate."
—KELLY VALEN, author of *The Twisted Sisterhood*

MWF SEEKING BFF

MWF SEEKING BFF

MY YEARLONG SEARCH
FOR A NEW BEST FRIEND

RACHEL BERTSCHE

BALLANTINE BOOKS
TRADE PAPERBACKS
NEW YORK

A Ballantine Books Trade Paperback Original

Copyright © 2011 by Rachel Bertsche Levine

Published in the United States by Ballantine Books,
an imprint of The Random House Publishing Group,
a division of Random House, Inc., New York.

BALLANTINE and colophon are registered trademarks
of Random House, Inc.

ISBN 978-0-345-52494-2
eBook ISBN 978-0-345-52495-9

Printed in the United States of America

www.ballantinebooks.com

2 4 6 8 9 7 5 3 1

Book design by Elizabeth A. D. Eno

FOR MATTHEW

AND IN MEMORY OF MY FATHER,
BILL BERTSCHE

Only connect! That was the whole of her sermon.
Only connect the prose and the passion, and both will be exalted,
And human love will be seen at its height.
Live in fragments no longer.

   —E. M. Forster, *Howards End*, 1910

Penny: *What's up with Ichabod?*
Leonard: *Oh, he's trying to make a new friend.*
Penny: *Well, good for him.*
Leonard: *Unless he makes one out of wood like Geppetto, I don't think it's going to happen.*

   —*The Big Bang Theory*, 2009

CONTENTS

INTRODUCTION

I've known my two best friends since I was 10 and 14. Sara was in the bunk next door to me at summer camp. She had chubby cheeks and came from Manhattan. Someone asked her once if she heard gunshots a lot. She had beauty products by FACE Stockholm and effortlessly cool stationery. She was allowed to walk alone around Greenwich Village. I guess we were friendly enough that summer—it was seventeen years ago, who can remember? What I do know is that sometime during the following school year Sara called out of the blue and invited me to her family's country house for the weekend. That's the defining moment for me.

Callie sat across from me during a math placement test for the high school where we'd be new kids that September. She wore saddle shoes, a term I didn't even know, and a short skirt. She was "funky," I thought. She wouldn't stop jabbering with a kid she clearly knew about their school play and, I learned later, her starring role in *Alice in Wonderland*.

The bestfriendships grew naturally, as they do when you're thrown together in relationship breeding grounds like high school and summer camp. They were my bridesmaids. On the night (or, I guess, morning) I found out my father was going to die from the cancer we'd thought was being treated, I called Callie. It was 3 A.M. but she picked up. "I don't know why I answered the phone," she mumbled. "It normally doesn't wake me."

A few nights later Sara borrowed her father's car to drive uptown, bring me a clean T-shirt, and sit with me while I stole a few hours of sleep at my brother's studio apartment. She just sat there, watching TV, while I slept. All those clichés about friends dropping everything when you need them? The ones about always picking up where you left off, even when you haven't talked in a while? When it comes to Callie and Sara, they're all true.

But summers, semesters, jobs, boys, and cities later, they're still in New York while I've moved to Chicago. Unlike our freshman hallway or Tripp Lake Camp cabin, the Windy City isn't rife with girls waiting to be my new best friend. In your late twenties, friend-making is not the natural process it used to be. In fact, as it turns out, I've completely forgotten how to do it. I'm too shy to approach a potential BFF at the local bookstore just because she too is caressing *The Things They Carried*. The ladies at yoga class already know one another and, for a discipline all about nonjudgment, seem oddly unapproachable. I'm not a mother, and won't be for at least a few years, so I can count out the Mommy-and-Me classes that are so obviously more for the mommy than the me.

Life was easier when playdates were set up for us.

There's no pity to be had here. I moved to Chicago with my boyfriend. We'd been doing the long-distance thing for three years since college and were very much over it. He had no interest in moving to New York, and I wasn't relocating to his hometown of Boston. We met at Northwestern University, so Chicago was the obvious choice. When he got a job at a law firm here, I started packing my bags. Sure, I'd be leaving most of my friends (despite going to school in the midwest, our college pals flocked largely to the East Coast), but I would finally be in the same place as Matt. I figured we'd get engaged in about a year, married in two. We'd do grown-up-people-who-live-together things like picking out art and making couple friends when we weren't doing really cool young-at-heart things like playing beer pong and Wii Tennis. It would be perfect.

Mostly, it was. We moved to Chicago in June 2007 and got married in August 2009. We bought a portable tabletop to play drinking games and framed a five-by-three-foot lithograph to hang over our fireplace. And it's not like I didn't know anyone in the city. I had a friend in town from college (who moved shortly after I arrived) and a cousin who I figured I'd get closer to. But there wasn't a Callie or a Sara. Not even a potential one. I found myself with no one to call on Sunday morning to see where we were having brunch, nowhere to stop by after work to watch *Project Runway*.

The truth is, I've always felt comfortable in groups. I know, so *Mean Girls* of me, but I'd argue it's true of most women. It's un-PC to use the word "clique," but most of us can name our "group of friends" pretty easily. And it's not necessarily exclusive. Just the opposite. Defined groups eliminate the hard decisions. There's no question of who to invite to a dinner party, where to sit during lunch. Yes, if there's a woman anxious to join your ranks and you ignore her, you're being a bitch, but I like to think that scenario ends after high school. Come adulthood, women don't sit around wishing they would be accepted by the popular girls. They have their own friends who are their own popular girls.

In fifth grade there were seven of us. We called each other LYLAS. Love Ya Like a Sister. We hung out on the playground singing in obnoxiously loud voices to En Vogue's "Giving Him Something He Can Feel." In high school, five of us shot our senior yearbook photos together. We took a "Senior Page!" picture at my wedding. By the beginning of my sophomore year of college, I could have told you who I'd live with when we were seniors. When that time came and we all moved into a house together, people started referring to us by our address. "Is 1113 coming?"

My office held a fitness challenge last year. I joined a team with four coworkers. We called ourselves The Transformers and took Booty Beat classes to, well, beat off our booties. Eventually, the dance classes phased out. The name stuck. We eat lunch together every day. There's another group of women in our department who also eat as a pack. We like them, they like us, but there's no room in the cafeteria to all sit together so we smile and wave as we pass en route to the salad bar.

Come the weekend, though, I don't have that goes-without-saying lunch date. Other than Matt, of course. But men, even husbands, aren't the same. They don't need to gab over drinks, analyzing every conversation, potential purchase, and awkward run-in they had that week. They're happy to silently watch sports over a beer. Guys hardly even look at each other when they hang out. Their buddy requirements are minimal.

Aside from my coworkers, I've made exactly one new friend since I moved to Chicago. Matt and I met Lindsey and her boyfriend at a wedding. I see her every month or so, when we gather for dinner with the bride and a few ex-Northwesterners we both know. They're fun, but even after two years we haven't reached that call-on-a-Sunday-morning level.

That's the bestfriendship test, I think. The "What are we doing today?" phone call. If you have that, you have someone with whom it is implied you will spend the day or at least an hour. That's the level of BFF I'm in the market for. At this point, I have girls in Chicago who I could email to set up a dinner date. But when Matt decides at the last minute to take a Friday-night trip to the casino, I use the time to catch up on *Grey's Anatomy*. When he has to work on a weekend, there's no one, save for my mom (who followed me, er, moved, here a few months ago), whom I feel comfortable enough to call and say, "What are you up to?"

Getting to that level is tricky. It's essentially dating. At what point after meeting a new friend is it acceptable to call "just to say hi"? When is it not overly aggressive to text "Pedicure in a half hour?" The first time I saw a coworker outside the office, we'd been texting on a Saturday about a work-related issue. When Lynn wrote, "If you're not doing anything, come over for Guinness and oysterfest!" I went into a tizzy. I wasn't doing anything! I'd love to come over for Guinness and oysterfest! But could I just say that? No one wants to be the pathetic girl sitting by the phone, waiting for an invitation. I wrote back a few minutes later. "Have to get lunch and run some errands . . . How long will you be there?" It wasn't entirely untrue—I did have lunch plans. With my 60-year-old aunt, my cousin, and my brother's girlfriend, Jaime. Easily cancelable, but made me look less eager. There were no errands.

This was big-time. It could be the transition from "work-friend"—Lynn sits in the cubicle next to me at the office where we are both web producers—to "friend." I wanted to play it exactly right. At lunch, Jaime laughed as I dealt with my nerves by asking a zillion questions. Did the outfit I'd thrown together for lunch look weekend-casual-but-cool enough? Was Lynn just being nice, or did she really want me to come over? "It's not like you're trying to hook up with her," Jaime said. "You'll be fine."

And I *was* fine. My T-shirt and yoga pants were perhaps a little more weekend-pajama than weekend-cool, but I walked the street fair with Lynn and her college friends, passing on oysters and Guinness in favor of a Bucket O' Fries. (Cool girls eat fries, right?) These could be *my* friends, I thought. I could infiltrate the clique! At one point, Lynn's friend Karen put her arm around me. I was awkward but tried to go with it. It was a great day.

Other than Lynn, I haven't seen any of them since.

Around that same time, Lynn was the friend-to-be I invited to join me for my first wedding dress fitting. Callie and my mom had flown in from New York for the shopping, but I was on my own for this appointment. My aunt was supposed to come, but a last-minute doctor's appointment forced her to cancel. Even though I knew it was a big step for our fledgling friendship, I was desperate.

"Are you doing anything Saturday?" I asked Lynn at work one day. "I have to go try on my wedding dress and would love your opinion. Do you want to come?" Bridal-related activities are usually reserved for VIPs, so I knew it was a monumental request.

"Just me?" she asked. The look on her face reminded me of the male lead in a romantic comedy when the girl says "I love you" too soon. It was a startling combination of fear and confusion and whoa-slow-down-there-lady. "Um, I'm not sure. I might have plans."

I tried to backpedal. "What? Oh no, never mind actually. I was just thinking, but actually I, well, I'll let you know. I probably won't need you." It was a poor exit strategy but Lynn took it.

It's possible that I read more into my coworker's reaction than was actually there, but I'd already psyched myself out. I didn't mention it again and a few days later I went to my fitting. Alone. But not before having a minor breakdown on the phone with my mom, devastated that I had no companion to tell me how blushing bride–like I looked.

All of this makes me realize one thing: I do not miss dating. Matt and I met freshman year of college. He went from friend-with-benefits to boyfriend to husband. My experience with all this courting and should-I-call-the-next-day is limited, and the thought of diving back in—even if only platonically— is seriously daunting.

My friend Blythe moved from New York to Portland six months ago with her boyfriend. She's funny and outgoing and I figured she'd probably found her Charlotte, Miranda, and Samantha already, so I shot her an email seeking advice. "Here in Portland, I have two friends, Eve and Julia," she told me. "Eve is dating my boyfriend's business partner. She's great, although I find myself thinking that she's not very much like me and if we didn't have the common experience of following boys we love to a place we have little interest in being, we might not have become friends. She's a finance geek. She's quiet and thoughtful. I adore her—but in other circumstances, I don't think we'd have connected. My other friend, Julia, is married to another of Max's friends. She's fun, lively, adventurous, and a Republican. When I was talking about Rosh Hashanah, she said, 'Who?' Right now, with work and all, these two seem to be enough for me. I would love to find some other girls to become friends with but I don't even know where to look. My yoga studio is filled with women, but how do you strike up a conversation? In the locker room when you're naked? I'm sarcastic and facetious. It's hard to find those people on first encounter. I can be nice, but I don't want nice friends. I want funny, gregarious, sarcastic, and smart friends."

It's so nice to hear you're not alone.

Journalist Valerie Frankel wrote in *Self* magazine about the types of friends a woman needs to be happy. "Psychologists have long described four major types of friendships," she wrote. "1) The acquaintance, someone you'd chat with on the street or at a local café, who gives you a sense of belonging; 2) the casual friend, a 'grab lunch' pal who often serves a specific purpose, such as a tennis or running partner; 3) the close buddy, an intimate, trustworthy comrade you can say anything to; and 4) the lifer, who's as deep and forever as family." Frankel's research found that women should have 3 to 5 lifers, 5 to 12 close friends, 10 to 50 casuals, and 10 to 100 acquaintances. I'm searching for someone who would fall in the close-friend category. If she became a lifer I wouldn't object, but I imagine the differentiating factor from one to the other is time. No one I meet next week is going to measure up to someone I've known since fifth grade. But I'm pretty chatty. I could get to the "say anything to" level pretty quickly. I do have close friends, it's just that they live in New York City, D.C., San Francisco, and Boston. I need someone who lives across the street rather than across the country.

I've been in Chicago for more than two years. Obviously, sitting around waiting for friends to emerge naturally isn't working. It's time to turn this mission up a notch. I'm looking for a Kate to my Allie. Six to my Blossom. Blair to my Serena.

No one's knocking down my door. If I want a new best friend, I'm going to have to go get one.

I could go the old-school route and take out a want ad. Craigslist perhaps:

"Married white female seeks best friend forever for last-minute brunches, TV-watching playdates, and general girl talk. An East Coast transplant newly settled in the Midwest, I work as a web producer by day though my first love is writing. I run and do yoga. I'm addicted to television, be it critically acclaimed *(Friday Night Lights)* or juvenile (everything on ABC Family, anyone?). I'm an avid reader with a soft spot for book clubs. I vote Democrat and drink too much Diet Coke. I grew up in a New York City suburb though I went to a private high school in the Bronx. At 27, I'm too old to stay out drinking until 3 A.M., but too young to start a family and move to the suburbs. Truth be told, I hope never to leave the city. In high school and college I had tons of close friends, but now it's not so easy. Research says female friendships are most at risk between ages 25 and 40, the career-building, child-rearing years. I'm looking for someone, locally, to stick it out with me until the big 4-0, so we don't find ourselves in fifteen years with no friends to rely on."

I know all about the Craigslist killer, and that's a lot of information up front, so I decide to start smaller scale. First I'll reach out to my entire social network asking to be set up with any and all friends they have in Chicago. Then I'll actually call or email the women I've met with whom I've exchanged the requisite "we should get together!" I'll approach the girl at the bookstore or yoga. Who cares if she thinks I'm trying to get in her pants? I'll wear my wedding ring; that should clear up any confusion.

For the next year, I will go on one new friend-date a week. Why a full year? Because when I first complained about not having any BFFs in Chicago, my cousin Elizabeth (who is from here but, alas, now lives in New York City) said, "It's like college, you need to give it a year." I saw her point. In college, people are initially friends with the kids who live on their dorm floor at first. Those are the friends by convenience. By the end of the school year, you unearth your actual friends—the ones you will keep in touch with over the summer or room with as a sophomore.

Twelve months from now, my contact list will hopefully be full of Chicagoans dying to join me at the farmer's market or movie theater. I've already got four girls to ask out: Hannah, a friend of a friend who I've been introduced to via email but never met. Kim, a girl in my cooking class foursome when Jaime and I took Seafood 101 eight months ago. She was there with her sorta-boyfriend and we exchanged email addresses. Neither of us ever used them. Becca, a girl I met at a bar when a mutual friend was in town. (She'd heard of me from that friend and said, "You should have called me!" *I'm* the new kid in town, I thought, *you* should have called *me*.) And the manager at the boutique on the corner whose name I don't know. I go into her store almost every weekend and we've struck up a friendly acquaintance. She knows I'm married and the exact style of sweater I like. She seems the most promising.

By the end of December, I figure one of three things could happen: 1) I could have a new best friend. She and I will talk on the phone as we run errands, balancing our cells on our shoulders as we carry in groceries and fumble with our keys. We'll meet for lunch to discuss Lindsay's latest meltdown or the new Nick Hornby book. 2) I could have fifty-two new ac-quaintances, with whom I'll chat when we run into each other on the street. I'll realize that I'm 27 (28 by then), not 14, and friendships will never be the same as they were back in the day. Blythe said she's "spent a lot of time thinking that you don't replicate your lifelong friends when you move somewhere new, especially with a boy. You can't presume to even come close." Maybe she's right. 3) I could come to the conclusion that I don't have the time or energy for these new friends after all. I'm married now, I work long hours and I spend a lot of time with my mom, who lives six blocks away. It's entirely possible that this project will convince me that Matt is my best friend, and the reason I don't have more close friends in Chicago is that I don't really want them. My life is plenty full already.

The only way to know is to get out there. Play the field. Dive into the world of serial girl-dating and just hope I emerge in one piece.

WINTER:

"I'LL BE THE ONE HOLDING A RED ROSE": SETUPS AND LONG-LOST ACQUAINTANCES

CHAPTER 1

FRIEND-DATE 1. As I approach the restaurant, there's a girl down the block walking in my direction. I squint to make her out through the January flurries. Average height, brown hair, peacoat. An everygirl. That's got to be her. When I enter Market, the new bar next door to my office, I do a quick once-over of the area near the hostess. Empty. The peacoat girl was definitely Hannah. She'll walk in the door in about 20 seconds. 19. 18 . . . My head starts spinning. When she gets here, do we hug? Or handshake? Hug is a little familiar for someone I've only met over email. But a handshake is pretty formal for potential buddies meeting for a drink. We did exchange "I feel like I know you already!" emails. And when you know someone, you hug them, right? 11. 10. 9 . . . I don't want to be overzealous in my hugging, though. Definitely don't want to be that girl. What if I lean in for an embrace as she sticks out her hand for the shake? We'll end up in one of those one-arm-around-each-other half-hugs. That already happened to me once this week, with a colleague. Yikes.

She's here. We make eye contact. "Rachel?" "Hannah?" She

goes right in for the hug. I reciprocate. Flawlessly, I might add. There's no sign I spent the last half-minute rehearsing this in my mind.

Let's back up. My inaugural girl-date and I exchanged our first email two months ago. She came to me via my best friend Sara. Actually, we should back up a bit further. Five years, to be exact.

After I graduated college, I moved home to New York and Matt moved to Philadelphia for law school. About a month into his Villanova stint, he broke up with me. I know now this is the natural course of events for post-grad long-distance relationships. Most of the women I know who married their college sweethearts went through the same thing. But at the time, I was devastated. I was quite sure Matt was out of my life forever and I was furious with myself for wasting years on him. I was lonely and frustrated and decided I needed a new social outlet to distract me. I started a book club.

I invited my other best friend, Callie, and Callie invited her cousin, Lauren. Then each of us invited two more people. The only requirement was that we bring in ladies the others didn't know. The idea was that if we were strangers, we wouldn't let gossip distract us from the book discussions. For three years, nine of us met every month. Over time, girls moved away and others were invited to replace them. Soon after I moved to Chicago, Hannah was called in as a relief book-clubber. After two years, and one bad breakup, she decided to leave Manhattan for Chicago, her hometown.

I was elated when Sara, who also belonged to the book club, emailed to tell me Hannah was moving here. "You guys will be great friends," she wrote. "She has a book club she can invite you into or she can start a new one with you." Amazing. I'd wanted to be in a book club since I arrived in Chicago but when I mentioned it to my friend from college, she said "How 'bout a dinner club?" I once even tried to finagle an invite to a coworker's book group when I overheard her mention the titles they'd read. "If you ever need another person, I'd love to join!" She looked at me as if I'd asked to join an orgy.

I sent Sara an email shortly before Hannah was due to arrive. "What's her email address? I want to grab her as my BFF ASAP." When I next checked my Gmail, I had two responses from Sara. The first had Hannah's email address. The second said "Oops. Didn't mean to cc her. I guess the ice is broken."

Sara is the smartest girl I know, but her fleeting moments of idiocy are made worse by the fact that she has no idea she's just been a huge idiot. After she typed Hannah's name in the TO: field to get her email address, she left it there. She thought nothing of this slight oversight, cc'ing her again on the "oops!"

She'd just forwarded my first potential girl-date an email in which I laid claim to her as my best friend *forever*! We'd never even met! Sara is as low-key as I am overexcited, so it all seemed peachy keen to her. I was mortified.

Despite our memorable introduction—we'll laugh about it one day?—Hannah wasn't scared off by the declaration of my intentions. We decided to meet for drinks.

So here we are. Hannah and I settle into our seats, order two glasses of wine and start chatting. When she starts to ask if I'm hungry, I shout "Yes!" before she finishes the question. I eat when I'm nervous.

The conversation is off to a comfortable start. We each explain how we're connected to the other book club girls, which leads to a wider-cast name game. Oh, you went to Tripp Lake, you must know Jill! You're from Glencoe? Do you know the

Bernsteins? We come from similar upper-middle-class suburban worlds. We know plenty of people in common.

Hannah grew up forty minutes outside of the city. It becomes clear, as she tells me about her recent move, that she already has plenty of friends in town. "So, you know a ton of people in Chicago?" I'm not happy with where this is going.

"Yeah, about a million."

A pause and then I hear myself saying, "I wish you didn't have so many friends."

Um, that was weird. Did I just say that? That's not what I meant. Well, it is what I meant, but I didn't mean to say it *out loud*. At least I caught myself before saying, "How many, exactly?" That's what I really want to know.

It may sound like the question of a crazy jealous stalker, but it's actually a logical inquiry. A person can only maintain so many social contacts. Facebook may trick us into thinking we have five hundred friends, but research shows there's a saturation point for actual interpersonal relationships.

It all goes back to the chimps. When British anthropologist Robin Dunbar was studying the behaviors of primates in 1993, he noticed their social groups were generally limited in size. Chimps, for example, could not maintain tribes of more than 50. For any species of nonhuman primates, Dunbar found the "mean group size is directly related to relative neocortical volume." In English, he's saying the size of your brain determines how many relationships you can maintain. Chimps can have about 50 friends. Since human brains are bigger, we can keep up a wider social network. The exact number Dunbar proposed was 148.4, but the Dunbar Number, as it has come to be known, is 150.

Social network means something different today than it did back in the nineties. Dunbar didn't care about the number of people who follow you on Twitter. He was talking about relationships "that depend on extensive personal knowledge based on face-to-face interaction for their stability." Reading someone's status update doesn't count.

When I came upon Dunbar's Number, I realized it was time to do some math. People don't have to be close friends to qualify as part of the 150. They just have to fit into your social group, even if you haven't spoken in a while. If you saw them, you might "have to do a lot of catching up, but they know you fit into their social world and you know they fit into yours," Dunbar told the *Wall Street Journal.* "You have a history." I whipped out my wedding invite list. Once I removed the guests who are exclusively Matt's friends, and the significant others who have since broken up with my friends or vice versa, I determined that I had sixty-four invitees who fit into my Dunbar web. Then I checked out the Facebook friends who didn't make the guest list. There were thirty-six people with whom I have communicated in the last year, or who I would actually stop and talk to if I saw them on the street. I'm generally a social person, but I've been known to run in the other direction to avoid small talk. Family falls under the Dunbar umbrella, too, if you maintain independent relationships with them, so I added another thirty—I've got a lot of cousins. That put me at 130. Twenty spots left for my new BFFs. I considered wearing a sign: 20 VACANCIES, NOW ACCEPTING APPLICATIONS!

You can see why I want to know exactly how many friends Hannah has here. If she has a big family and a large network of buddies in both NYC and Chicago, she may have already hit her 150. If she has reached friendship saturation, what am I doing here?

Three girls about our age sit down at the table next to us. As if trying to prove just how popular she is, I see a spark of recognition flicker across Hannah's face.

Suddenly, "Hiiii!"

One of the girls who just sat down is squealing at the sight of my date. Hannah looks at me sheepishly ("I wasn't kidding!") and gets up to greet this long-lost friend. As they briefly catch up, I stare at my food. I can't help thinking of an article I just read about a British journalist. She struck up a friendly conversation with a man who then told her he had no vacancies for friends. He maintained a one-in, one-out policy. Six months later, she got a card notifying her that the guy was now open for friendship. But Hannah agreed to this dinner, so she must at least *think* she can handle a new friend. A new *best* friend? We'll see.

Once she settles back into her seat, Hannah tells me about her recent breakup. She'd gone to law school in Boston while her boyfriend was in Manhattan. After graduation she moved to New York City to be with him and took the state bar, only to have him dump her a year later. "Does Matt know any single guys I might want to date?" I rack my brain. Most of the people we know here are coupled off. There is this one guy . . .

"Who is he?" she asks. "I bet I know him."

I tell her David's name.

"Who are you? Who are you and where do you come from?" Those are her words, and I fall a little bit in friend-love. She's witty! She's quick! Could this search really be so easy?

My friend David, it turns out, is her close family friend. They've known each other since the womb. The setup is not an option, but the coincidence has us laughing. Ever since she moved to Chicago, her friends have been trying to set her up. "I told them I had a girl-date tonight . . . 'cause this is a girl-date, you know?" Uhh, yeah, I know. "They keep telling me 'Screw girl dates. You need to go on *boy* dates.'"

I wonder if this will be a common theme. Single women my age are more interested in meeting potential boyfriends than potential best friends, though I would argue the latter's a lot harder to come by and plenty more emotionally nourishing. A husband is wonderful, and Matt makes me laugh. He makes me feel beautiful, loved, protected, cared for. But when I need to talk my feelings to death, really sit and analyze why I am confused/lonely/ecstatic, he's just not up to it. It's not for lack of trying, but men can only go over the same thing so many times. They don't understand that, as women, we crave having someone validate our feelings. And then do it twice more.

When I first moved to Chicago, I took a job that turned out to be a disaster. I was to be the senior editor at a new luxury magazine. The job, and the magazine launch, kept getting pushed back until the company decided to have me "train" in their Florida office so I wouldn't up and quit. For six weeks, I spent Monday through Friday in Miami, working as a glorified intern and utterly miserable. I had just relocated to end a long-distance relationship and here I was, in a city I hadn't signed up for, and farther away from Matt than ever. When I finally decided to quit, I needed to run the idea by anyone and everyone whose opinion I valued. Matt's response was "I can't tell you what to do, but I will support your decision regardless." A textbook answer. Such a good guy. But what I wanted was someone to talk it out with me for hours. To say, "You should quit" or even, "You shouldn't." Callie, who herself had quit a job recently, stayed on the phone and walked me through the different scenarios, letting me talk out how I would make a living if I put this Miami disaster behind me. Sara said, "Of course you should quit. You're miserable! You're young! Work at a bakery." I needed someone who would listen as I repeated myself in case a new thought came up. Someone who would tell me what they already knew I wanted to hear so that I would be more confident in my decision. Though Matt said everything right, I got the emotional support I needed from my friends.

I don't tell Hannah about my search—I haven't yet worked out the ethics of disclosure—but when we talk about leaving Manhattan I deliver my usual line: "I don't miss the city, but I miss my friends." I explain that while I do know some girls in Chicago, I haven't made close friends like the ones I had in New York. In the three years I was in our common book club, the nine of us became extremely tight. We'd gone from casual acquaintances and reading buddies to real-life let-me-tell-you-my-problems friends. That's what I miss, I tell her.

The good news, which she told me when we first emailed, is that Hannah was recently invited into a book club and got me an invite, too. In the meantime, she says, I should come to her friend Leah's house for dinner on Wednesday.

"*This* Wednesday?"

"Yeah, she's having some girls over for a get-together."

It's Monday. Wednesday seems a little quick. Doesn't the two-day rule say no post-date communication for forty-eight hours? Seeing each other again that soon must be a definite no-no. But friend-dating doesn't have the same rules as romantic-dating. In fact, it doesn't have any rules at all. I can probably write my own. Still, tomorrow night is yoga and Thursday I have plans with my Mom, so Wednesday is my only weeknight to go home, watch *Modern Family*, and spend some quality time with Matt. On top of that, being the only stranger at dinner with a group of girls who are already close friends doesn't sound appealing at all. I'll have to pretend to laugh at stories I don't get about people I don't know. I'll probably stuff my face just to have something to do while they all gab about their ninth-grade English teacher or some other inside joke that makes me feel like an outsider. It's hard to know how to behave in those situations. You can jump right in, asking "Who?" and "Where was this?" or you can sit back and let them have their laughs. I almost always opt for the latter, sometimes to my detriment. What I think is letting them have their fun, they might take as she-thinks-she's-too-cool.

I think back to my stack of research. In the "How-To" pile, I have three different instruction manuals for how to make a best friend. Thank you, Google. EHow.com says I need to join clubs and online social networks (I've got the upcoming new book club and am already knee-deep in Facebook, LinkedIn, and Twitter); go to after-work functions (I always do, but they happen rarely); move to a new neighborhood (not going to happen, we bought our condo six months ago); participate in my child's school (*definitely* not going to happen soon); and make the first move (pretty much what I'm doing this entire year). It says nothing about being the new kid in an already established group. WikiHow *does* say that in order to make a best friend I should get to know her friends, and PsychCentral .com suggests stealing other people's friends. Wednesday's dinner could be a great site for friendship burglary.

I decide to not decide now. I'll see if Hannah actually follows up and make the call then.

As the friendship manuals go, I'm really into wikiHow. It bills itself as the "The How-To Manual That You Can Edit" and is definitely the most spot-on of the three. It's very explicit in its instructions to be friendly but not too friendly, lest you be perceived as creepy. "Get their phone number and call them once in a while," it suggests of trying to make someone your BFF. "Don't call on the same day every week; try to pick a random day or keep it unpredictable." Noted. "Ask if one day they can come over to your house, or do something fun together. Make sure you've known this person awhile first, though. If you know someone for a day or two, then you ask them to come to your house, they may find this a bit strange." So true. "Do not go for the 'popular girl' in class. This is a given, and looks like you're trying something."

I'm starting to think the "You" that has edited this manual is in middle school. My suspicions are confirmed when I read the world's sneakiest trick, one that could have only been conceived by the most conniving of adolescents—a seventh-grade girl. "Tell the person a secret that you wouldn't mind too much if they revealed, since sharing secrets builds trust. If the person tells the secret, you will not have lost much, but you will have learned that they cannot be trusted as your best friend. If the person keeps the secret, you can tell them a slightly larger secret. Soon, your friend may build a track record of trust by keeping all your secrets, and you will know that this is a person you can share your deepest thoughts with." Wise stuff. I need to get me some secrets.

I make a mental note to implement these steps. Middle schoolers have all sorts of weapons in their arsenal, both for making friends and getting rid of them (which, you never know, I may have to do this year). My father was a middle school principal. Oh, the stories I've heard.

When dinner is over, I give Hannah a ride home. We play some more of the name game—it's like "how's the weather?" talk, an easy silence filler. When I drop her off, she says she'll email me about Wednesday (we haven't exchanged phone numbers yet). "It was a great girl-date," she says. "Next stop, boy dates."

I call Sara on the way home. Then Callie. Neither pick up. I run into the house. "I made a friend!" I tell Matt about the hug, our many mutual friends, that she likes to play poker and loved *American Wife*, that she is a family advocate lawyer and only ever missed one book club . . . and it was because she had to visit a client in the psych ward at Bellevue! I mention, too, her possible friendship saturation and calling us out on our girl-date. Matt seems to think it's funny, so I pretend to as well.

Come Wednesday, I haven't heard from Hannah. I'm relieved. Now I can go home to *Modern Family* without feeling guilty. I'll see her in three weeks at the book club anyway, so this friendship is just getting started. Being new together at the meeting will forge a bond. We'll be comrades-in-arms, equipped with *Loving Frank* and plenty to say about it. I envision picking her up on my way from work, driving together up to Andersonville. It will become our monthly ritual.

At 4:06 P.M., a bolded message in my inbox: "Tonight?" She invites me to her friend Leah's for baked ziti with five other girls. I've already planned my dinner and told Matt I'd be home. Excuses, but I take them. I'll blame my no-show on the office. That's always an easy out. Plus, wikiHow specifically says that one should "try not to visit your best friend like every day, she may find it annoying and may think you're getting in the way." (Of what, I'm not sure.)

"I DO want to come!" I write. "But unfortunately, I'm stuck at work. Booo. Sucks. But the other night was so much fun (this is really starting to sound like a post-date email). Let's definitely get together soon!"

Try hard much? I am going to scare this girl off. I know it.

She writes back, two days later, that she's sorry I couldn't come but "to be honest there were already two Rachels involved ☺." I'm pretty anti-emoticon, but I look past it. This is no time to be picky, and I'm on the losing side of that battle anyway. We make a plan to see each other at book club.

And now, only fifty-one more dates to go. I've got a city full of women to scour.

CHAPTER 2

At yoga class, I make my first attempt at friend-flirting.

I'm two deep breaths into side angle pose when the instructor tells someone named Carrie to drop her shoulders away from her ears. In an attempt to remain Zen, I tune her out. She repeats herself. Twice. When I glance to the middle of the room, I see my teacher is staring at me. Clearly I haven't made much of an impression on this yoga community. I correct her, release my shoulders, and continue to twist my chest toward the ceiling as instructed.

As I roll up my mat after class, the girl who had been chaturanga-ing next to me introduces herself. "I'm Zoe. What's your name again?" Someone's trying to pick me up! I get ready to woo her in return.

"Rachel."

"Are you Jewish?" My name and my curls usually give this away.

"Um, yeah."

"Cool. Me too. Shalom!" And with that, before I have a chance to pick my jaw up off the floor, Zoe wanders off.

Did she really delve into religion before we'd even exchanged last names? If that was her pickup line, Zoe might be worse at this than I am.

Before this girl-dating year started, another fellow yogi showed more promise. I'd been checking her out for a few weeks because she looked about one nose job away from someone I'd gone to summer camp with. Eventually, sleuth that I am, I reviewed the sign-in sheet. Sure enough, it was Sloane. I approached her before class and introduced myself. She stared at me blankly. "We went to Tripp Lake together? You were on my team when I was the captain of color war?" Nothing. I was shocked. Camp was where I thrived—my coolness peaked at age 16—and I've always been delusional enough to believe that anyone who was there in the nineties would remember me. After some prodding and mentioning the girls she was friends with (she was an age group below me, and I have a weirdly good memory) I got an "Oh, yeah . . ." that was clearly out of pity. But I'm not too good for pity. Later, we chatted about camp, her job as an inner-city kindergarten teacher, and our mutual experience as East Coast transplants. We talked for so long that the studio closed and we had to move outside to the parking lot. We even exchanged phone numbers.

At home I looked up Sloane on Facebook. Nothing. More than five hundred million users and she was nowhere to be found. Perfect. Still, I figured a few more post-class chats and we'd be in prime position to transition to actual friends.

Well, she wasn't there the next few weeks. When Sloane finally showed up, she looked right through me. We passed on the stairway and as I started to say hi, she didn't even make eye contact. Not a hint of recognition. What's wrong with this girl? She's like my grandma with Alzheimer's (if without the slurred speech). Perhaps I should greet her the same way I do

Grandma Betty, shouting exactly how we're connected every time we come in contact. Since this was all pre-friend-dating, I was too shy to push the issue. Now I'm taking a proactive approach. She's been added to the little black book.

I can't look at another female without assessing her BFF prospects. The girl at Bloomingdale's Home who told the saleswoman that she plans to return everything on her registry for cash, but that she has to register for plenty of different price points for the Midwesterners who won't write her a check? Definite possibility. Same goes for the clerk behind the register who I met while shopping with Matt. She was the perfect mix of friendly and sarcastic—we shared great banter about the tragedy of Chicago weather making it tough for girls to dress up as slutty nurses and schoolteachers on Halloween. I thought we could have something special. I returned to her store three times, ready to chat her up and perhaps schedule drinks, and she was never again behind the register.

She's the one that got away.

I'm still not sure how it came to this. When I was a kid, I had friends within days of being somewhere new. Two years in Chicago and I'm still floundering in a sea of best friend prospects. My 57-year-old mother, on the other hand, has lived here for three months and already has a pal with whom she's planning to go on cruises. (It's unclear if said friend has been informed of these plans.) Born thirty years apart to the day, my mom and I have found ourselves on parallel journeys. Both in the beginnings of a new life stage—Rachel, marriage; Harriet, widowhood—in a new city, having left behind our closest friends to be with the people we love. The person I love is Matt. The person she loves is me.

I am, of course, thrilled that my mother is having an easy

time making new friends. She's never been a burden to me, but at first I couldn't help feeling a twinge of guilt when I declined her offers to take Matt and me to dinner when we had other plans. Her very best friend in the world is her older sister who lives only blocks away ("I want to live walking distance from you and Gail," she told me when she was looking for an apartment), but I think it's healthy for Mom to have a social life independent of family. She does have some friends of her own—she grew up in Hyde Park and her two oldest pals live in Chicago—but if there's one thing I've learned it's that when it comes to friends, more is more.

My father died when he was only 58, so I'm intent on having my mother around for a long time. A large network of friends, it turns out, is a powerful deterrent against an early demise—even more so than close family ties. The evidence is overwhelming. Most notable is a 2010 study that found that social integration improves a person's odds of survival by 50 percent. Researchers found that having low levels of connection is comparable to smoking fifteen cigarettes a day or being an alcoholic, more harmful than not exercising and twice as harmful as obesity. Another study, this one of Australians aged 70 or older, found that participants with a large circle of friends were 22 percent more likely to survive the next ten years than those with fewer friends. Having a spouse, close relatives, or even lots of loving children, had no impact on survival. I figure the more friends my mom makes now, the more she'll have when she's 70. The more friends she has when she's 70, the more likely she is to live to 80. On top of that, widowhood doesn't even put her at a disadvantage (although, who knows, she could be remarried by then—I've heard rumblings of JDate). The correlation between friends and survival was there even in people who'd lost spouses or family members.

The more research I find, the more it feels as if it was done specifically for my mother's benefit. Breast cancer runs in my family—my maternal grandmother and aunt are both survivors. So when I come across a study of women with breast cancer that found that those who had ten or more close friends pre-diagnosis were four times more likely to survive than women with "low levels of social integration," I take note. (Not coincidentally, my aunt and grandmother have always had tons of friends.) Again, being married had no impact on survival. My mom, so far, has been cancer-free. Still, this study makes me want to round up the neighbors and drag them to her apartment until she's weaving friendship bracelets with ten other middle-aged women. You can't be too careful.

My mother's mother, long after beating the breast cancer, developed dementia and eventually full-blown Alzheimer's. Again using the "let's show why Harriet Bertsche needs tons of friends" model, Harvard researchers studied the effect of large social networks on brain health as we age. Surprise! "Social integration delays memory loss in elderly Americans." This, too, holds up against my anecdotal evidence. My grandmother didn't start to really lose it until she was about 85, while the average age of diagnosis is around 80.

Maybe my BFF search is selfish. Perhaps I should be going on mother-daughter double-dates. I can just picture it. As if writing almost-strangers and asking them out isn't bizarre enough, imagine being on the receiving end of an email that says "I'd love to get together sometime. Oh, and can you bring your mom? Mine needs someone to play with."

But like I said, I'm the one struggling, not my mother. When I first realized how much I missed having a best friend nearby, I was concerned for my emotional welfare. Now I know my physical health could benefit from some face-to-face friend-lovin', too. It's not just about living until I'm ancient. Studies show that having more friends will help me sleep, stave off colds, improve my immune system, and lower my blood pressure and cholesterol. Researchers haven't yet uncovered exactly why friendships influence physical health so strongly, but I can surmise some logical explanations. My friends are the people I vent to when my stress reaches insomnia-inducing levels, and I'd rather do it over drinks than over the phone. Talking through my issues helps reduce that stress. Less stress means better sleep, better immune system, lower blood pressure and cholesterol.

More friends also means more people to convince you to quit smoking, get that weird mole checked out, put down the ice cream, and drag yourself out of bed before the bummer of a breakup turns into full-fledged depression.

The Australian researchers make another convincing point: "Friends can have effects on depression, self-efficacy, self-esteem, coping and morale, or a sense of personal control, possibly through social engagement by reinforcing social roles or because interactions with friends stem from choice or selectivity." Blood might be thicker than water, but friends are people we've chosen. That doesn't explain the spouse thing, as these days most of us are picking our own husbands, but it speaks to why having children and relatives didn't really help the old Australians make it through the decade. Maybe they didn't want them there in the first place.

FRIEND-DATE 2. Sally moved here from Manhattan a few months ago to be with her boyfriend. She's a college friend of my high school classmate and only knows one other girl in Chicago. Considering our how-we-got-here stories are exactly alike, I'm confident the date will be a slam dunk. We met a few times back in New York and for our girl-date we try out a restaurant in Chicago's Greek Town. She's a sweetheart, if perhaps a little flighty, though I don't feel the you-could-be-the-one spark that I did with Hannah. Our conversation never takes off after the obligatory "Where are you from? What does your boyfriend do?" chatter. Still, when Sally invites me out to dinner the following Saturday, I gladly accept. Matt is in Vegas on a boys' trip with his high school buddies and I figure this search means giving every potential BFF a fighting chance.

"It's going to be you, me, Chris, and his sister," Sally says.

"Sounds good." Agreeable is always a good trait in a friend.

Sally and Chris pick me up at home and we drive to his sister's apartment. It's a small place with a carpet made of toys. I watch her 2-year-old son play with a plastic baseball bat while Chris and his brother-in-law recount the joys of going shooting.

I wait until we're alone to corner Sally.

"When they say shooting . . ."

"Yeah?"

"They're talking about actual guns?" I ask.

"Oh, sure. The range is fun!"

Suffice it to say, I feel a little out of my element.

FRIEND-DATES 3 AND 4. The next two weeks bring drinks with Lauren, who did my makeup at my wedding, and Heidi, another former camper. Lauren couldn't be nicer, which in this case seems to be the kiss of death. The conversation is forced, the silences awkward, and neither of us makes any false promises to call the other when we part. As for Heidi, we ran into each other last year on a flight to LaGuardia and I had been meaning to write her an email ever since.

Two days before our scheduled girl-date, she emails to tell me she invited Michelle, her own BFF (who also went to our camp) along.

Sitting across from me, Heidi and Michelle look like they could be sisters. Both are in jeans and fitted cashmere sweaters with their shiny hair blow-dried stick straight. It's that same flat-ironed look that made me insecure about my curls for the first nineteen years of my life.

I'm a bit off my game during dinner—it was a rough day at work—but that can't be entirely to blame for our lack of connection.

"Who do you guys still keep in touch with from camp?" I ask over a bowl of edamame.

"Just Michelle," Heidi says.

"The girls and I text all day long," Michelle says. By "the girls" I know she means the same group of five friends she bunked with summer after summer.

"Oh, that's great."

"Yeah."

And then . . . nothing. Silence. I fiddle with my chopsticks just to have somewhere to direct my attention.

I can tell Heidi and Michelle interpret my interest in making this friendship happen as pure desperation. And it feels like it from my end, too. To fill one long pause, I find myself asking Michelle, "Soooo, what TV do you watch?"

As I tell Sara during our recap phone call, if TV or books don't come up organically, we're really not meant to be.

On Tuesday morning, the three of us exchange "We should do it again!" emails. But considering that when I took Mi-

chelle's phone number she didn't ask for mine, I'm not holding my breath.

###

Having ruled out 75 percent of my potential best friends after
only a month, I need to home in on exactly what I'm looking
for. What is a BFF, anyway? Most people lump bestfriendship
in with love, one of those you-know-it-when-you-feel-it intan-
gibles. But I can't continue blindly on this quest looking for
something even I can't define. I'll wade through the year like
Goldilocks—this one was too grumpy, that one was too old. If
I'm lucky, I'll find the girl who's just right, but trying to cast
someone in a role is a lot tougher when you don't know what
the part calls for.

If I take the *Bartlett's Familiar Quotations* route, a friend
is both someone "before whom I may think aloud," (Ralph
Waldo Emerson) and who lets me have the "total freedom
to be myself" (Jim Morrison). She "leaves footprints on my
heart" (Eleanor Roosevelt) and "gets me a book I ain't read"
(Abraham Lincoln). Which is why I can't stand quote books.
These definitions all sound lovely, but don't provide me with
any actual help. If Abe had his way, librarians would be the
most popular people in the world.

It turns out that while we may think best friends are people
with that magic something we can't put our finger on, researchers have fairly accurately defined the traits that propel someone
from acquaintance to friend to BFF. Journalist Karen Karbo details this ascent up the friendship ladder in *Psychology Today*. In
order for someone to move from girl-date to friend, she says, we
need intimacy. Not intimacy in the turn-the-lights-down-low

sense. Friendship intimacy starts with self-disclosure—sharing personal information you wouldn't tell just anyone—and reciprocity, meaning if you tell her your secrets, she better tell you hers. But it's not just about disclosure. Friendship intimacy calls for whoever is on the receiving end of the information to offer "hefty helpings of emotional expressiveness and unconditional support." Yet, as Karbo points out, they can't be too opinionated. So if I'm enraged that Matt canceled our Friday night plans, again, she better huff and puff and agree it was lame of him, but she would never say "He's such an ass. I've never liked him." Such are the unwritten rules of friendship.

In order to move from a regular friend to a best one, I will need über-intimacy but also what researchers call social identity support. That is to say, my best friend is someone who will reaffirm my social role in society—as a wife, a writer, a pop-culturist—and thereby boost my self-esteem. Sounds a bit self-indulgent, sure, but who am I to argue with science?

Given these criteria, I see why only Hannah so far has been deemed a potential bestie. She's the only one with whom I felt comfortable mentioning my father's death and the unfortunate timing of my father-in-law's lost battle to pancreatic cancer two weeks after my wedding. She listened, said "that's horrible," and didn't harp on it enough to make me feel sad. In turn she told me about her parents' divorce and the challenges of moving back home. Intimacy and reciprocity. That she invited me to join a Chicago book club told me she respected me as a true reader—social identity support in action.

There are steps I should take to nurture this budding relationship. According to psychologists Debra Oswald and Eddie Clark's research, there are four necessary behaviors to make a friendship stick. Self-disclosure, supportiveness, interaction, and positivity. I've got the first two down. Interaction is pretty self-explanatory. Call, email, and accept invitations to dinner instead of declining so I can watch *Modern Family*. As for positivity, no one's going to want to be my best friend if I spend all our time together complaining about having no friends.

These four steps are important. They're not all that different from what I found on wikiHow—tell secrets, invite her over—but they have the weight of actual research behind them. They are proven friendship guidelines—no matter your age—and will be integral for both building new friendships and maintaining old ones. Now I just need to translate science into action.

■ ■ ■

I'm meeting University of Chicago professor and psychologist John Cacioppo this morning to discuss my predicament. Now that I've started to pinpoint, scientifically, what a best friend is and why I need one, I'd like an expert's take on just how I should go about finding her. Cacioppo is the coauthor of *Loneliness: Human Nature and the Need for Social Connection*. Since he's an authority on people *not* having friends, he probably has some insight into how to reverse the problem.

Scheduling an appointment with a college professor to ask for help making friends does feel a bit, well, sad. And formal. It's not like higher educators have a reputation as the most social beings. As I wander the halls searching for Cacioppo's office, I'm feeling self-conscious. Like my bestfriendlessness is showing on my face, seeping through my pores. I try to adopt the strut of someone with too many friends to count. Confident, head held high, a knowing grin on my face as if I'm remembering an inside joke with my closest pal.

I'm not sure why I'm putting on this show. The building is

empty save for one janitor, and I can't imagine he cares about my social life.

I arrive at Cacioppo's office at 7 A.M. I'm not usually fit for conversation this early in the morning, but Cacioppo wears a warm smile under his thick mustache that perks me right up. I wonder if studying connectedness all his life has made him especially attuned to friend-seekers like me. His voice is gruff but quiet and, as I jabber on, he's got that encouraging psychologist's nod that makes me feel like I could talk forever. I give him my entire I-need-a-local-BFF spiel.

But suddenly I'm wondering if I really do *need* a local one. I want one, obviously. My lack of nearby buddies has affected me enough to spur this quest. But the research I've read seems to indicate that long-distance pals do the trick. The physical and mental health benefits of friendship exist regardless of whether your friend is next door or across the country.

"Full-threaded contact is important," Cacioppo tells me. "This is why social networking sites can exacerbate loneliness. People use them as a substitute for interaction. The person who hides behind four thousand Facebook friends probably feels very isolated."

Cacioppo says that when it comes to technology, Skype is better than the phone, and the phone is better than texting. "There's a lot that goes into personal interaction. You have a much richer understanding of someone when you are physically present with her than if you are talking over the phone or email."

"So how do I find someone to be physically present *with?*" I feel like an overeager golden retriever, panting at the feet of my master until he's ready to throw me a bone. Cacioppo seems to hold the answers to all my life's problems.

"Well, you're already doing the first thing right. You're

going out and looking. But selection is critical. You need to find people with similar values, attitudes, and outlooks," he says. "Think about what's important to you, then find others in the same boat. Join those activities, troll those sites. Then relax. Be your generous self. You'll meet others like you."

Sensing my let's-get-out-there-right-now attitude, Cacioppo issues a quick warning. "If you are looking too urgently—if you've got to find your best friend *today*—it probably won't go as well. You may find people who will betray you or disappoint you. A person can tell the difference between someone who desperately wants to be her friend and latches on right away and someone who seems cool and laid back about it." Was he on my date with Heidi and Michelle? "You have to have the right frame of mind. Give it time."

Not to worry, I tell him. I'm giving myself a whole year.

Once I find people I connect with, Cacioppo says one of the best ways to upgrade the relationship from friends to best friends is to venture out of our natural habitat. "It's like marriage," he says. "Too often we fall into a routine that makes a relationship stale. Research suggests doing things that are ridiculous. Sharing that kind of experience promotes bonding. The same is true for friendship. You might meet friends in the places you enjoy—like a book club—but then you want to get them outside of that safe environment. Go bowling or dancing. Those are the kind of friendship-building activities you need."

Got it.

As for my master plan, the whole fifty-two-dates-over-a-year thing, Cacioppo is skeptical. "It's a lot to take on," he says. "Friendship brings responsibilities and obligations. If you're tending too many, you may not have time to get really close to any of them."

Too many friends? That's what I call a high-class problem.

Cacioppo adds a final thought. One that is apparently supposed to make me feel better. "Finding a best friend is a low probability for anyone. But you only need one or two to ward off loneliness. What you're doing is smart, but it will be hard."

Believe me, I know.

■ ■ ■

Just after my date with Hannah, I somehow landed an invitation to a second book club. Matt's coworker Natalie, who I met at a wine-tasting fund-raiser, organizes this one. She mentioned it at the benefit and Matt immediately chimed in.

"Rachel's been looking for a book club," he said. "She's obsessed." Obviously he'd forgotten that I just found one.

"You should come," Natalie told me. "We're reading *Olive Kitteridge*."

Committing to two clubs a month seemed ambitious. My schedule is getting pretty full between the weekly girl-dates, my yoga classes, and, hopefully soon, follow-up dates. Making friends is a full-time job. The problem is that I already have a full-time job. And let's just forget crazy notions like spending time with my husband during our first year of marriage.

Against my better judgment, I agreed. I can read two books a month, and double the book clubs means twice the potential BFFs.

As I read through people's responses to the next meeting's Evite, I get the feeling I'm going to be the youngest person there. By about ten years. "I'll be there if I am feeling well and Bill can watch the little one," says one member. "Sorry, we're taking the kids to meet their great-grandparents," says another.

I was wrong. I'm the youngest person here by only five years, but they feel like important ones. Three of the members have two children (one woman brought her five-week-old while I brought two bottles of pinot grigio), one is a school principal, another mentions her upcoming tenth anniversary. There's lots of chatter about breast-feeding, composting, and second children. I chime in when the conversation turns to *The Biggest Loser* and *Twilight*.

Eventually one woman, Anne, starts talking about the guy she's dating, a law student. Much more my territory. They finally had the age talk she says, which had been weighing on her for weeks.

"What do you mean the age talk?" I ask. "How old is he?" I assume she means he's too old to want kids.

"Well, how old do you think I am?"

Yeah, right. I know this game.

Natalie jumps to my rescue. "Anne looks so young," she says before directing attention back to the conversation at hand. "How old is this law student?"

Anne explains that he's 29, six months older than her last boyfriend. That she's counting his age by months is a tip-off, but if I were to have answered her question I would have guessed 33. Maybe 35. She's tall, blond, and has a dancer's body. I'd kill to look like her at 35.

"I'm 41," she says. "But it's not like I'm a cougar. I just tend to like younger guys."

When talk turns to the book, I finally forget I'm the baby of the group. Those of us who've read it have a stimulating discussion. Anne is actually quite fabulous—she sews yoga mat bags and has a contagious laugh. The fact that she's fourteen years my elder is much less an indicator of our friendship potential than is the fact that she owns her own dog-sitting and -walking business. (I'm not an animal person, but three of the women here refer to their dachshunds as their babies. As in, "My baby has a yeast infection in her ear.") And while allergies alone would never allow me to go to her apartment—she houses up to eight dogs at a time—she seems to have BFF potential. She too loves *Les Miz* and eighties movies, and clearly she believes age is nothing but a number.

What a cute buddy trio we could be. Twenty-seven-year-old me, Natalie, who's 32, and Anne. I can see the women's magazine spread now: Best Friends Span the Decades. There'll be a *Real Simple*-esque black-and-white photo of us laughing together about that time when Anne told Rachel she wasn't a cougar. Ah, the memories.

Natalie's taking me under her wing. I can feel it. She says she's going to send me an invitation to her friend's upcoming cookie party, where each guest must bring three dozen homemade cookies. I laugh to myself at how Suzy Homemaker it sounds, then realize that cookie parties are the kind of thing people in the market for friends can't laugh at. There was a time when I would've scoffed and made some snide remark about cookie parties being for moms in the suburbs, but I guarantee that some of the guests are, in fact, moms in the suburbs. And, I have to keep reminding myself, there's nothing wrong with that.

I've spent much of my life with an us-versus-them mentality. Us: the young, hip urbanites who would never leave the bustling city for the station-wagon lifestyle of the 'burbs, who are too young for kids and would never give up our careers for babies and the stay-at-home life. Them: the family folk who've settled down and have two ear-infected dachshunds, composters, and cookie parties. It's like I always say to Matt, "It's so weird that we're married. We're too young to be married. Marriage is for grown-ups."

Or, us: the too-old-for-going-out-on-weeknights worker-bees, who laugh at the drunk college kids yelling outside the bar. Them: the just-out-of-college workforce who arrive at the office hungover because, I mean, it was Thursday night.

I'm straddling the line, slowly becoming a grown-up without ever having realized it, while still keeping a foot in the post-grad life. And beggars can't be choosers. If I limit my best friends to an age or life-stage, I'll probably be pretty lonely in eleven months.

I tell Natalie to count me in.

The morning after the book club I receive an email subjected "Catch Up." I see that it's from Rebecca, the former office intern who my coworkers called a virtual mini-me. Mostly because she has the same brown curly hair as I do and goes to Northwestern. Rebecca is seriously wrapped up in college life, saying things like "It was just me and my sixteen best friends," or, "If you went to Northwestern now, you would *totally* be in Kappa."

Now that she's a senior, I know Rebecca's especially eager to stay in touch with those of us who might be able to hire her in six months. I can't blame her. Six years ago, I *was* her. In her email, she asks if I'm available to get "dinner or something" before her break. She has no idea what she's in for.

I hit reply. "Are you free tomorrow night?"

CHAPTER 3

FRIEND-DATE 5. At 7:45, fifteen minutes after Rebecca the intern and I agreed to meet, I get my first indication that this bestfriendship isn't meant to be. I'm waiting at the bar of a local sushi restaurant and haven't heard a peep from her about a late arrival. Tardiness is my pet peeve, but tardiness with no phone call or text I'm pretty sure is just rude. Could I be getting stood up? By my *intern*?

When she finally shows—"my midterm ran, like, so long"— we settle in and catch up on office gossip.

"Dave quit," I tell her.

"I heard!"

"And Tim," I say.

"I know, so crazy."

She's as informed about my office politics as I am.

Most of the evening is spent going over the finer points of job searching. I give her some insider tips, share a website I found invaluable, and spend half the meal trying to convince her that no matter her qualifications, getting a publishing job six months before you're available to start working is impossible.

Rebecca's life, one that still includes those magical words "Spring Break," is pretty far removed from mine. Probably too far for a true friendship to blossom. It's not merely that we're six years apart—at 31 and 37 we could be a perfect fit. It's that she lives in a college bubble, the same one I happily inhabited myself. I don't begrudge her the sorority parties and dance marathons, they just don't interest me anymore. I don't care which fraternity raised the most money for the charity ball, and though I admire the work she does in her Investigative Journalism class, it doesn't inspire much conversation between us other than how it can help her get a job. And given that she checks for texts/emails/BlackBerry messages whenever I utter words like "in-laws" and "wedding" and "mortgage," it's clear that the life of a married woman is one she'd rather gouge her eyes out than have to hear about all the time. It's a total lack of social identity support. I don't validate her role as college student, and she seems to think that being a wife and homeowner makes me something of a sellout.

But the night isn't a total bust. I promise her that if I ever do start writing full-time, I'll take her on as a research intern and it'll come with no pay or benefits. She promises to accept such a position. Everybody wins!

███

On Friday night, I'm alone in my kitchen with my Empire Red KitchenAid stand mixer (God bless registries), making the one recipe I swore I never would: two batches of my mother-in-law's Mandelbrot. It's Matt's favorite dessert and his mom has been baking it and sending care packages to his various places of residence since I've known him. When he first offered it to me in his freshman dorm room I resisted. Same when it came from the fraternity house or the senior year off-campus dump or the law school apartment. But when I eventually visited his family's home in Cape Cod, fresh with the smell of just-baked cookies, I caved and never looked back. Mandelbrot, for the gentiles out there, is a Jewish version of biscotti. My mother-in-law's version has chocolate chips and is covered in enough cinnamon-sugar to kill a diabetic. Delicious.

When I first started dabbling in the kitchen, I warned Matt not to even ask for Mandelbrot. I would never be able to make it as well as his mother does, and I wasn't interested in hearing my husband whine, "It's not the way mom makes it." Just the thought of it gives me flashes of *Everybody Loves Raymond,* and not in a good way. Still, Natalie has invited me to her friend's cookie exchange and accepting invitations—interacting—is part of the process. So tomorrow I'm expected at a party, as are three-dozen homemade cookies. Since 1) Mandelbrot are the only cookies I know how to make, 2) I'm fairly certain no one else will bring them, and 3) each one is small enough that thirty-six doesn't seem like such an undertaking, I am breaking my own vow and baking his beloved dessert. On a Friday night.

I want to believe that this cookie exchange could present me with my new best friend forever, but I don't. The next day, standing outside my apartment, holding two Lululemon bags full of my mother-in-law's specialty, I feel like a phony. Cookie exchanges are more her speed; I'm a *Law & Order: SVU*–marathon kind of girl.

This isn't what friend-making should be. I need to be true to myself, not some super-smiley dessert-wielding chipper version of myself, which is probably expected of someone at a cookie exchange. But "being true to myself" is perhaps just a self-indulgent way of saying "hiding in my comfort zone," so when Natalie's car pulls up to my apartment, I'm all grins.

We enter the home of the cookie master. It's like a cozy winter wonderland. The entire downstairs, made up of a dining room, kitchen, living room, and enclosed back porch, looks like something out of a Martha Stewart magazine. The cookie table displays beautiful treats—frosted sugar cookies, giant peanut butter bars, and oversize classics like chocolate chip and oatmeal raisin. My own offering looks dinky in comparison.

The affair is filled with grown-ups. The 38-year-old host's parents are here. Her in-laws are here. There's a small gathering of grandmothers in a corner admiring the desserts. There's a fire burning in the back room and an itty-bitty baby asleep on the couch. The kitchen has two pots of heavenly smelling soup, phyllo dough appetizers, and a champagne-spiked punch. The soundtrack is set to classical music. I had pictured a loud gathering of 20- and 30-something women laughing, gossiping and eating, but this party has more of an afternoon tea vibe. It's the single most refined event I've ever attended socially. That doesn't automatically disqualify it from being the bearer of best friends, but, looking around, I'm not hopeful. Unless there's someone else who showed up and was caught totally off guard. I stand in the corner downing my punch as I scan the room for such a girl. She's not here.

If this were an evening event there might be more mingling, but at noon on a Saturday this party is more of a family affair than a friend one. Considering I don't even know the host, I wonder if everyone in the room is thinking, "Who the hell is *that* girl?"

When Natalie first told me about the exchange she explained it as "such a fun girl thing," but she and Anne are sitting in a corner by themselves. I settle in next to them. Rather than making new friendships, I'll use the party to keep building these two.

A few hours later, my Lululemon bag is full again (the guests think it's hilarious that the rookie didn't know to bring Tupperware), this time with a variety of cookie flavors. I've met and actually talked to only Melanie, who lives in Wisconsin but comes to Chicago some weekends. Not BFF-qualified. It's time to get out of here, and I feel perfectly satisfied that I put forth my best effort. There's only so much talking to Grandma and gazing at a newborn I can take. Anyway, my friend—my *real* friend—Chloe is in town and I need to get home to greet her.

As I leave the party I think about my ideas of us versus them. I do think I could be close friends with a woman in a different life-stage, but between the date with Rebecca and this cookie party, I've come to realize that finding her may not be easy.

So, Chloe. She's one of those effortlessly gorgeous friends who, no matter what she wears, looks fit for the pages of *Vogue*. She makes jeans and a T-shirt look fresh. She pulls off berets and sequined blazers and wears them so easily that I wonder, "Why haven't I spent a hundred and fifty dollars on a sequined blazer?" And then I do. And then it sits in my closet. And then I give it to Goodwill, tag still attached. Where does one even find the occasion to wear a sequined blazer? But, anyway.

Chloe is Sara's best friend from college and when we both lived in New York, we became friends ourselves. She's smart and silly and whenever she visits we stay up late chatting on the couch like 12-year-olds at a slumber party. Chloe is in business school in Philadelphia now, and she came to Chicago Thursday night for a job interview. The rest of the weekend, she's staying with me.

I'm elated that Chloe might move here but I'm not planning our life together just yet. She's teased me like this before. About a year and a half ago Chloe almost enrolled in Northwestern's business school. I was skipping around town thinking my friendship problems had been solved, picturing our Sunday brunches, when she called to tell me she'd chosen Penn. I can tell Chicago's a second choice for her this time, too, so I try not to get my hopes up.

But still, my hopes are a little up.

"Take a breath," Matt tells me on our way to dinner. "You two have all night together."

Chloe and I are talking so fast I'm not sure either of us can hear the other, let alone break for air. She's telling me about business school dances and yesterday's interview and I'm yapping about our 8-month-old nephew and plans for a one-year-delayed honeymoon. I'm a giddy schoolgirl, in a car with Matt *and* a close friend. I have it all! It feels as if, finally, I can stop trying. I'm talking about anything and everything—work, family, *Top Chef*—without a filter. It's so natural and I feel so . . . light. It's as if I was totally unaware I'd been lugging around this burden until it was lifted. The weight, I guess, was the heavy load of loneliness, though I loathe that word. It reminds me of those "Depression Hurts" commercials, the black-and-white ones where everyone is gazing out windows. People are always doing that in movies, staring out windows to signify their hardships. I've tried a few times, but it was pretty boring. I'd vote couch for a good bout of the blues. But that's not the point. The point is that I'm *not* depressed, and to even think the word "lonely" sounds so . . . sad.

The psychological definition of loneliness is "perceived social isolation." As John Cacioppo told me, "Loneliness isn't being alone, it's feeling alone." If we're going strictly by the book then I guess I am, in fact, lonely. I'm certainly not alone—aside from Matt, I'm surrounded by coworkers and family, and the two of us do have plenty of friends. When we throw a party, we pack the house. But obviously I don't feel enough of a meaningful connection with any of them, or I wouldn't have launched this yearlong search.

There's also what social scientists call "social comparison" working against me. The gist of the theory is that we evaluate our own circumstances by comparing them with others. It's why researchers say loneliness peaks during the holidays—inundated with images of Christmas parties and loved ones gathered around the tree, our own small dinner party feels not good enough. Because I watch so much TV, and my favorite shows are the likes of *Friends, How I Met Your Mother, Sex and the City,* and *Entourage,* I'm socially comparing myself all year long. If those are the models I live by, I should have three or four BFFs who I meet for coffee or beers or cosmos every single day, sometimes twice.

But now that Chloe's here, I'm feeling super–socially connected. We spend Sunday laughing, eating, and trying on clothes. She's my favorite shopping buddy because she buys with abandon and encourages me to do the same. Probably Matt's worst nightmare, but whatever. She's only here for the day.

"You need to get it," Chloe tells me about a gray cotton vest with a shimmery trim.

"Really? It doesn't make me look like Charlie Chaplin?"

"No! If it doesn't feel girly enough, pair it with skinny jeans and heels." I never wear skinny jeans and heels.

"Okay. But if you come back in a year and I've never worn it, I'm giving it to you," I say.

"Deal."

We go through a few more rounds like this. When we get home, I've got a new cable-knit sweater, a plaid button-up shirt, a little black dress, and the vest in question.

"I had so much fun," Chloe says as she packs her suitcase full of purchases. "I'll keep you posted about the job."

"Please do," I say. We hug goodbye. "Our second bedroom is always ready for you."

Matt's in the office, so after Chloe leaves I plop on the couch to check in with my DVR. I think about her visit, about how purely happy I was, and how I don't have that relationship with any girl in Chicago. The potential for how happy I *could* be, versus how happy I *am*, is clear for the first time. Which is weird because I've had friends visit before without these kinds of epiphanies. Only five weeks in and this project has me all hyped up on friendship. It's worse (er, better?) than crack.

I'm not *un*happy in Chicago, it's just this idea that I could be so much happi*er.* For the first time in two and a half years, I wonder if Matt and I could have made it work in New York, if he really would have been as miserable as he thought, and what life would have been like to have him and my best friends all in one place. I picture us living in Brooklyn, inviting Callie and Sara over to watch the Golden Globes or eat Thai food. I don't want to even think it, but I wonder, could we have made a mistake?

It's a moot point. We're here, and we love this city. It's not like I didn't want to move to Chicago. I was the one who pushed for it because it was the one place we both wanted to be. But still, I wonder.

When I wake up beside Matt the next morning, the questions are lingering. Will I ever find the pure giddiness I felt with Chloe with someone nearby? Will there ever be a time when I feel like nothing is missing? In New York, Matt's absence left a deep void. Here, the hole that should be filled with friendships is a bit shallower, but it's there, like a manhole you don't notice until you've fallen and are knee-deep in sewage.

"What are you thinking about?" Matt asks.

"Just Chloe's visit."

"What about it?"

"Just that I was so happy, it was so fun, and I never have that here. I was just, you know, wondering, if—even though I know we didn't—if we maybe made a mistake when we moved here." The minute the words are out of my mouth I regret them. This will turn into a fight.

"You think we made a mistake?" he asks. "I'm sorry, I thought we were happy. We love Chicago, we love each other, we have an amazing life. Then your friend comes for one day and you think we made a *mistake*?" Oh, no. Now *this*, this was a mistake. "I don't have that many best friends here either, Rachel. But I don't let that make me question my entire life here. I have *you*."

What Matt's saying is actually quite kind. That I make him happy, that all he needs in life is me. Or something like that.

"Of course I'm happy with you. I was just thinking, I don't know. That I miss having them . . ." There's no easy way for me to articulate my feelings, mostly because I know Matt can't understand them. A man's well-being isn't as dependent on friendships as is a woman's, and his needs really are different. Psychologists say that women have face-to-face friendships, while the male kind are characterized as side-to-side. Women like to engage in conversation, men like to bond over an activity. It's not that novel a discovery. Anyone who's seen men sit and watch the game while the women gab in the kitchen knows this to be true.

The fight escalates. There are tears (mine) and heavy sighs (his). Matt says I've become obsessed with this friendship thing and have let my search spiral into the notion that my life here is empty when we actually have a lot going for us. I yell something about how I know I have friends but not the friends I need, and that it's not a reflection of my feelings for him.

I'm worried this last point might be hard for my husband to believe. Research has found that both men and women get more emotional satisfaction from their relationships with women. Studies show that men think their wives are their best friends, and women think their best friends are their best friends. When marriages break up, social scientists say it's the men who have the harder time. They're suddenly left with no one. Women, usually, have friendships to fall back on that are nearly as intimate as the romantic relationships that failed them.

While I can help Matt stave off loneliness, my own protection must come in the form of some local BFFs.

There are, of course, plenty of people—male *and* female—who tout the idea that "my spouse is my best friend and the only one I need." It's one of those romantic notions that has been perpetuated by our mothers and grandmothers and every movie in the Meg Ryan canon. It's a myth that has probably been responsible for thousands of unhappy marriages. Imagine the sense of failure a woman must feel when she enters into this covenant, expecting to be rewarded with a whole new level of bestfriendship, only to realize that her husband will never be her Callie or Sara. It's enough to make her feel far lonelier than when she was alone.

A husband can fill many vital roles—protector, provider, lover—but he can't be a BFF. Matt is my most intimate companion and the love of my life. But I can't complain about my husband to my husband. That's what friends are for.

It's like what journalist Ellen Tien wrote in *O, The Oprah Magazine* about her self-proclaimed "mid-wife crisis." "Your husband is not your best friend. Your best friend is your best friend. If your husband were your best friend, what would that make your best friend—the dog?"

Or as an old colleague once told me of her significant other: "He can't be my girlfriend, he's my boyfriend."

I'm not sure where the husband-as-best-friend myth came from, anyway, but I imagine it began as a story women told themselves to ease the pain of giving up friendships for marriage. Loneliness in matrimony isn't a new phenomenon. Back before women were liberating themselves and taking back the night, they were doting on their husbands and children 24/7. That didn't leave much time for BFFs. "Wives are lonelier now than they ever used to be," wrote Nora Johnson in "The Captivity of Marriage," her 1961 *Atlantic Monthly* article. "Great numbers of friends are a luxury she can no longer afford; old friends often diminish in importance, which she is sorry about. But there is a limit to her capacity for giving affection, and maintaining old friendships at their original intensity requires an effort she hardly has the energy for. Besides, she is often forced into unwanted and demanding friendships with the next-door neighbor, the boss's wife, or the ladies' club chairman, and she must learn to cover up her real feelings . . . It can be painful to find oneself isolated, in marriage, with problems that have always been shared with mother or girlfriends, and to realize that there are some things that even one's husband cannot be told."

I can't necessarily relate to being forced into friendship with anyone at a ladies' club, but the isolation Johnson writes of is still very real almost fifty years later. The problems that I've always shared with girlfriends cannot be foisted on Matt. Not because he doesn't want them, but because I need to sort through them in the female, face-to-face manner.

And, anyway, these days friends are a luxury women *can* afford, so I want to embrace the "have it all" mentality. Marriage and bestfriendship. They're not one and the same, nor are they mutually exclusive. And, as it is with work and life, I need to find a balance.

When I started this project I told Matt that I'd found the perfect man, now it was time to find the perfect girl. He encouraged my quest so that I could find a way to be happier here, not so I could decide we should move back East. Hence, the fight.

It's become one of those arguments where halfway through neither of us knows what we're arguing about. Matt does make one point that sticks with me. "It was just a visit," he says. "You were with Chloe for less than twenty-four hours. If she lived here it wouldn't be like that all the time." He's right. Maybe I'm letting the idea of having a best friend here cloud the reality of it. I'd still have to go to work. I'd still want to spend time alone with my husband and veg out on the couch solo once in a while. I'd still have family obligations. And if, say, Chloe were here, she'd have her own life, too. We wouldn't have sleepovers and stay up late every night. People are busy, people travel. It's likely that if she lived in Chicago, we'd only actually see each other once or twice a month.

Matt and I leave for work. While I'm at the office, I get a call from Chloe. She didn't get the job. Well, that was quick.

Back to the drawing board.

The workday separation gives Matt and me time to breathe. When I come home, things are okay. We apologize. Matt knows I don't regret moving here with him, I know he just wants me to be happy where we are. That's what I want too. After all, I can find a new BFF in Chicago. I can't find a new Matt in New York.

FRIEND-DATE 6. Fight or no fight, there's no time to dawdle at home. I have a date to get to. My coworkers and I have planned a group date of sorts. We're all fans of musicals, both the High School and Broadway varieties, and Kari found a coupon for thirty-five-dollar tickets to *In the Heights*. We decided to make it an event. Kari, Ashley, Joan, Lynn, and I gather at Ashley's for dinner and drinks before the show. These four are currently my closest friends in Chicago, hands down. After two years of lunches together, they know I hate strawberries and mint, send me any and all links related to *How I Met Your Mother*, and agree that Rachel Bilson should play me in the movie of my life even if my hair is closer to Keri Russell circa *Felicity*. There are a few problems though. First of all, they've lived in Chicago longer than I have—Joan, Ashley, and Lynn are all from here origi-nally—so they already have their own best friends. I figure that's not too big an issue. I've already entered their Dunbar circle, I'm just fighting for higher status. If I earn a spot, they can add me to their BFF list just as I'm looking to add to mine. The larger problem is that we spend most of our time together gos-siping about work. As we grow closer that's fading, but it's still our common thread and dominates the conversations. I want time with my best friend to be an escape from office politics. Then, of course, there's the fact that since we spend so much time together on weekdays, we hardly call or see each other on weekends. When we do, it's for a group activity like dance class. I can't imagine any of us will share a one-on-one "want to get brunch?" call until we've moved on to new jobs.

But this year is about building relationships. I'm not going to make a best friend overnight, so this is a date with long-term potential. Every time the five of us have a real-life playdate we move another step closer to being friends independently of the office.

There's a pretty large collection of research about workplace friendships, both pro and con. Some experts say you should keep office relationships separate from the real-life kind. In her book *Friendshifts: The Power of Friendship and How It Shapes Our Lives*, sociologist Jan Yager says coworkers should adhere to a "three-year rule," taking that long to turn coworkers into friends. Even then, she says, you should keep the relationships casual.

Three years? That's absurd. That's about how long I stay in any one job. We live in a world of high employee turnover, so why make office friends at all if you're going to leave by the time the relationship is established? And how do you time that, anyway? If I say five words to my cube neighbor every day, it will be just enough to make us buddy-buddy in three years? That's crazy talk.

Personally, I side with author Tom Rath. He's the Global Practice Leader for Gallup (you know, the company that conducts all those polls). His book, *Vital Friends: The People You Can't Afford to Live Without* celebrates the office BFF. The numbers he presents are staggering. Rath's research found that while only 30 percent of employees report having a best friend at work, most people would opt for an office bestie over a 10 percent raise. And the lucky employees who do have a best friend at work are seven times more likely to be engaged in their jobs.

I believe it. If I had no officemates to make me laugh or with whom to talk celebrity gossip when I need a break, I would have checked out long ago.

Most of the existing research focuses on how office friendships affect the productivity of the workplace, but I'm not worried about my department's well-being. I'm worried about my own. Rath says people with three or more friends at work are 96 percent more likely to be satisfied with their lives. That's no small thing. There's little information out there about how to transition a work-friendship into a real-life one (only 20 percent of employees ever do), but I know plenty of women who've made it work. "Lost is the generation that didn't mix business with pleasure," one friend tells me when I ask for advice. "Once I realized I worked with girls who were my age and were also going out most weekends, we'd all go out, text each other, and ultimately meet up (a few drinks helps). You just have to be up for anything, anytime and put yourself out there."

The more people I ask, the more I'm told the same thing. Start with something small or group-oriented, then jump in. "If you really enjoy the person's company, you just have to go for it," my college roommate says. "Be aggressive about it."

But not too aggressive, I note. To elevate work-friends to the next level, text messaging seems to be the communication method of choice. Phone calls bring up all sorts of unnecessary small talk, plus the possibility of getting screened if she thinks you could be calling about work.

I've compiled a work-to-life friend playbook:

1. Ask potential friend(s) out for after-work drinks. Keeping it on a weekday seems less invasive of her personal time, but gives you a chance to establish your off-hours relationship. A few drinks help clear the cloud of professionalism that might be looming.

2. If it still feels too soon for one-on-one time, plan a group outing. A friend of mine says the women in her office do a "Tour de Brunch," once every couple of months. It makes for a slow transition, but, you know, slow and steady and all that . . .

3. If bi-monthly group dates are getting old, go for the text message. Take matters into your own hands. Try, "Doing anything fun tonight? Want to meet up?" In the worst-case scenario, you don't hear back. No biggie. It'll at least get the ball rolling. If you're office friends, it's likely she's just as happy as you are to take it beyond Big Brother's walls.

As for my big transition, the whole night is easy.

About halfway through dinner, talk turns to standard 9-to-5 gripes—late hours, frustrating colleagues, all that good stuff.

"No work talk," I announce. There are nods all around and we return to a much more interesting topic: Men.

Tonight feels more like a gathering of old friends than a girl-date. We weigh in on the plans for Lynn's wedding, analyze Ashley's dating dilemmas, and enjoy a song-filled few hours in the theater. These aren't off-the-clock BFFs (not yet, anyway) but strong weekday friendships are pretty fulfilling for eight (or, who are we kidding, nine or ten) hours a day, five days a week. And in my new hometown, this is my one and only clique, the one group of girls where I fill a niche—I'm the goofy one!—and it feels like home.

What a difference a day makes.

■ ■ ■

The work outing was just the boost I needed. If the sub-par dates since Hannah and my visit with Chloe had me down, the fun with my coworkers has me reinvigorated. I start my second batch of invitations.

Looking back at my emails to Lauren the makeup artist and Heidi the ex-camper, it's clear why they read my discomfort on the page. I'm not exactly used to writing women I hardly know and asking them to dinner. I worried they'd be turned off if I emailed out of the blue, so I buffered my solicitation with "I've lived in Chicago for about two years now, but some-times I still feel new in town and am always eager to make a new friend." It's like asking a guy to dinner by saying, "I'm still single, but I'm always looking for a husband!"

For this next set, I've revised my tactic. Instead of taking the Needy Girlfriend approach, I'm going for Confident Fun Woman Open to New Things. I send out a round of six emails: to Jen, a fellow Northwesterner who I've run into at a few bars around town (she's also best friends with Matt's ex-girlfriend, so that should add an interesting twist); Sloane, the yogi and fellow camper who forgot me a month after we met; Margot, the bridal consultant who sold me my wedding dress a year ago; Hilary, a friend of a friend who I met my first weekend in Chicago; Becca, another second-degree connection, who I met six months ago when a mutual friend was in town; and Kim, with whom I made paella in a cooking class nine months ago. In all of these cases, we vowed to get drinks "one day" and never did. So I remind them. "We talked about getting together, which I'm finally making good on." That's not desperate, that's follow-through.

Within twenty-four hours, I hear back from everyone but Sloane with some variation of "So good to hear from you! How's next week?" I'd be lying if I say I'm not a bit shocked. I figured some of them would take me for a charity case they didn't have time for. But maybe everyone could use a new friend. Screw Dunbar.

(Sloane never writes back which, given our last encounter, I kind of expected.)

Hilary's the first responder. No surprise. I actually messaged her via Facebook, which, given the frequency of her status updates, appears to be her preferred method of communication. She loves her some Facebook. We've met only once, at a bar-hopping outing organized by my college friend, but there was a friend request in my in-box first thing the next day. In the two years since, here's what I've learned about her: She loves to work out. And post smiley faces in her status updates. And call every one she goes out with a "hot date." And by "loves to work out," I mean her status update every weekend is some version of "It's 7 A.M. and I've got a 17-miler under my belt! Now just a 4-mile swim to go. Super Saturday :)"

Her online profile doesn't give me much hope for us.

"Why are you asking her out if you're already not into her?" Matt asks. Damn him and his logic.

"I have to do fifty-two of these things! Do *you* know fifty-two people? I need to go out with everyone I know in this town and I can't rule them out until after the date."

"She sounds all wrong for you," he says.

She does. But I need to keep an open mind. We set up a dinner for next Monday night.

As I suspected, finding a best friend really is like finding a man. At least in the beginning. There are the wardrobe changes before the first date (I go for nonpolarizing casual cool—jeans tucked into my new gray boots, a cozy sweater), the clumsy hellos and goodbyes, the "so nice to see you" next-day correspondence that only sometimes leads to a second invitation.

So far I've noticed only two real differences: We're just friends, or trying to be, so we always split the bill. Also, women have no problem inviting other friends along. Since there are no sexual prospects, I guess girls figure they can get in a date with two for the price of one. It's driving me batty. I don't want a chaperone.

This has happened to me twice now. When Heidi invited Michelle to dinner, I felt like I was on an audition. They were already best friends, so with every glance that passed between them, I wondered, *Do they think I'm funny? Will they let me in? Did I just make an ass of myself?* Michelle drove Heidi to dinner, so when they got back in the car I was sure they were mocking my desperation. The worst part was that Heidi and I hit it off, but there was something amiss between Michelle and me. We weren't in sync. Had Heidi and I met alone as I had intended, we could be exchanging witty banter this very minute. Instead I think our future, or lack thereof, is sealed. Michelle and Heidi, best friends forever. Is there a word for the friendship version of cock-blocking? There should be.

Now Hilary's done the same thing. On Sunday, she sends me an email to firm up plans and mentions that she invited her "really awesome friend Claire, too. She is one of the nicest people on earth." What are these people doing to me? Don't they realize I am looking for a best friend here? If the chances of wooing one girl are slim, getting two at once feels impossible. It's almost enough to make me wish this *were* real dating. No one would stand for a first-date threesome.

The good news is that as pessimistic as I am about Hilary, I'm equally as hopeful about my budding friendship with Hannah, date number one. She's like my wedding dress. The first gown I tried on was perfect, but I slipped on thirty more to be safe and each beaded monstrosity made me more confident in the tulle number I wore down the aisle. Since our first meeting we've only seen each other once, at book club, but we've been trying to set up a second date for weeks. The problem is that she's studying for the Bar exam, which pretty much guarantees a person won't see the light of day for at least a month. But in our emails back and forth about schedules, we've chatted about books and weddings and boys. We're pen pals, taking it slow.

FRIEND-DATE 7. When I arrive at English, the upscale pub Hilary chose for dinner, she's waiting for me at the bar. She's blond, with the tiny body you'd expect of someone who runs seventeen miles before 7 A.M. on a Saturday.

"Hey hottie," she says.

We sip our cocktails—me a pinot grigio, Hilary a vodka tonic—as we wait for Claire.

"The last time we met we were at this same bar," I say. It had been a fun, and funny, evening. Fun because it was my first girls night in Chicago, funny because it was July and the air conditioner was broken at the bar where we started the festivities. Imagine five 25-year-olds trying to look sophisticated while sporting dresses covered in sweat stains. Like I said, funny.

"That was probably the last weekend I went out on the town," Hilary says. "I'm usually in bed by ten."

"Me too! I'm more of a homebody," I say. "Definitely."

This is good. Connection.

When Claire shows up we grab a table. Suddenly, before I have a chance to overanalyze the situation, something crazy happens. Hilary and I click. It starts with Hilary telling Claire how we connected—my college roommate used to live across the street from her—which leads to a gossip fest about another mutual friend and her husband, who neither of us particularly likes. The conversation reminds me of a study that found people are more likely to connect over a common dislike of someone than a common fondness for him. It's called the negativity bond, and it's hard at work here. There's also a girl who goes to Hilary's gym who we both know and find completely objectionable. That helps. Suddenly we're running our mouths about local restaurants, East Coast upbringings, the fact that she dated a contestant from *Survivor*.

"Um, you're kidding. *Survivor* is my favorite show," I say. "Jeff Probst is my celebrity crush."

"Oh jeez. You should have dated this guy. I've never seen the show in my life."

It turns out Hilary is training to qualify for the 2016 Olympic trials, which makes the status updates more forgivable. That she's the first to mock her own obsessive posting earns her even more points. I can accept the updates if, when we are eventually BFFs, I'm allowed to tease her about them.

Claire's nice, too. I don't think we'll establish an independent friendship just yet (and every time she speaks to me she grabs my arm, which makes me want to scream something about personal space), but she's plenty friendly and, for now, that's good enough.

"You're a reader, right? I think I remember that from the last time we met," Hilary says to me.

"Yup. Or, at least, I like to think I am."

"You should totally join our book club," she says.

I have to decline—I draw the line at two—but it leads to a great discussion about what we've read (*The Spellman Files*) and what we've loved (*The Help*). From there, we move on to movies and television.

This is what I meant! TV, books, organic conversation. Finally.

"You ladies want to take a shot with us?" There are three men at the bar shouting over to our table.

"It's Monday night. We'll pass," Hilary says.

We take this as our cue to leave, but not before Hilary and I make plans to go to yoga tomorrow. I hop in a cab, excited and surprised that the night was so much fun. There's a warm and fuzzy tingling I don't recognize. Could it be an inkling of friendship? The realization that between Hannah and Hilary, I might have two new, local friends? That are all mine? I look out onto the skyline of my not-so-new city and for the first time I feel like a Chicagoan. Like, just maybe, I belong.

CHAPTER 4

The next day, I'm on a post-date high. I'm so pleased with how my evening went that I'm not even fazed when Hilary texts me to bail on yoga. Something about dinner plans she couldn't change. I should be disappointed—our first follow-up and she's already canceling—but I'm too encouraged by the fact that my Judgy McJudgersonness was off base. For the past seven weeks I've been sizing up the prospects before we'd even met: She lives in a fancy neighborhood, must mean she's trendy and too high-maintenance; she posts smiley faces on Facebook, must be a saccharine dud. The fact that Hilary turned out to have big-time potential makes me think that my having so many preconceived notions of who my BFF would be is exactly why she doesn't yet exist.

Going forward, I'm vowing to approach each date with an open mind. I can't completely rid myself of natural tendencies, but just being aware that I tend to write people off too early should help matters. I'll say yes to every invitation (when they start pouring in). Sure, I'm shy and judgmental when it comes to meeting new people, but things can change. Hilary surprised me. Who's next?

FRIEND-DATE 8. I'm especially excited about dinner with Jen, an old Northwestern classmate, because after just a few emails I've scored an Evite to her birthday party. I'm glad to have penetrated the outer circle, but that's the easy part. Now I need to see where exactly I belong on the friendship ladder. I've already told Matt we'll be attending the shindig, to which he responded with a halfhearted "Okay." I expect to be met with more reluctance closer to the date, but I take note of the fact that, whether he was listening or not, he agreed. It's not that Matt hates human interaction or anything—he's great in a crowd, a real charmer—but the group of people at this party will undoubtedly be his ex-girlfriend's crew. We're married now, and she's engaged, so in theory we've all moved on. But still, it could be weird.

In the planning stages of our dinner, I suggested Jen invite her friend Alison. Yes, I know this goes against everything I stand for—I'd be the first to march the anti-threesome-date picket line—but I've known Jen and Alison, as a duo, since college. Asking one without the other feels wrong. So I don't.

The three of us meet at Flat Top, the downtown location of a stir-fry restaurant we loved in college. Jen and Alison are your quintessential Midwestern BFFs. Pretty, blond, totally wholesome-looking. They could be cover girls for *Today's Chicago Woman* or, better yet, *Windy City BFF Weekly.*

While playing catch-up, we exchange updates on all our mutual acquaintances. I try to nonchalantly get in some questions about Matt's ex.

"So, when's Molly getting married?"

"Um, like, January?" Phrasing statements as questions is a sure sign of discomfort. I ignore this.

"Oh, that's nice, where? Georgia?" I'm trying to sound cavalier, and Molly's from Atlanta.

"Yeah, I think so." Jen looks to Alison for confirmation. Or maybe a bailout.

"Gotcha. Well do you have a lot of bachelorette parties coming up?" I'm putting on a bad show, pretending to ask only because we've talked about their whole college gang and not because, eight years later, I'm still irrationally wary of Molly. But Jen and Alison know I've always been disturbingly fascinated with their friend.

They're both noticeably tight-lipped. Either they've had a falling-out, or Molly has told them not to even utter her name in my presence. Both scenarios are plausible, but from where I'm sitting she's starting to feel like the elephant in the room. I decide to let it go. For now.

Other than Molly's looming presence, the dinner is great. I really like them both. I liked them in college, too, but we were in different groups of friends and, given the fact that I competed with their BFF for Matt's affection sophomore year, a close friendship was never in the cards. Maybe things are different now. We talk TV, their new book club (what is it with this town? For two years I couldn't find a book group anywhere and suddenly they're slapping me in the face), career goals, and Jen's upcoming party. We laugh a lot. Eventually they ask about our wedding and, because they knew Matt so well in college, I tell them about his father. Then I mention my own father's death, only in reference to how bittersweet it was that I could be there for Matt in such a real way.

At the end of the evening Jen turns to Alison. "Can you drive me around Saturday so I can pick up some stuff for my party?"

The request is so nonchalant. Just a favor between best friends. There was no "This is probably a huge pain but . . ." or "Can you do me the biggest favor in the world?" Just "Can you drive me around?" No big thing. That's what I want! I want to drive someone on errands! *That* is friendship. I think about offering to be said driver, but bite my tongue. "Hi, I know this is the first time we've hung out in, like, ever, but I'll give up my Saturday to be your chauffeur!" I've learned to avoid overt signs of friendship desperation.

The next day, I get on Facebook to do some detective work. A quick peek through Alison's pictures tells me she went to visit Molly in Atlanta not too long ago. There was no falling-out. I wonder what this means for our relationship. Will it be impossible for us to be close? Maybe, but probably not. Molly lives far away and if they've been told not to mention her, at least they haven't been asked to avoid me. Or if they have, they didn't listen. They probably just don't want to betray their friend. I can respect that, even if I'm denied not-at-all-valuable-but-still-fascinating information. It speaks highly of how they'll treat me if this friendship develops. As Joseph Epstein writes in *Friendship: An Exposé,* "Considering the obligations owed to genuine friends, at a minimum I should say that loyalty, or at least the absence of betrayal, is among them."

The biggest barrier to bestfriendship with these two is the fact that they've already got a tight-knit local group. There are two other girls from their college crowd in town, plus Alison has a twin sister. Their friendship slots might call for impressive résumés.

FRIEND-DATE 9. Becca. Friend of a friend. Actually, she's the friend of two friends. On paper, she's just like me. Similar upbringing, except she was raised in a Chicago suburb rather than a New York one. In person, she's . . . nice. Still, the most exciting part of the date was my Asian chicken salad.

Moving right along . . .

On the night of Jen's birthday party, Matt and I are among the first to arrive. We set up shop near the kitchen and chat with Alison and other former classmates. It's a pleasant low-key evening. On our way out, I stop to say goodbye to Jen. She pulls me aside. "Just after we had dinner, Alison's father died," she tells me.

"Wait, what? After we had dinner *last week*?" I ask.

"Yeah, I know. It happened the next day. We're trying to support her, but we don't really know what to say. I thought maybe, since you've been through it . . ."

"Of course. I'll reach out."

On the way home, I think about the news. How was Alison at the party only a week later? What happened? I think about how strange it is that I mentioned my dad, and Matt's, at dinner, and how unfortunately this is probably my in. It reminds me of the *Grey's Anatomy* episode that aired just after my own father died, when Christina welcomes George into the Dead Dads Club. It's not a fun crowd to belong to, but there's a bond between members. This really does feel like social identity support in action. Somber as it may be, I identify among the fatherless. In my twenties, I don't have many friends who can relate.

On Monday morning, I send Alison a condolence email. After the standard "I'm so sorry," I write: "I know you have tons of close friends here in Chicago, but if you ever want to talk to someone who's been through the same thing pretty recently (twice, sorta), I'm always here. Or, if you want to sit around and watch *The Office* and not talk about it, I'm good at that, too." Researchers say you're more likely to find satisfaction from supporting others than from getting support yourself, and in this moment I recognize how true that is. Alison may not be my best friend, she may never be, but it feels good to engage in some real friendship behaviors. To lend a hand and say, "Hi. I'm here."

I get a message the next day that, yes, Alison would love to get together. "I meant to tell you Saturday, but there's no easy way to do it, especially at a party," she writes. "It would be really nice to talk to someone who's been through this. Everyone has been really great, but most people (thankfully) can't relate and so I find myself not talking about it a lot when I probably should." We make plans to have lunch.

Because the universe is bizarre, that same day I notice the Facebook status of another former college classmate, Katherine. It reads: "Dad's final mention in *The Washington Post*. Fitting it should be above the fold." The link brings me to her father's obituary. Katherine and I weren't good friends at school, but we worked on a group project together and had always liked each other. Just a few months ago I ran into her at our college reunion and she made some vague reference to getting cupcakes together at the bakery on my corner sometime. I decide to write her an email, and then immediately feel like a dirty ambulance-chaser. Is this my friend-making approach? Find people whose fathers have recently kicked the bucket and prey on their need to talk? Ew.

I write the email anyway. Even if my motives are 75 percent selfish, I appreciated all the messages I got after my dad died, and extending an offer of support is the nice thing to do. If I get a new friend out of it, so much the better. I compose a similar email to the one I wrote Alison. I hit send. I never hear back.

When Alison and I meet for lunch, we share some small talk before getting into the deep stuff. She tells me, clearly embarrassed, that even though it has been two weeks she still thinks about her father every day.

"Alison! Two weeks? That's, like, zero time," I say. "And it doesn't go away, at least not for a while. My dad died three and a half years ago and I still think about him at least once a day."

She seems both disappointed and pleased to hear it. Her father's death was sudden, he wasn't sick for seven years like my dad was, so she hadn't prepped for this grief—if one can ever really prepare for such a thing. Alison wells up as she talks about her dad not walking her down the aisle, I mention how bummed I am that my kids won't have a Grandpa. We laugh at how uncomfortable people get even saying the word "father" in our presence. Just last week a coworker said to me: "I went home and was watching TV with my dad—oh, God, sorry . . ."

It's a nice, if sad, meal. We part with a hug and my reiteration that she can call or email if she ever wants to talk. I don't know if she'll reach out, but I do feel like we've made a small connection.

Jen and Alison. Add them to the promising pile.

The thing about the ever-growing list of potential friends is that that's all it is. After two months, Alison's the only best friend prospect I've gone out with more than once. I've spent time with Hannah at book clubs, but everyone else has so far been a one-hit wonder. I had this idea that once I reached out and got the first girl-date on the books, it would get easier. I made the first move, so they'd make the second. Reciprocation is a primary rule of friendship. But here's the thing—these people aren't my friends yet, so the rules don't apply. I can't expect them to start calling me for brunch dates after only one meeting. It'd be nice, but it's not required. When it comes to friend-dating, I think I've been screwed by romance. Women are used to being the askees, not the askers. You can tell me twenty-first-century women are a different breed, but not the women I know. We want to be pursued. It's flattering to feel like we're wanted. But what happens when two women are trying to build a relationship? Then what? You've got two BFF-wannabes, waiting by the phone for the other one to call.

There's a theory in social psychology called the familiarity principle. The more you see someone, the more you'll like her. It kind of makes me want to stand on the corner near Hannah's and Hilary's apartments and coincidentally bump into them on their way to work. Every day. Except I think that's called stalking.

The familiarity principle is a good argument for why I need to keep pursuing the friends I'm interested in. If they don't reach out, it's not that they don't like me (well, not necessarily), but that I'm not top of mind. I need to be more familiar.

I decide to institute a new plan. For the friends with potential, I will follow up at least once. Two or three times if I really want this bestfriendship to happen. At that point, if she still isn't reaching out I can give up. It can't be a one-way street forever.

FRIEND-DATES 10 AND 11. The common thread with potential best friends one through nine is that I shared a mutual acquaintance or network (school, camp, book club) with each. I figured this would be helpful in forging a bond. It's always nice to have a friend in common, a way to assure ourselves that the maybe-BFF isn't a serial killer. That's why the name game is usually one of our first exchanges when I meet someone new. It puts the other person in context and gives me somewhere to go for the real scoop. "What's the deal with her husband?" "Is she open to new friends?" "Is she my type?"

Research backs this up. In the early 1900s, a German sociologist put forth the theory of triadic closure: that one's friends will find it easy to become friends with each other. These days, scientists use Facebook and the like to prove the theory's validity. They say triadic closure helps explain exclusionary social cliques and why we tend toward building social networks rather than a smattering of individual friendships.

That's all great, and makes good sense. But I'm getting tired of mutual friend setups. They may help widen networks, but they come with baggage. Stories we've heard about each other, judgments that have been passed, endless chatter about people and places in common rather than any substantial conversation. My next two dates, Margot and Kim, are totally new. There are no preconceived notions of who the other one is. I met Margot over a year ago. She was the salesgirl on duty when I bought my wedding dress. We clicked and exchanged emails dancing around the topic of getting together, but it never happened. The same was true of Kim. We met in a cooking class, hit it off, exchanged contact information, and then never used it. I've sent each of them my "I'm finally following through" email and they seemed genuinely pleased to hear from me. Kim even wrote, "It will be refreshing to hang out with someone new." Score.

Now I've got plans with both and am jumping out of my

seat at the idea of meeting people with a completely clean slate. I'm like a kindergartner at the bus stop on the first day of school. We have no mutual friends in Chicago that we'll feel obligated to invite along when we want to hang out. Our opinions of each other won't be tainted by any rumblings from others that Margot's "nice but ditzy" or Kim's "awesome but a selfish friend" or Rachel's "funny but snappy sometimes." Good or bad, we can find it all out on our own.

Basically I want a BFF to myself. Again, I'm like a kindergartner on the first day of school. I'm not interested in sharing.

I feel like these new potential buddies bring the possibility of a whole new Chicago. After only two months I'm eager, not nervous, to meet virtual strangers. I think they call this progress.

The date with Margot is first. We arrive at Market, the restaurant next to my office, at 6:30. We don't leave until 10. At dinner, she chats up the waiter until we've been blessed with free drinks. I'm in awe. I'm the girl who's overly polite to waitstaff, lest they hock a loogie in my soup, but I'm no good at, nor have I ever really tried, befriending them. I feel a little like the nerdy kid in school who's been adopted by the cool girl, even if Margot is three years younger.

Other than the fact that we're both white, Margot and I couldn't be more different. She's a pastor's daughter from Ohio, the middle child of eight kids. She got engaged at 18, then broke it off before meeting the boyfriend with whom she moved to Chicago. She sells wedding dresses and knows pretty much every style number by heart (I learn this when I test her, as I've been trying to identify a dress I tried on that Callie wants for her upcoming wedding. When I show her the iPhone picture of me wearing it, she says, "Oh, Angel Sanchez, style #n3006." Impressive).

"So, then, do you love *Say Yes to the Dress*?" I figure we

should get to the important stuff first and I've been known to waste hours in front of the TLC reality show.

"I can't watch it. Too close to home," she says. "But I can tell you it's absolutely accurate."

We discuss religion. "I am, I think, an agnostic Jew," I tell her. (If I'm not even sure of that, does that make me an agnostic agnostic?) "You?"

"I'm . . . spiritual," she says. "I definitely believe in God, but I don't love organized religion."

Then Margot throws me for a loop. "Oooh, I've got a great one," she says, bouncing in her seat with excitement. "Do you believe in soul mates?"

You mean, like us?

I don't actually say that. But I want to. Instead I spend a moment formulating my answer, as if the fate of our friendship rests on my response. I decide to quote one of my favorite movies, *Kissing Jessica Stein*. "I don't believe there's just one person. I think there are, like, seven." She agrees. Phew.

Jessica Stein was referring to romantic partners, but her wisdom applies to my search, too. When I tell family and friends about the plan, they always ask: "What if you meet the one at, say, date ten? Will you stop?" The answer is no. There's room for more than one best friend in my life. I could have, like, seven. Just as I don't want to put everything on Matt—I need a BFF so I *don't* dump everything on him—I'm nervous to invest everything into one friend. What if she moves away? I start a new search? A few supertight friendships would be ideal. If I come out of this year with five women I'm comfortable calling just to say hi, I'd consider it a great success.

The dinner with Kim is in some ways a repeat of Margot. We're back at Market, though at the bar rather than a booth. (I think the waiters and hostess are beginning to recognize me. They must either think I'm the most popular girl in Chicago or a lesbian seriously looking for The One. Either option is far less embarrassing than the truth: "I'm here auditioning best friends forever!") Because we have no common social network, Kim and I discuss career goals and relationships. She's as great as I remember. The day we first met, I called Matt on the way home to brag. "I got a number!" Back then, I'd just gotten engaged, so now I tell her about my wedding and she tells me about the guy who accompanied her to that Seafood 101 class. "Turns out he was a loser," she says. Okay then.

One of the great differences between Kim and me is that she's African American. Before my dinner with Margot, almost all the girls I'd met were Jewish, and all of them were white. Not by choice, but I guess when you're set up by friends who fit that description, often *their* friends fit the same bill. I'm white and Jewish, most of my closest friends are, too, so it's not a huge shocker that early in my search that's who I ended up meeting. But ten dates in I need some change. And I'm not particularly proud of the fact that I have only a few black friends, so I'd be thrilled to add some diversity.

I'm not alone in having a limited number of friends outside my race. In 2004, only 15 percent of Americans reported having at least one confidante of another ethnicity (up from 9 percent in 1985). Among college students arriving on campus, race and living proximity are the two strongest indicators of who your friends will be. I'm not out of the ordinary in my same-race friendships, but in this case, I'd like to be the unusual one. That statistic isn't very encouraging. I'm not going to befriend someone I wouldn't otherwise, solely based on skin color. But would I be happy if one of my best friends ended up being black? Or, just not white? Yes.

Kim has a friend in town from college so when he arrives, I take my cue to leave. I don't want them to have to catch up while simultaneously babysitting a new pal. And I'm heading out of town this weekend, so I've still got to pack.

As I head to my car, I think about the last two girl-dates and that old adage, "don't talk about politics or religion around the dinner table." It's oft-given first-date advice, but science has proven it invalid. A recent study, which looked at how happiness correlated with conversation topic, found that the happiest people in the experiment engaged in one-third as much small talk and twice as many substantive conversations. I certainly found that to be true with my last two dates, though it's important to acknowledge that they shared my politics, if not my religion. Had we fallen on opposites sides of the Sarah Palin fence, I could be telling a whole different story.

I guess it's a risk-reward thing. When you go on a friend-date with someone completely disconnected from your life—where there's no triadic closure—there's a bigger risk that the date could be a bust. There's no third party saying "You two will make a good fit." No one's vouching for her sanity. But what you stand to gain might be greater than what you can get from a setup: Instead of widening an existing social network, you could be creating an entirely new one. Instead of spending the first half hour playing the name game, you could have an entire evening of substantive conversation. Both types of friends have merit, of course. There's no saying that a friend of a friend can't be The One. But my dinners with Margot and Kim were decidedly different than with Hannah and Hilary and Jen-Alison. Still, they're all on the follow-up sheet.

A few days later, I'm ditching cold Chicago and heading to Miami for a friend's wedding. Emily was one of my best friends in high school. Back then, we were the only two of our crowd who lived in Westchester, a suburb of New York City, rather than in the city itself. We drove to school together every morning, had "*Dawson's Creek* Parties" on Tuesday nights, and showed up at a moment's notice if anything went wrong. She was the one by my side the night my high school boyfriend broke up with me, which, at the time, I believed was the single biggest tragedy to ever befall my existence. She still lives in New York City, of course, and hangs out with plenty of friends from high school. Callie will be there with her fiancé, Nate, as will my close friend Jill.

Matt had to cancel on the trip because he got called to Cleveland at the last minute for work, so I'm anxious to use this weekend as old-friend catch-up time. One of the side effects of spending my life trying to make new friends is that I miss my old ones even more. It's hard to insert someone new into your life history, so no matter how close Margot or Kim and I become, they'll never have known me when I was 14.

I've already asked Callie if Nate is going to mind my constant presence.

"Nate? No, he's used to it when we see each other," Callie says. Love that guy.

It turns out poor Emily chose the coldest, rainiest weekend Miami has ever seen. There was no need to pack my bathing suit. Instead of the pool, I spend all day Saturday at The Cheesecake Factory.

Over Thai chicken and a Diet Coke, I tell Callie and Jill about the search. "It's good. I've met a lot of girls with potential," I say. "I don't have a new best friend, or even a new good friend, but I could eventually. It's hard because I'm not the most patient person in the world, and apparently making friends takes time. And work."

"This is why I'm never leaving New York," Callie says. "I'll deal with new friends once everyone moves away and leaves me." She says this because Jill might relocate to be with her boyfriend, who lives in Pennsylvania, but there's really no need to worry. Callie grew up in Manhattan and left only for college. She has more friends in New York than I can count. She's also a best-friend magnet. I've always said she'll have trouble picking a wedding party because she's one of those people who has a million friends, each of whom considers her their BFF. She's really good at talking on the phone, too, which makes it easy for her to stay close with many people at a time. (Mental note: Work on phone skills.) So, no, she'll never find herself on a friend search in New York.

Throughout the weekend, there are casual references to Callie's birthday party, or Jill's new apartment, or that night at that bar where that crazy thing happened.

"What crazy thing?" I ask.

"Oh, it wasn't even that funny," Callie says. "It was just that . . . It's a stupid long story, never mind."

Instead of taking comfort in my friends, I feel left out. I'm frustrated with myself for not appreciating the time we have together. I know I'm being childish, but it's hard not to notice every little thing I'm missing.

"I swear, you're really not missing anything," Callie says while we're watching MTV in the hotel Sunday morning. "I don't see everyone as much as you think. I'm in Brooklyn, they're in Manhattan. Jill's in Pennsylvania most weekends. Emily's busy with school. I promise." Well, now I just feel sillier, because I'm an adult and my best friend is sitting here promising me she doesn't see her other friends that often. As if it would be cheating. There's something very wrong with this.

"No, obviously you should see people," I say. "It's not that,

I just wish I was there sometimes." Not having Matt here is making it harder for me to not get jealous. He usually keeps me in check when the crazy-wheels start spinning.

This is the same thing that happened when Chloe was in town. It seems my moments of friendship insecurity are strongest, strangely enough, when I'm actually with my best friends. Sitting with everyone in Miami, talking about the wild nights I've not been around for, that's when it hits me. Friend envy. Or, as I like to call it, frenvy.

In their book *The Lonely American,* psychologists Jacqueline Olds and Richard Schwartz discuss this very feeling. "Seeing the love between others can make someone feel left out, even if he knows that the others love him as well," they write. "No one has to *be* left out to *feel* left out; a person simply has to believe that the bonds between others are more alive or intense or intimate than their connection with him."

Jealousy in friendships is usually studied in terms of one friend being envious of the other's success. She met a great guy, lost five pounds, or landed a great promotion and you smile on the outside but secretly wish it was you. Psychologists say this kind of behavior is what turns a friendship toxic.

But that's not the jealousy I'm dealing with when it comes to my specific breed of frenvy. I want my friends to have success, I just want to be there to share in the celebration.

I'm not living in New York, by my own choosing, so I. Must. Stop. Acting. Insane. I tell Callie not to worry about me and we turn our attention to the matter at hand. *MTV Teen Cribs.*

Heading back to Chicago, my plane is delayed three hours. I sit at the gate, and, like a PI in a detective movie, hold my *Marie Claire* just below eye level while secretly scoping out my fellow passengers. Is my new BFF here? Could I spot her even if she was? How would I approach her? Bitching about the airline is always a good start, and the opportunity arises when the gate agent announces our flight has been moved to an entirely different terminal. There's a collective groan as a mass of people gather their bags and start streaming down the corridor. We look like the Bitter Parade.

"What gate did he say?" A girl who looks about my age is talking to me.

"I think E Six? I figure if we follow the crowd we'll end up in the right place." This is where I would usually stop talking, look down, and pick up the pace so we aren't awkwardly walking next to each other.

But I continue the conversation. She looks like friend material. "Do you live in Chicago? Or just visiting?"

"No, I live in Miami. But I go to school at Notre Dame, so I'm driving once I get to O'Hare."

"Oh, what year are you?" Please say graduate school.

"Freshman."

Huh. That means she's 18. I thought maybe 28. I would make a horrible bouncer.

At the new gate, she pulls out a magazine and we part ways. I don't think an 18-year-old student in Indiana is what I'm looking for. Still, it's clear I'm getting friendlier. She's the second person I've chatted with in a situation where I would normally give a terse response and run. The first was at the gym, when a 20-something girl in the locker room asked me what I paid for my membership. Turned out she was on the family payment plan with her boyfriend, who recently broke up with her, and she was trying to figure out if she could afford to still belong.

"We bought our condo together, too," she said. "We were so young and stupid. I was twenty-one and he was twenty-four. Now my credit is shot, and my parents had to co-sign my new lease and they're totally freaking out." This is more information than I would usually want from a stranger, especially at 7 A.M. My workout has always been me-time. But instead of cutting the conversation short ("Well, good luck! Gotta grab a treadmill!") I told her about my apartment-buying hassles. I've developed the "you never know where your best friend will come from" mind-set. Nothing came of it, but I was flexing the talk-to-strangers muscle. It's a vital exercise in its own right.

After seeing what I'm missing in New York, I'm even more determined to turn one of my dates from potential-friend to friend. So when I get an email Monday about a film screening that Wednesday, I stop myself before calling my mom. She's my go-to for romantic comedies since Matt's not the rom-com type. She'll always say yes to a last-minute movie. But that's how I got into this predicament. Now, with a handful of almost-friends, I figure it's a perfect follow-up date. I email Hannah, but she already has plans. I try Hilary. She has a training run. Margot, who's in school part-time, has a test the next day. Kim has work.

Wow. People are really booked. I guess when they have workouts, job, errands, and school to attend to, going to a weekday movie with a friend seems a bit luxurious. It doesn't feel productive.

Teenagers spend nearly 33 percent of their time with friends, but that number drops to less than 10 percent for adults. When we do have time for friends, most people would rather spend it with already-established BFFs than having to be "on" with a possible new one. Because when we're not busy, we're tired. And even though 85 percent of adults feel less stressed and more energized after they've spent time with friends, the couch is still much more inviting after a hard day's work. In his book *Bowling Alone,* Robert Putnam wrote, "Visits with friends are now on the social capital endangered species list." Sad.

Even though I'm dedicating my year to making a new best friend, the potential BFFs aren't. I respond to all the declines to my offer with a counteroffer. Want to have brunch this weekend? Drinks next week? Go to another cooking class or yoga Sunday night? Making the second round of plans takes another exchange of back-and-forth emails, but I get a dinner with Margot—plus our men!—on the books, and a potential brunch plan with Hilary. The ball is rolling.

I end up bringing Becca, the friend of a friend who was just . . . nice . . . to the movie. First dates can be uncomfortable, and we have two friends in common, so maybe we were merely out of sync last time. During pre-movie chatter, she asks if I have anyone to set her up with, so I throw out my friend David, the same guy I mentioned to Hannah weeks ago. Becca's intrigued. I promise to investigate his relationship status.

After the girl talk, we fall silent. We're both looking around the theater quite purposefully, as if the reason we're not speaking isn't because we have nothing to say, but because we absolutely need to catch the eye of the cute guy in the third row or the texting girl two seats back. Finally, the lights start to dim. Thank God.

Later, as we part, there's an awkward hug and a "We should do this again sometime" that clearly means we probably won't.

Two days later I get a text. "Did you find out about David?" I did, and even though I gave him a glowing description— Becca may not be right for me but she's very much his type— and Matt verified her good looks, he's not interested.

"I looked her up on Facebook," he emails me. "I've dated too many of her friends."

Oy. This is why I don't set people up. I text her that it appears he's dating someone—that seems a better excuse—but will keep her posted if anything changes. It's clear her new-relationship energy is dedicated to the romantic kind. Totally understandable. But given that she has a plethora of childhood friends in Chicago and I'm saving the third follow-up for the most promising contenders, I doubt I'll reach out again and I don't expect to hear from her. Oh well.

FRIEND-DATE 12. On Thursday I have a blind friend-date that Callie set up. My mystery woman is named Muffy, and all I've been told is that she's really pretty and went to Yale. Given the name and background, I'm picturing someone with Upper East Side glamour. Pearl earrings, Tory Burch flats, straight-leg ankle-length pants. When I arrive at the bistro she suggested, I tell the host I'm meeting someone.

"Who?"

"Um, Muffy?" I feel silly saying her name aloud.

"Oh, sure, Muffy's here all the time." Wow, this is going to be even more *Gossip Girl*-y than I thought. She's a regular! The whole thing feels very un-Midwestern. He seats me at the bar, and when Muffy arrives, she's as glamorous as I imagined. She's approximately eight feet tall, with short bobbed hair, and is wearing some sort of fur stole. I'm feeling very plain.

"Should we get a table?" I ask.

"I don't think they let you sit at tables if you're only getting drinks." Oh. I guess we're only getting drinks. I try sending Matt telepathic messages to not eat dinner without me.

Another date, another nice time. We have a drink—I get a white wine, she gets her "usual," a dirty martini with blue-cheese-stuffed olives—and dish our backstories. She's from Little Rock, but her husband is from Chicago so they moved here six months ago. She lived in New York after college, then in London for a year working for Burberry. Now that she's in Chicago, she's trying to figure out what the next career move will be. In the meantime she bides her time serving on women's auxiliary boards all over Chicago.

Callie tells me later that Muffy wore a huge sun hat to her wedding. Of course she did.

Twelve dates in, I still haven't put my finger on exactly what makes one date click and not another. Joseph Epstein wrote that friendship is "affection, variously based on common interests, a common past, common values, and, alas, sometimes common enemies." I've read that each common interest between potential friends boosts the chances of a lasting relationship, and also increases an individual's life satisfaction by 2 percent. Commonalities certainly seem important, but I can find something in common with everyone I've met. A common upbringing or religion, a shared love of books, similar politics, a mutual friend. There's got to be a reason why I never noticed the time during my three-and-a-half-hour dinner with Margot, but checked my watch with Muffy, despite having a nice enough evening. Certainly the ease of conversation is a big factor, as is synergy. John Cacioppo told me that "the relationships that seem to fuel people are synergistic, they produce more than the sum of the parts. You're investing in a way that you're getting more returns than you're putting in. As soon as you see it that way, you focus a little bit differently on who's a friend, because it's not about you getting what you want. It's about both getting more than you're putting in." That is to say, the friendships I'll gravitate toward aren't just the ones that have a lot to offer me, but those where I bring something to the table as well.

It's nearing the end of March. Almost a quarter of the way through the year, it's time for a temperature check. Do I have a BFF? Clearly not. I don't even know if I'd go so far as to say I have new friends (Merriam-Webster defines a friend as "one attached to another by affection or esteem," and none of these relationships involve attachment just yet). But I have new acquaintances, plenty of whom, over time, I'm confident will become friends, and—fingers crossed—maybe even best ones. I have high hopes for Hannah, Hilary, Margot, Kim, and Jen-Alison (they're a twofer). Given Hannah's wide network, and Jen-Alison's tight-knit group, I'm not sure we'll ever reach that "I'm calling just because I need someone to vent to" level, (they have their own friends for that, so we may never get the synergy right) but I do think that real friendships are possible. As for my coworkers, they certainly are friends, but as long as we work together I think our friendships will remain mostly 9-to-5, with off-hours activities generally five strong. I'm fine with that. Having good friends within earshot five days a week is pretty amazing.

I do feel like I've mastered the art of the first date. No longer is the should-I-hug-or-handshake dilemma. There's no right answer really, though I tend toward the hug. Certainly a hug on departure.

I've fine-tuned the email to a long-lost friend: "We talked about getting together and I'd love to make it happen," yes. "I've lived here two years and am still looking for friends," no.

As for setups, I opt for the mutual friend introduction. When Callie fixed me up with Muffy, she sent one email to us both: "Rachel, meet Muffy. Muffy, meet Rachel. You're both newish to Chicago, and my friends, so I thought you should meet!" It's an easy way to get things moving. All I had to say was "Hi, Muffy! I'd love to get together. How's Monday?" If I'm Facebook friends with the BFF-in-waiting already, as I was with Hilary, I'll send the initial message that way. Feels more casual. More, well, friendly.

On a personal note, my loneliness is dissipating. It's not gone—hence the bouts of jealousy when I saw Callie and Jill—but with weekly friend-dates and yoga and monthly book clubs, there's hardly time to be alone, certainly not to feel alone. Only three months in, I'd count that as success.

SPRING:

"BFFLESS SEEKING SAME": TAKING OUT A WANT AD

CHAPTER **5**

In February, I wrote an essay about my search that was published online. I figured serial killers are unlikely to troll the Internet for want ads hidden within an essay, so if I was too nervous to post on Craigslist this would be the next best thing. After laying out my backstory and explaining why Matt wasn't enough to quench my thirst for friendship, I put it out there: "MWF Seeking BFF: Must live in Chicago. Must not bring her dog to lunch dates. Fluency in *Entertainment Weekly* preferred but not required." It wasn't easy to distill my BFF requirements into three short sentences, especially since there's so much more I want out of a BFF. But how do you say, "Looking for someone to call on a moment's notice, who will watch TV, talk books, laugh at nothing, and analyze others (from Charlie Sheen to my mom) with me when necessary. Someone who will talk me off the ledge from time to time. In return, I will support you in all you do, drive you to the airport whenever you need, and be up for a playdate always"? Well, I guess you say it just like that, but it might be coming on a bit strong. My twenty-three-word classified got to the heart of who I am and, I thought, might attract someone similar. (To be clear, while I'm not an animal lover, I am not a complete hater. I wouldn't disqualify someone for having a dog. However, I really don't like being licked while trying to enjoy a nice turkey burger. It just feels wrong.)

Within days I was getting emails from Chicago-based strangers in the same boat. The first was from Jodie, a single mom who's also new to the city. "It's like you have been following me around the city somehow sucking the thoughts out of my very frustrated mind," she wrote. "I want a friend here in Chicago that I can grab a coffee or drink with at someplace casual or fabulous occasionally. Someone who will laugh with me about the crazy things we hear women talking about in the locker room, or the latest scoop picked up from some television show we know we shouldn't be watching because we have five hundred other more important things we should be doing."

Kaitlin wrote, "Thank you for writing the article—I truly felt I was going crazy trying to make friends lately."

Gina said, "I can completely relate! You gave me a sense of relief that I'm not the only one looking for a BFF."

A steady stream of similar notes filed in for weeks.

I was shocked. I knew I couldn't be the only woman on the prowl, but while I hoped one or two brave souls might track me down, I never imagined the onslaught of notes that ensued. The emails all carried a similar message: "I'm in the same boat." "I thought there was something wrong with me." "I was so relieved to see that someone else is going through this. I'm not crazy!"

I was flattered and excited by the response, but also kind of disheartened. There are so many women on this same quest—

maybe not as overtly as I am but certainly internally—and no one talks about it. Popular culture has made it okay to yell "I want a man!" from the rooftops, so why are we still embarrassed to say, "I want a best friend"?

When you tell someone "I'm looking for new friends" what they hear is, "I have no friends." They're drastically different statements, but in today's world, you don't go seeking out new best friends unless you have none. Why would someone waste the time? Letting on that you could use a new BFF implies loneliness, and if you say you're lonely you might as well say you're a shut-in. In *The Lonely American*, Jacqueline Olds and Richard Schwartz write, "Talking about loneliness in America is deeply stigmatized. We see ourselves as a self-reliant people who do not need to whine about neediness. If a person is going to complain, far better to complain about what someone has done to him (abuse, coercion, rejection) or what diagnoses and addictions he is saddled with; to wistfully describe how lonely he feels is not socially acceptable." It's true, but it sucks.

And yet despite—or perhaps because of—this resistance to talking about loneliness, the amount of socially isolated Americans is on the rise. Between 1985 and 2004, the number of confidants Americans reported feeling close to—someone with whom they discussed important matters within the last six months—dropped from three to two. Startlingly, the number of people who reported having no one to talk with about the important stuff tripled in that same time period. In 2004, people who claimed to have zero confidants made up nearly 25 percent of the fifteen hundred respondents to the national General Social Survey, which is conducted biannually by the National Opinion Research Center at the University of Chicago. We are simultaneously feeling more socially isolated and less willing to talk about it. Sounds like a recipe for disaster.

But don't confuse loneliness with depression. I did, and I was wrong. People often think that if you're lonely, you must be depressed, or at least socially inept. But loneliness and depression are two very different things. They may have a high frequency of co-occurance—people who are depressed report feeling lonely more often than the nondepressed—but Professor John Cacioppo says they are in many ways complete opposites. While loneliness is a trigger that tells someone she needs to reconnect socially, depression makes her apathetic. Loneliness, like hunger or thirst, evolved as a signal to tell someone when a biological need—in this case the need for social connection—is not being met and to cause her to change behavior. "Loneliness propels us forward," he told me, "depression holds us back." So, while someone dealing with a mild case of loneliness might, say, embark on a yearlong quest for a new best friend, if she were depressed she'd stop caring altogether.

I responded to the emails as fast as my little digits could get the words on the screen. Some women had asked me out, others just said, "I feel your pain and I'm in Chitown too," so I made the first move. Suddenly, getting to date fifty-two didn't seem all that difficult.

FRIEND-DATE 13. Originally I had a soft spot for Jodie, the first woman to email me. Her note was enthusiastic but not crazy. She seemed smart, funny, normal. Here's what I knew: She's 40-something, has a 13- and a 10-year-old, and moved here from Los Angeles after a divorce. I was intrigued by her explanation of why she moved here: "That in itself offers enough material for your next article," she wrote. I forwarded her note to my mom with a message of my own: "Don't try to steal her from me!"

But as the date has grown closer, I've started to second-guess this pairing. What kind of friendship is really possible with a mom of puberty-crazed children? I'm almost embarrassed—how are we going to look, me and the mom? Am I going to have to go to high school volleyball games and dance recitals if this works out? I know, rationally, that it doesn't matter how we "look," whatever that even means. It's not like we want to have kids together. But we're having lunch next door to my office. What if my coworkers see us? I'll have to explain why I ditched them. For a stranger. Who's, like, a grown-up.

This isn't like the setups, or the reconnections with long-lost acquaintances like Margot or Kim. I have no idea what to expect. It's the closest I've ever come to online dating and it doesn't help that everyone I tell thinks it's hilarious that I'm meeting a stranger who has more than a decade on me.

I'm not entirely sure why I'm so hung up on the age and kids thing. Maybe I'm trying to hold on to my youth. Like being best friends with a woman about thirteen years closer to middle age would make *me* seem closer to middle age. Maybe I'm scared it will be further evidence that I'm not a young fun post-grad anymore. While friends with babies seems doable, friends with teenagers just sounds, well, old. It's a life phase I'm not ready for yet.

Lunch is only an hour, I tell myself. If it's horrible, you'll be done in sixty minutes. You are an adult. This is not that big of a deal.

I get to the restaurant first, grab a seat, chug water, and play with my iPhone—my Words with Friends app is a lifesaver—as I wait for Jodie.

I keep one eye on the door, waiting for her entrance. I've gotten pretty good at spotting my dates even without a physical description. There's a universal look of eagerness and confusion when a woman arrives at a blind friend-date and scans the room for her match. Once you're both there, you make eye contact for a second, do a half smile and point as if to say "Is it you?" and then laugh at the strangeness of it all.

At 12:35, she walks in. Long brown hair, diamond stud earrings, a Coach purse. She definitely looks 40-something, but a good 40-something.

"Thanks so much for emailing me," I say after official introductions. "I'm so glad we could do this."

"I know, it's so funny, but I had to reach out."

I dive right in with questions: How did she end up in Chicago? Is she working? Where do her kids go to school? Does she like the city?

"Well my husband—sorry, my *ex*-husband—got a job offer in Indiana, and asked me to move out there so the kids could still be close. So I was planning to do that."

"That was nice of you."

"Yeah, I know that now. And when I realized he was moving in with his twenty-four-year-old girlfriend, I had second thoughts. I didn't want to be the woman scorned. You know how people talk. Chicago was a nice compromise."

She isn't working, though she's thinking about maybe doing an internship one day. I'm getting the impression that a day job isn't really necessary for her. Lucky.

Her kids go to a private school I've never heard of. Her son, the 13-year-old, is big into soccer while her daughter is a musician.

I tell her my story—at least the part she hasn't read online. How I got married last August, no kids yet, and have a great job but hope to write full-time one day.

The conversation at this date is, just, polite. There's no deep connection. If friendships that work are about each coming away with more than we put in, I don't think Jodie and I have a real shot. Other than company—which is something—we don't have much to offer each other.

How can I tell? The early indicator is usually the talk that comes after we share our histories. It's about recognizing a dialogue versus two monologues. I'm starting to tune in to this simple difference in my dates. Do we have an interchange of ideas, or are we both just telling our own stories?

In her email Jodie mentioned that she belongs to the East Bank Club, a fancypants gym in Chicago that I've always wanted to visit. I tell her I've heard plenty of stories of members who belong and never work out but go for the food and the dry cleaner. (Both of which cost extra, of course.)

"I'll take you one day," she says. Girl-dates, all dates probably, are funny like that, the way we make plans for the future, even if we're not sure there will be one. But what else was she supposed to say?

At the hour mark I'm getting restless, though it seems like Jodie could chat all day. That's one nice thing about the people responding to my essay. They also put a high premium on friendship. They're in the market, too, so this time I don't feel like the desperate one. We're both the desperate ones.

I start to bundle up my napkin as if to say "It's about time I head out" and Jodie gets the message. We pay the check—actually, she treats (this *is* like a date!)—and walk back to my office. I direct her to a street a few blocks down where there are cute stores and we part ways, but not before she says "Let me know if you want me to take you to East Bank!" I thank her, for the offer and for lunch, but make a conscious decision that I won't reach out again. I feel like a jerk, but if I'm going to do fifty-two of these, I need to focus on the dates with real BFF potential. Jodie was nice, but aside from not feeling the synergy, our schedules are totally conflicting. She's a single stay-at-home mom so her weekdays are free while her afternoons and weekends revolve around soccer tournaments and parent-teacher conferences. Evenings and weekends are exactly when I do my socializing. I worry I'm being picky, like suddenly I'm the mean girl casting potential friends aside, but there are only so many hours in the day. It would be impossible to pursue a deep friendship with fifty-two different women. Plus, I'm confident that if I didn't feel a strong bond, she didn't either. If she reached out to me again, I'd say yes (how would I even say no? "Sorry, I didn't think we hit it off"?) but, for now, I think this ship might have sailed.

■ ■ ■

That Friday, Matt and I meet Margot and her boyfriend, Daniel, for dinner. Earlier in the week I'd broken the news to my husband that he was being called on for his second stop on the BFF tour.

"Friday we're going to dinner with Margot and her boyfriend, okay?"

"Which one's Margot again?" I've been on thirteen of these dates, with nineteen girls, and the only ones Matt has ever met are Jen and Alison, who he knows from college and their friendship with his ex, and my coworkers. As the list keeps growing, and follow-up dates are now taking up the rest of the week, he's having increasingly more trouble keeping them straight. (If you are, too, check out the who's who of friend-dates on page 345.)

"She's the wedding dress girl." I expect Matt to agree to the dinner, but begrudgingly.

"Oh, right. Okay."

"Maybe you can make a BFF, too." Though he hasn't put

up even a hint of a fight, I feel the need to make it sound worthwhile for my husband. Like there's something in this for him. It's not like Matt signed up for a friend-quest, but being married to me he's become an unwitting participant.

"Awesome." There is his signature sarcasm here.

"Don't you want to get to know my potential friends?"

"I already said okay. You don't need to keep selling me." True. I stop talking.

I'm excited that Matt's meeting one of my most promising prospects. For the last three months it's felt like I was leading a double life. Friend-dater by day, wife by night. Or, really, office worker by day, friend-dater by night. Wife when there's time. But some of the potential friends—Kim, Margot, Hannah, Hilary—have become like characters in our house. Matt's bad with names—bad as in: He asks me if my cousin's fiancé is named Jason or Teddy when his actual name is Peter—so they're often referred to as Cooking Class Girl or Wedding Dress Girl.

On the drive to dinner there's a lot of "Okay, Margot and who again?"

"Margot and Daniel. Margot and Daniel. Just keep repeating it in your head."

When we get to the local Vietnamese restaurant Margot chose, they're already seated.

"You guys picked a great spot," I tell them. "We love it here."

"Aren't you in Vietnam in your Facebook picture?" Margot asks me.

"Me on the elephant? Yeah, we took that trip a few years ago." My Facebook profile photo, of me riding a baby elephant, is in Laos actually, a three-day stop during the Vietnamese vacation we took after Matt finished the bar exam. This leads to a riveting discussion of how to pronounce the traditional noodle soup, pho. It's actually "fuh" not "foe," which we learned when we stayed in Hanoi and ate pho every morning for breakfast. On the street. In ninety-degree heat. Sitting on plastic baby chairs with our knees at our chins. Here the seating is much nicer but the soup doesn't hold a candle.

After the waiter takes our order, I tell Matt and Daniel how Margot scored us free drinks on our girl-date. "She totally buddied up with the waiter. I was one hundred percent the dorky friend."

"I was so worried I got too drunk! I got home and told Daniel that you probably thought I was crazy and would never call again, " she says.

I laugh this off, but kind of love hearing that Margot was as "will she call or won't she?" as I'd been. I secretly pat myself on the back for following up. Just as I suspected, we'd both been waiting for the other to reach out. My pursue-the-good-dates rule is paying off.

Daniel is a chemistry student at the University of Chicago. He does cancer research, and tells us about some pharmaceuticals he's investigating that will assuage some of the side effects of chemotherapy.

Just like at my first date with Margot, talk turns to politics and the struggling economy.

"It's our parents' fault," Margot says. "They got us into this mess."

"Well, that's not true," Matt counters. This is when I get nervous. I don't need any heated battles at my first couple-date. "It's way more complicated than that."

"You think? I'm not so sure."

The discussion continues, and I listen, mostly quietly, nervous that this could escalate. There's no real disagreement happening—we all live on the same end of the political spectrum—and even if there were, I know it will be fine. It's just that tension makes me uncomfortable. I guess this is what they mean when they say not to talk about politics on the first date. Still, Matt's a lawyer, he likes a good debate, and Margot seems to as well. We're all adults, I remind myself. (This has become my friend-date mantra. I go into my yogic place and repeat it in my head whenever I get nervous. *We're all adults. We're all adults.* It's funny how much trouble I have remembering.)

Also like my first date with Margot, the evening lasts more than three hours. Everyone hits it off, and at the end of the night I can tell Matt enjoyed himself. I love it when he gets all fired up, and he was good and chatty this evening. Matt's always a people person, but I can tell he is extra well-behaved for my potential best friend. He wants me to find a match nearly as much as I do.

Matt and Daniel may not become independent friends, but that's fine as long as they get along. Matt and I have plenty of couple-friends where, as a group, we work, but the other wife and I don't have strong individual relationships. It's bound to happen. When you meet in the context of the two of us getting along with the two of you, it can be tough to extract a one-on-one friendship.

It would be great, however, if Margot and I could be besties and the four of us could do dinners every now and then. Studies show that couples with couple-friends have happier and longer relationships—spending time in a foursome forces you to talk about issues other than the mundane logistics of your day-to-day life. Happy and long are two adjectives I'd really like to describe my marriage down the road.

Experts say couple-friends are harder to make than the girl-on-girl kind. After all, to become best friends only two people have to hit it off. To become couple-friends, you need four people on board. As psychologist Judith Sills told *Ladies' Home Journal,* "Good friendships are a rare phenomena in any case. Good couple friendships are a rare phenomena squared."

The next morning I get a text from Margot, "We had such a great time. Need to do this again soon." Swoon.

One good follow-up isn't enough. This weekend I'm doubling my efforts, though the more aggressive I get about this search, the louder I hear the voices of the detractors in my head. You see, for all the personal positive feedback I got from my essay—the invitations to dinner and notes of "I've been there"—there were an equal number of anonymous comments from people who think looking for friends is the exact wrong way to find them. "You can't go look for a new best friend. Best friends just happen," one wrote. "This is your classic story of a stalker case," said another.

The perception is that being proactive about making friends is inauthentic. That you aren't going to meet your true BFF unless it happens organically. And of course it's fantastic when a friendship "just happens." Callie just happened. Sara just happened. I figured that's what would go down when I moved to Chicago. But it's also great when romance just happens, and yet there are millions of people online dating, or speed dating, or going to singles mixers because they know what they want and are going after it. You've got to kiss a lot of frogs before you find your prince, right? Or in my case, princess.

I'm continuing, full steam ahead, but can't help wondering if these girls I'm emailing are reading my propositions of a follow-up brunch or movie or dinner and thinking, "This is your classic story of a stalker case."

There's no time to worry about that now. After Friday

night's double date, I have Sunday morning brunch plans with Hilary. I should be excited, given how much I enjoyed our first meeting, but planning this date has been such a hassle that I've lost all enthusiasm. After she declined the movie last week, I suggested grabbing a bite sometime. In response, she wrote, "I would say brunch would work next Saturday, but I have my long run. Sunday would normally work, but I'm trying not to overcommit myself for once and already have a run with a friend visiting from NYC, yoga, and dinner plans."

I responded that it sounds like she's swamped on weekends, how about a night next week? To which she told me that if I wanted to try out her yoga studio, she could maybe go with me and maybe get dinner with me.

I decided to give up. It seemed that unless I wanted to run with her, or plan my life around her workout schedule, a two-way friendship wasn't in our future. The whole situation frustrated me. Who writes "*If* you will try out *my* yoga class, then *maybe* I'll be able to hang out with you"? I'm happy to make the first, second, third move, but I'm not okay with feeling as if my schedule is irrelevant. And yes, I like to run and do yoga, but the gym is my morning routine—I do it early to get it out of the way—and I'm not the marathon runner that she is. I couldn't keep up even if I wanted to, and, to be honest, I *don't* want to.

After I got the last note I was sulking around the apartment, frustrated with this follow-up attempt. "I'm not going to chase her around town," I told Matt.

"You shouldn't," he assured me.

"I'm just going to email her something about how I know training is a priority for her right now, and I'd love to get together when her schedule clears up. Is that okay to say? I'm just not going to suggest a date or a time anymore."

Matt laughed at me. "You realize you're planning a breakup speech, right? You've only met the girl once."

Huh. "Sounds like your schedule is too busy for me." "We have different priorities right now." Those *are* some classic get-out-of-jail-free lines.

As if on cue, an email popped into my inbox. Hilary changed her Sunday night dinner plans to brunch ones, could I join? I was still soured by the I'll-meet-you-on-my-own-terms exchange, but agreed nonetheless. I adored her when we met, I reminded myself. Just go eat an omelet.

So Sunday morning, tired and not at all in the friending mood, I drag myself out of bed, pull on my comfy leggings, and meet Hilary at a brunch spot near her apartment. Her friend canceled so it's just the two of us and nothing's changed. We still click. Once again, I leave feeling much sweeter on her than I did when I arrived. Maybe she's one of those friends who is a total pain to make plans with but is awesome when you're together. Is the work worth the payoff? We shall see.

FRIEND-DATE 14. My second want-ad response date is with Kaitlin, who in her email explained that while she's in the same boat as I, her journey to the BFF search was different. "Many of my friends have married or moved away and now I literally have one best friend who is a gay male. While he is great for emotional support, whenever we go out people assume we are together as a couple instead of seeing me as a possible candidate (I am single) and, honestly, there are some days when a female simply needs another female's company."

It's been fascinating to read how each potential friend found herself in the BFF market. Some, like me, have recently moved—for love, for work, for school. Others have lived in Chicago forever, but their friends have all shipped off to the suburbs with spouses and babies. One girl travels for work so hasn't had the opportunity to make more than surface friendships. Another, a new mom—of twins!—is suddenly looking for someone to have exchanges with in a language other than baby talk, but isn't into the Mommy-and-Me scene. And perhaps the funniest—or saddest?—part of all is that even though my essay clearly states I'm searching for friends, that I plan to take on the world one potential BFF at a time, the women who email still couch their notes in caveats. "This is not something I would normally do." "I feel weird writing this email." "I know this sounds cheesy but . . ." "I'm not psycho!"

Once upon a time—or a few months ago—I, too, felt the need to add a disclaimer to my invitations. The unfortunate truth is that we live in a society that's not only suspicious of people who declare they're looking for friends, but thinks friendliness in general must be qualified. We're worried that an overt show of camaraderie will be taken the wrong way. Fourteen weeks in, I've found that friendship advances are generally received positively, but as the asker we worry we're imposing. The last person we want to be is *that girl*.

Remember back in the day, when we'd knock on neighbors' doors to see if Betsy could come out to play or if Sharon had a moment for a cup of coffee? Those days are long over. Unannounced guests were once considered gracious; today they're a nuisance. I can't help but think of *A Streetcar Named Desire*'s Blanche DuBois, how she "always depended on the kindness of strangers," and wonder how she'd fare in today's world. Although, I guess that didn't work out too well for her in 1947, either.

When I arrive at the Asian restaurant Kaitlin has suggested, I'm totally frazzled. I drove to dinner from work and am running late. I couldn't find parking, so eventually gave up and settled for a spot in a paid lot, then had to walk a block in the lovely April showers, sans umbrella. When I sit down at the table I'm feeling guilty about being late and spewing out small talk without coming up for air while simultaneously struggling to dry off, catch my breath, order a drink, and take off my coat. This often happens when my timeline gets thrown off, especially when it's by my own doing. I turn into Grace Adler, TV's most lovable—or annoying, depending on who you are—neurotic. Though now that I think about it, perhaps that's not just when I'm late. More than one person has told me I remind them of the kooky redhead.

Kaitlin seems the exact opposite of Grace, other than the gay best friend part, but appears amused enough at my crazy. She has short brown hair with an edgy uneven cut and is wearing big hoop earrings and clogs. She appears unusually calm, not even flinching as I barrel into the restaurant and try to get my bearings. I get the sense that she's artsy, but not intimidatingly so. When I'm finally settled, white wine in hand, she says, "How many of these meetings have you had?"

I note her choice of words. "You make it sound like an interview," I say.

Kaitlin shrugs, as if to say, "Well, isn't it?" Given how this date came about, we're both acutely aware that we're sizing each other up, looking to see if there's a bestfriendship at the end of the rainbow. The same was true of my lunch with Jodie. With the shared emphasis on friendship comes the added pressure of "Are you The One?"

Psychologists say that within ten minutes of meeting a person, you decide what kind of relationship you hope to have. Ten minutes in, I don't think Kaitlin and I are going to be best friends. This is different than judging. I didn't know at the outset that we weren't going to click. There was nothing to indicate as much in the emails. But with some people there is easy conversation and not enough time in one meal to get out everything you want to tell her—all the things you didn't know you'd been holding in until you're suddenly confessing to Facebook-stalking ex-boyfriends and how nerdy you are for coveting the iPad—and with others there is that subtle but heavy weight of constantly trying to think of what you might say next to avoid an uncomfortable silence.

What Kaitlin and I have in common is work. She's a graphic designer, I'm a writer, and we've both just started blogs, so we have an interesting discussion about the intersection of social media and creativity. While I don't think we'll be best friends, she might make a good "let's do artistic things together" friend. People who fill specific roles—a yoga or cooking pal, someone who'll join me when a fascinating speaker is in town or a documentary about musicals comes out—are important. According to Dunbar, I had twenty friendship openings when I started this project. I am not going to make twenty new BFFs. I probably won't even make twenty close friends. But remember the tiered friendships? Like the food pyramid, they ascend from acquaintances to casual friends to close ones to lifers. I'm building acquaintances in abundance. Perhaps Kaitlin and I will be casual friends, to be called upon when there's a blogging workshop in town. Or something.

As we exit the restaurant, there's that brief moment on the street where it's unclear what form this farewell will take. So I, always one to make an awkward moment more so, say "I'm going to give you a hug." Had I hugged her without announcing my intentions, I might cringe less in retelling this story. But I said it. And she said, "Oh okay . . . we're doing this." And there was a hug. A painful one.

The next day I get an email that Kaitlin is "willing to get together again." Gee, thanks. Maybe she wasn't so amused by my neuroticism, er, I mean *enthusiasm,* after all.

■ ■ ■

Keeping in touch with old friends is as important as making new ones, so I recently made plans to get together with an old friend and his boyfriend. Kevin and Patrick live near my office and accompanied me to an opening weekend showing of *Harry Potter and the Order of the Phoenix,* but I hardly ever see them due to conflicting schedules. Matt and I were supposed to go to their apartment, eat bruschetta and meat loaf (an unusual combination, yes, but when someone's cooking for me I don't complain), and play some Wii tennis. Sounds like an ideal evening. But on the eve of our date I get a Facebook message that Patrick has a tennis match (the real-life, not video-game, kind) and is it cool if we reschedule?

All I could think to say was, "Thank you."

As I get further along on this journey, I get busier and busier. I've taken it upon myself to follow the four steps to lasting friendship—self-disclosure, supportiveness, interaction, and positivity—with the ladies I'm most interested in. I've been especially heavy on the interaction. Without it, the others are impossible. So while I'd love to have a casual night with Kevin and Patrick, I feel as if they've given me the overscheduled's equivalent of a gorgeous Balenciaga bag—a night of nothing to do.

■ ■ ■

Speaking of keeping in touch, I'm beginning to worry that my long-distance friendships are taking a hit. Given my new schedule, it's harder and harder to pencil in phone time. And the more time that passes between calls, the longer my friends and I need to catch up. So when someone like Sara appears on my caller ID, I usually screen it and plan to call back when I have an hour. Which is almost never. Suddenly the person I miss most is the person whose calls I ignore repeatedly. And even though my reasons are sincere—Sara deserves a chunk of undivided attention—it doesn't change the fact that I'm talking to my friends less and less.

Sara's worse at phone communication than I am, but just last week we finally connected. She started to tell me about a guy she just broke up with, to which I said "What guy? I haven't even heard of him. It was serious?"

"He's been around a little bit. I mean, the people in my everyday life knew about him." Ouch. She didn't mean it as a jab, but it felt like one.

An unintended consequence of this search is that I'm suddenly even more aware of how much I need my old friends. Going on girl-dates, even the good ones, takes energy. With old friends, it's easier. Less exhausting. So late that night, after feeling like a bonehead because of the Sara call, I email Brooke, my New York City roommate and another lifer. "Can we talk soon? I miss you. I'm learning that interaction is key to friendships and we haven't interacted!" Yes, I'm spewing friendship jargon, but good friends are rare so they shouldn't go unappreciated. Plus, research shows that those who've told a good friend how much they value her friendship in the past month are 48 percent more likely to report being "extremely satisfied with the friendships in their lives." So I redouble the staying-in-touch-with-old-friends effort. If I lose my old friends while trying to make new ones I could very easily end up with none at all.

* * *

FRIEND-DATE 15. Sometimes, you ignore the signs. When you're trying to keep an open mind, a red flag suddenly seems like just one more piece of evidence that you're too judgmental. That you don't give people a chance.

The first email was fine. Quite nice, actually. Three weeks ago, Gina read my essay and wrote, "It was just such a relief to find I'm not the only woman out there, a little west of Chicago, who needs a BFF." She lives in the suburbs with her fiancé and works from home, so the girls' night invitations, she said, have been dwindling. "If you are still looking," she wrote, "please consider me!"

To some (to me, even) the wording may have come off as overzealous—I'm not actually accepting applications—but it was certainly in the spirit of openness and friendship. I'm the one who posted the want ad, so who am I to fault someone for treating it as such?

I wrote back thanking her for the kind note and checking when she might be able to meet. "Do you come into the city much? If you have any plans to make the drive anyway, we should plan around your schedule, otherwise we'll figure something out." Considering she responded to a want ad that very clearly sought out Chicago-based friends, this didn't seem such a stretch.

Here's what I got in return: "I'm going to be totally honest with you: I'm a country mouse, not a city mouse. Though I have been to the city many times, I don't go frequently, and the only time I tried to go down there alone, my train hit someone and was delayed for hours. I want to warn you that I am not very public transportation savvy." This does not sound promising.

She wrote that she lives in Morris, Illinois. A Chicago suburb, fine, but hardly "a little west." It's about sixty miles away.
When I asked a coworker, she said it takes about an hour,
maybe an hour and twenty minutes, to get there.

In that same email, Gina wrote, "I'm not sure what your
thoughts are on meeting in public, but you're welcome to
come to my place if you'd like." Um, my thoughts on meeting someone who found me over the Internet in public are
very positive. I'm sure she was just trying to be friendly, but I
wanted to write, "I'd actually rather not come to your house
sixty miles away from my husband and family so you can chop
me up into pieces in your basement, but thanks for the offer.
I've seen that episode of *SVU*."

Instead, I suggested we meet somewhere in the middle. In
daylight. Surrounded by lots and lots of people. We settled on
the Orland Square Mall in Orland Park, a forty-minute drive
from my house.

A few days later I got another email: "Can I ask you for
some advice? Can we just pretend that we're best friends already and that you can't wait to give me advice?"

You've been the one showing blatant signs of desperation before, I remind myself, don't get put off by her eager-beaverness.
Stop. Judging.

She asked me what she should do about waning friendships with coworkers. Something about how she didn't go to
college, can't sympathize with her school-loan-ridden friends
and instead flocked to coworkers twice her age who she thinks
might have been using her as an excuse to go out to bars and
cheat on their husbands. And then there was something, unrelated maybe, about the other ladies in the office ignoring her.

"So, do you think that they are stereotyping me as a young
party-girl type like I stereotype people my age as such?"

Whoa there, lady. I don't even know you. I can hardly even follow what you're talking about.

So much of making friends is about tuning in to social cues. "Coming on too strong, oblivious to the other person's response, is the quickest way to push someone away," John Cacioppo and William Patrick write in their book *Loneliness*. Gina is doing exactly what Cacioppo warned me not to. But I shall not be pushed! Sure, she was self-disclosing like a mad woman way too soon, but it's such a complicated dance, this friend-making.

She was probably nervous. And lonely. And excited to meet someone new.

I put off responding for three days. What do I know about her reputation? Eventually I wrote back that while I'm no expert—I'm advertising for friends on the Internet, don't forget—it seems to me that life-stage is more important than age when it comes to BFFs and that "people do grow apart naturally, that's part of life, but the hope is that we can find new people to connect with." Apparently I'm a therapist.

Then I said something about the older generation being less open to work-friends than the 20- and 30-somethings. I have no idea if this answered her question. I hardly know what the question really was.

There were a few more back and forth emails. On top of the general intensity of her friendship advances, I was starting to rethink the geography thing. Is a friend an hour away any better than one a plane ride away? I'm not so sure. We wouldn't be able to grab a last-minute lunch. We would probably only ever meet at Orland Square, or in Morris, since she's scared of coming into the city alone.

While proximity isn't necessary for maintaining friendships, research shows it's a key factor in making new ones and a primary indicator of which of those will stick. I make a mental note to befriend someone in my apartment building. We could borrow a cup of flour from each other, grab cupcakes down the street, lie out on the communal deck . . .

But back to the matter at hand. I'm going in with an open mind. At least an ajar one. I've heard stories of friendships unlikelier than this one, and potential friends on whom I'd pinned low expectations have surprised me before. So tonight, Thursday, I wrote her an email: "Hiya! Are we still on for Saturday?"

And I've just received this:

> Hi, Rachel,
>
> I'll be honest, I kinda have mixed feelings about it. It's really a downer that we live a little farther apart than is optimal to be BFFs. And I like corresponding with you via email, but I'm not sure that a pen pal is what I'm looking for, or something that you have time for. I know you're a busy lady.
>
> What are your thoughts on this? I'm not opposed to meeting, but I'm not thinking we're going to be each other's BFF. I'm weary of meeting someone I'm not confident that I'll really get to know or be friends with. Sounds like friendship heartbreak to me!
>
> Know what I mean? Or am I nuts?
>
> :-/
> Gina

Oh. My. God. I just got dumped! I can't believe this. She's breaking up with me before we've even met. I know that I had the same issues with the distance, and a part of me is relieved, but still, yikes. I figured that we'd work it out—or not—in time. And while yes, the ad said I was seeking a BFF, I don't *actually* think we will become best friends forever on first meeting. It's as if she's saying "I don't think we're going to get married, so we might as well not go on the first date."

"This is good," Matt reminds me. "Now you don't have to schlep out to Orland Park. We can get breakfast together."

Did I do something wrong? I know the last email was from her to me, but it didn't call for a response, did it? Is she mad at me for not writing back? Why doesn't she like me??

"You're really worked up considering you weren't anxious to meet her in the first place," Matt says when he sees that my hands are shaking.

"The last time someone dumped me it was you! Five years ago! It stings."

I write Gina a polite and formal email in response. I tell her I understand where she's coming from. That I hope I didn't do anything to offend her. That distance is hard for friendships. I use my business sign-off. "Best, Rachel." I know we've never met—this doesn't even qualify as a real friendship breakup, the truly heart-wrenching kind—but a part of me feels like we should be splitting up the good china.

In a response I will never live to understand, she writes, "Haha! You're really funny!"

What? That was the least funny email I have ever written. Girls are so confusing.

So far, when it comes to want-ad dating, I'm zero for three. Maybe this wasn't the best idea after all.

CHAPTER 6

FRIEND-DATE 15, TAKE TWO. I have a girl crush! I swear if I were in elementary school, I'd be writing our names on my binder: Rachel + Jillian = BFF 4-ever. Or maybe I'd buy us those necklaces. You know, the ones that are each half of a heart pendant, two pieces that fit perfectly together. Like us.

Let me start at the beginning. The good thing about Gina giving me the heave-ho was that I'd been trying to figure out a date to meet Jillian, a friend of a friend who wrote me after she read my article. Our mutual friend posted the piece as her Facebook status, Jillian saw it and sent me a message. "I also live in Chicago, have a shortage of female friends that do not require a plane to get to, and am an avid reader. I read *Entertainment Weekly* cover to cover every week." So when Gina kicked me to the curb, I emailed Jillian to see if she could swing dinner that week.

Going into our date, here's what I knew: Jillian lives in Andersonville, a Chicago neighborhood twenty minutes north of mine, is an assistant principal in Gary, Indiana, and has twins.

(True, when this all started, I thought all mommies fit in a social mold that didn't work for me yet, but I'm learning. Maturing.) She's from Connecticut, went to college in Manhattan, and used to teach in the Bronx. Our mutual friend is one I first bonded with over book talk, and she told me her friendship with Jillian blossomed the same way, so that was promising.

The night of our dinner plans, I had some time after work so I stopped at home to change clothes before walking to the neighborhood sushi spot that has become my other girl-date go-to. I put on black leggings and a long navy blue waffle shirt with small black polka dots.

"Is that what you're wearing?" Matt asked me as he scanned my outfit. Never a good sign.

"Why, should I not?"

"Well, it's a girl-date, I don't know what one wears to first girl-dates," he said. "If you want to wear your shirt that looks like a pajama top, you definitely should."

Understood. I changed into a bright blue sweater that could not be confused with something I'd wear to bed.

When I approached Sai Cafe, a girl on her cellphone gave me a wave. I did the "is it you?" point, she nodded, and I stood on the sidewalk sizing up my date while I waited for her to finish the call. She wore a long skirt and a loose blouse, a sort of hippie-chic-meets-theater-major outfit. I spotted a tiny nose ring, a subtle shimmer next to her full cheeks, which were rosy from the chill. (Yes, there is still a chill in mid-April. This is Chicago.)

"Sorry," she said as she hung up. "That was my brother. He was telling me he might go to The Wizarding World of Harry Potter."

That she said it with a hint of jealousy tells me she's a Harry fan like me. Point Jillian. "Sounds like heaven. I'm dying to go," I tell her. "I've been talking about taking a trip there with my two best friends when we all have kids, but now I'm thinking it might be more fun to go before that and just drink ourselves silly with Butterbeer."

"Yeah, Paul and I are the same way." Paul is her husband, I guess. "We're total *Harry Potter* nerds. I can't wait to start reading it with the boys. When I was pregnant, I told everyone we were going to name them Fred and George," she said, referencing the series' lovable Weasley twins.

That is totally something I would do.

"I love that," I said. "So did you?"

"Ha, no. Josh and Jeremy. But people definitely thought I was going to."

"I always say that if I have a girl, I really love the name Grace. But I'm probably going to name my son Will, after my father—he died almost four years ago—and then it hit me. They'd be Will and Grace! I love that show enough, people would actually think they're named after the characters."

"That's hilarious. Grace is a favorite of mine, too."

I was slowly falling under her spell. I have a lot of respect for other adults who openly adore Harry like I do. And I've long been obsessed with the idea of having identical twins, a wish most people say is crazy but Jillian, whose boys are almost two, thinks is awesome. And I love that when I mentioned my dad she did a sympathetic quick head nod but just listened and didn't interrupt me to say "Oh, I'm so sorry." That's the usual reaction. It's nice, but it always jolts the flow of conversation. I usually find myself, mid-sentence, uncomfortably saying, "Oh, thanks, it's fine but I was just saying that . . ." Jillian just listened and laughed when appropriate.

But back to the twins. "Do they have a secret language?"

This is the single most fascinating element of twinship, I

think. That unbreakable bond that allows them to communicate with each other before they can even speak.

"I don't know if it's a language, but they definitely have a baby-talk partner." Tomato, tomahto. "I think that's why they started speaking later."

One of the reasons Jillian wrote me is that she wants to join one of my book clubs. Since I'm still pretty new to the groups, I proposed we meet so I could vouch for her when I made the suggestion. So, after a few pieces of salmon-avocado maki, talk turned from babies to books, and more specifically, young adult fiction.

"On top of *Harry Potter, Little Women* is my other all-time favorite," I say. "I want to be Jo March."

Jillian is a middle-school administrator, so she suggested some other young adult novels I might like. Her office, she said, is wallpapered in YA covers. As she told me about school, and her latest adolescent troublemaker, a small smirk took over her face. It's clear she gets a kick out of her students and finds their antics amusing, even if she'd never admit as much to them.

We exchanged adult book titles, too. I told her what we'd read in book club—most recently *The Space Between Us*—and she told me about her book-buying addiction and the three-foot-high to-read stack next to her bed.

Over the course of the meal we shared three sushi rolls and each downed two glasses of wine. We conducted a deep analysis of the tabloid headlines and also our shared love of cooking. Jillian took our discussion of the latest celebrity romance as seriously as the talk of her sons' speech pattern. This is my kind of girl.

When the check came, we were nowhere near ready to go. We sat for another hour, conversation pouring out of us. She has a brother named Alex. I have a brother named Alex! Her father is William. My father was William! I've always had a thing about coincidences—not that I believe in fate, per se, but I usually take it as a sign when I share a lot of random similarities with someone. (I still remember when I first met Matt at Northwestern and learned we both had brothers at Syracuse. I thought it meant *everything*.)

It was the first time I legitimately wondered if I could call off the search. I know I said I'd like to have a handful of new best friends, but maybe I'd rather just free up my time to hang out with Jillian and her twins every week. I could send out an APB. "A BFF has been found. Resume your regularly scheduled programming."

But then, amid talk of how we're both East Coasters who migrated west, Jillian dropped a bomb. "Paul's taking classes this summer so he can apply for Nursing programs. We're thinking of moving to Philly."

And we're back. This is why I can't stop the search for anyone, even the most promising candidates. No matter how great a potential best friend is, there's always a but. She's perfect but she already has ten local best friends. She's perfect but she's too busy working out to make plans. She's perfect but she might move to Philadelphia.

The moving thing could be a big obstacle for me. Americans are the most mobile people in the world, moving on average every five years. And while fewer of us are relocating these days—the total number of families who changed residences in 2008 was the lowest since the 1940s, probably due to the recession—those who do move are largely in their twenties and thirties. And according to the U.S. Census, Illinois had the third largest annual outmigration—people moving out of the state—between 2000 and 2004, with an average of 72,000 people leaving per year. (New York, perhaps not surprisingly, had the highest average outmigration at 183,000.) It's got to be the winters. Damn sub-freezing temperatures drive everyone away.

Alison told me she's applying to grad school. Kim might move back to Missouri to be closer to family. Now Jillian. No one has it all. Things happen. I need to hedge my bets.

It's just further evidence of my more-is-more philosophy. Yes, quality is important, and you can only have the highest-quality friendship with a select few. But the closer you get to satisfying your Dunbar 150, the better off you'll be. It's not about quality over quantity. You need quality *and* quantity. More friends means better health, higher likelihood of living longer, better chance of surviving breast cancer. On top of that, making more friends today protects me against loneliness later, when someone like Jillian moves away.

I tried to hide my disappointment. The move wouldn't be until the following summer—Jillian's already signed on for one more school year—so no need to focus on that now.

When we parted I promised to let her know about book club ASAP. She said we should work out a time for me to meet the boys. We hugged completely not awkwardly.

And now I'm pretty much skipping home. I'm as surprised as anyone that my girl-crush is a mom. With two kids and a demanding job an entire state away, I can't imagine she'll be a meet-me-in-thirty-minutes friend, but suddenly that doesn't faze me. We're technically in different life-stages—I'm a newlywed, she's six years in and has twins nearing the terrible twos—but I don't even notice. It's the first indicator that I may need to change my friendship test. Maybe best friend and spontaneous friend aren't the same at all. Jillian made very clear that while she may have two children, adult time is important to her. Our values are aligned, our interests are similar, and though she could probably never drop everything to go grab a pedicure, she seems the type of friend I might feel comfortable—eventually—calling to say, "What are you and the boys doing? Can I come over?" That might be enough.

When I open the door to my apartment after the three-hour date, I approach Matt with a big smile. "I'm in friend-love!"

He's wearing a big grin, too. He'd been anticipating my good mood. "I knew it must be great. You've been gone so long. Put her on the board!" Matt really enjoys likening my search to a sporting event. To him, it's a horse race and he provides the play-by-play regularly: "Hilary's losing her lead, Jillian and Margot are neck and neck . . ."

I settle in next to him on the couch. After I tell him everything about the woman he has deemed front-runner there's still time for an episode of *How I Met Your Mother*. It's the perfect evening.

When I first started this friendship quest, I worried that such a personal project might place a huge burden on my fledgling marriage. A part of me wasn't confident in testing the relationship only four months into year one. I certainly didn't want this to turn into a lifelong cycle—spend one year concentrating on friendship to the detriment of marriage, next year do the opposite, then flip back and forth forevermore—and spending twelve months keenly focused on friendship would mean I'd be busy with things that didn't involve Matt. We'd spend significantly less time together than we were used to.

I'm delighted to see that the opposite is true. My already-good marriage is getting better. Now, when I get home from a girl-date, Matt and I are excited to see each other. On the rare weeknight when neither of us has anything planned, it feels like finding a twenty-dollar bill in my back pocket. And because I'm hyperaware of how hectic my schedule is, I carve out time, usually on weekends, dedicated to being with my new husband. We schedule date nights. When we braved the tourists at Navy Pier to see *Avatar* at the IMAX last month, I looked over at him wearing those ridiculous 3-D glasses and felt, more than anything else, grateful.

Before this year, Matt and I spent almost every evening together. The nights had become so routine that when we went to bed I'd realize we'd hardly had a substantial conversation all evening.

Things are different now. On friend-dates, the dish most often served is girl-talk. We discuss issues big and small, from hunting down the right dress for a black-tie wedding to where we see our careers in the next five years. I need an hour of this talk daily like I need seven servings of vegetables. I can survive without it, but I'm at my best when I've filled the quota. And when I go a long time with none at all, my health eventually starts to suffer. Back pre-search, when Matt and I spent the majority of our nonworking hours together, I tried to unload my girl-talk on him. It was like trying to get my vegetable servings from a french fry. When Matt didn't respond with the long, thoughtful, "I hear you" that I'd expect from a girl-friend, we'd suddenly find ourselves in an argument.

"You're not listening to me," I'd say.

"I heard every word," he'd respond.

"Well then say something!"

"What do you want me to say?"

"I want you to say what you think."

"I did already!"

"You did? Explain it again. . . ."

"I can't keep repeating myself."

Then the nail in the coffin. "You're my husband. You're supposed to care enough to talk with me about this as much as I want."

"You're impossible."

"You're mean!"

Good times.

But now I'm doing the analyzing and reanalyzing with other women. I don't need that from Matt anymore. In *Vital Friends,* Tom Rath warns against committing what he calls "the rounding error" in relationships—expecting one person to satisfy every need. I used to think a husband should be my sounding board for every aspect of my life. Now I realize it's not that *he* needs to be my sounding board, it's that someone does, and, until recently, Matt was the only one nearby.

FRIEND-DATES 16 AND 17. Ellen and Lacey. Two more essay readers. Ellen, a consultant, has a number of surface friends but says she struggles to take it to the next level since she travels so much for work. Lacey moved to Chicago from Kansas City for work *and* love but says her girlfriend has her own set of friends, so she's trying to make some, too. (She tells me she's a lesbian mid-sentence: "My girlfriend—it's a girlfriend that I have, not a boyfriend—she's from the South Side." In our email exchanges she exclusively used the term "my better half." I can't help but wonder why. If I were some nasty homophobe, wouldn't she rather I know early and bail on dinner than have to deal with me all night?)

They're great. In both cases we have an easy, friendly dinner (Ellen and I meet at Market, one of my usual spots; Lacey and

I go to a sports bar halfway between our apartments) and afterward I offer rides home, which makes me realize that a) I must
be getting more comfortable—there was a time I'd worry I
was coming on too strong—and b) they might think this is all a
ploy to drive them to a torture den in an undisclosed location.
But they accept, and I'm careful not to lock the doors as soon
as they get in the car. Like I said, I've seen that episode of *SVU*.

■ ■ ■

My least favorite part about living in the Midwest is that we
have to fly pretty much everywhere. Unless we're going to
Michigan or Wisconsin, which we never are, taking the train
is not an option. O'Hare is like a second home, and anyone who's seen Matt take a nap on the floor in the middle
of the gate—yes, he's that guy—can see how comfortable we
are there. Usually, while we wait for our flight, Matt does his
sleeping on the floor thing while I read, and nobody bothers,
er, talks to, us. But this weekend Matt and I are visiting his
brother, sister-in-law, and 10-month-old nephew, and something's different. Instead of flipping through *Us Weekly* with
the same do-not-disturb intensity that the Hasidic Jew next to
me is dedicating to his bible, I'm looking around the gate for
a new potential friend. Flights are the perfect friend pick-up
spot. You and Potential BFF are together long enough that
if you start chatting early, you can be old pals by the time
you deplane. There's a good chance you're from the same city.
And there's something poetic about the fact that you're on
the same journey, literally. (For anyone who ever finds herself on a plane next to me: Don't worry. If you put on your
headphones, bury your nose in a book, or make any naplike
gestures, I will leave you be.)

While I'm sitting there, gazing around at my fellow passengers, two—yes, two!—people start chatting with me. Unsolicited. Maybe I'm projecting, but I really think more strangers are talking to me than ever before. It's not just the airport folk. The other day a woman at the salon struck up a conversation about the vacation she was taking with her daughter. Then someone on the street stopped me to ask about my boots. With these airport women, I can see Matt smirking over on the suitcase bed he has fashioned himself, but I couldn't care less. Something big is happening. There's a new warmth in my demeanor that's signaling to people: Talk to me! I'm nice and open to meeting new friends!

My outsides are starting to match my insides.

FRIEND-DATE 18. I've been going on so many of these outings, I'm starting to notice every one of my dates' little quirks—a tendency to touch my arm, a fidgety hair flip. Amanda, another essay responder, curses. A lot. I don't mind it really, but I notice. An aspiring musical theater actress, she tells every story with the requisite animation and a side of jazz hands. She also tells me a very strange story regarding John Ritter's testicles. As in, "I remember watching *Three's Company* after school every day and he wore those tight shorts and I couldn't stop staring at John Ritter's balls. And I would think, those are John Ritter's balls." I'm not sure if those three words have ever been uttered in the same sentence, let alone repeatedly. It's a strange story to lead with. "That's when I really started noticing boys." Weird, yes, but a decent ice breaker.

The most important lesson of the evening came earlier in the night, though, when, while making small talk, I said, "So, you just moved to Chicago?"

"No, I've lived here five years." Oops. The potential friends

and their emails are starting to run together. I need to pay better attention to the dossiers.

Despite my inability to retain the simple facts she shared in her
introduction, Amanda sends me a Facebook request the next
day. I accept. Social media friending is step one on the path to
real-life friending. On her page, I notice she has a blog. Like
any good Facebook stalker, I check it out. The first sentence?
"I haven't really written much about this, but I am going on
a Blind Friend Date tonight." Oh my god, this post is about
me! I can't believe it. If I needed any proof that making friends
might be different in the digital age, here it is.

I shouldn't be so surprised. After all, I have a blog. There are
seven to ten million active blogs on the Internet at any given
time, so I'm bound to meet other women who are publishing their every thought on the World Wide Web. Still, when
you spend your time observing other people, it's a surprise
when you suddenly realize someone out there is watching *you*.
Amanda wrote about being nervous for our meeting, her con-
cerns that it would feel like an audition, and the necessity of
going after what you want. After getting over my initial shock,
I did what any self-respecting blogger-slash-friend-dater would
do. I blogged about her blog. And when she posted her reaction to our date—"Our time was fun, easy and interesting.
Nothing like a job interview, or even like a real blind date,
where there might be awkward lulls or uncomfortable staring
contests across the table"—I posted about that, too. Suddenly
I was blogging about her blog about the unnecessary nerves of
her first blog. It was all very meta.

Reading Amanda's blog and Facebook page, I feel like something of a voyeur. Suddenly I know that she loves Susan Boyle

and *A Wrinkle in Time* and has a job interview next Friday, even though she didn't share any of that when we met. It makes me wonder if social media actually makes it easier or harder to get to know a new friend. I see how it might be easier in the sense that you can gather tidbits about her life before you even meet. You might know her favorite TV show, have seen pictures of her wedding or baby. If she's a frequent status updater you may even know what she did last summer. Or last night. It's like you can fast-forward through the could-we-be-friends stage and arrive immediately at the meat of the friendship-building.

But isn't that discovery process what friendship building is all about? Sharing those bits of trivia—I know every word to "Stayin' Alive," she can recite Shel Silverstein's "Whatif"— isn't just a means to an end. Getting to know everything about a potential BFF might be more vital to the friendship than actually knowing everything is.

What if I see that a potential best friend's favorite shows are *Planet Earth* and "everything on the History Channel"? Will I (subconsciously or not) try to appear the type of person I imagine she'd like? I could tell her, honestly, that I own the *Planet Earth* DVDs. But I might leave out the part about how I got them for free at my last job and have only watched bits and pieces. I could memorize talking points about the History Channel miniseries *America: The Story of Us,* and tell her that while I thought its intentions were noble, "some measurable amount of conceptual sophistication would have been welcome, and a good deal less huffery, puffery, and gimmickry." She probably wouldn't know I was quoting *The Washington Post*.

It's a slippery slope, knowing too much too soon.

And now that I've gathered so much intel about Amanda, I'm worried I might let something slip the next time we see each other. Because while we all Facebook-stalk, protocol is to not admit it. I might know, from status updates, that a potential friend swims laps every morning, but it'd be creepy to say "Don't worry about eating that doughnut, you deserve it after all those calories you burn!" Instead, I check out her profile and she reviews mine, but then we meet and pretend to know nothing. And I'm no actor, so it would be a lot easier if I actually knew nothing.

This Wednesday marks my 28th birthday. Cinco de Mayo. A few of my new pals have noticed the occasion on Facebook and asked what I'm doing to celebrate. I've decided to lie low. We'll go to dinner with my mom—it's her birthday, too, I was born on her 30th—and my brother and his girlfriend, but that's about it. I was torn at first because I know all these new people suddenly. I could invite them out for dinner or a night of drinking, but we're still teetering on the edge of real friendship. I'm not ready to ask them to give up a Friday night for me yet. Next year. For now, I'd rather have a small celebration with my family and continue to focus on building the friendships. Anyway, 28 is not a very exciting age.

Though I may not have a lot of friends in Chicago yet, I do have a lot of family here. Matt and I spend a good chunk of our time with my cousin Ben and his wife, Amy, and this Sunday we head over to their place to have brunch, gossip (me and Amy), and watch golf (Matt and Ben). On the drive home my phone rings. I'm surprised to see Hilary's name pop up on the caller ID. Until now we've been exclusively email and Facebook message communicators, so it's exciting to see we've graduated to phone calls. My natural reflex is to hit ignore—I feel rude taking calls when I'm with other people—but this is a special circumstance. "Hi!"

"Hey, what's up?" Hilary is nonchalant, as if we talk on the phone all the time.

"Not much, just driving home with Matt. We were at my cousin's."

"Oh nice. Do you want to do something? My friends want me to meet them at a sports bar but I'm not in the mood and I need to get out of my house. I want to go somewhere fun. Like roller-skating."

This is what I've been waiting for! That "what are you up to, let's go on a playdate" friend. And though scheduling brunch with Hilary was next to impossible, maybe she works better last minute. My plan had been to go home and catch up on *Desperate Housewives,* but this sounds far better. Plus, when I met with University of Chicago professor John Cacioppo at the beginning of this search, he specifically said I should try to go on adventures with my new friends. Expanding outside your comfort zone is where you bond and make memories, he told me. Roller-skating would definitely qualify.

"Sure. I've got nothing going on," I tell her. "Though I don't know where one goes roller-skating in Chicago."

"Me neither. I'll look it up. Or maybe we could go bowling. Or to the batting cages."

"I'm up for whatever. I love a good adventure. I just need to drop off Matt, then I'll pick you up and we can decide?"

I arrive at her door thirty minutes later. "I've decided we should get our fortunes told," Hilary tells me as she enters the car. "There's a place on North Avenue in Old Town."

"Really? Okay." Roller-skating would've been more up my alley. I've never been to a fortune-teller. They sort of creep me out. But it will certainly be an adventure. There will be a story to tell. A memory. Hilary and I will always be able to say, "Remember when we went to that fortune-teller?"

When we arrive at a building distinguished only by a small sign that says FORTUNES out front, we ring the bell and are told to go to the second floor. I'm picturing some patchouli-smelling darkness with plenty of hanging beads and crystal balls, but when we let ourselves in, we're in a really nice apartment. It seems we've crashed some family's lazy Sunday. There's a baby that may or may not be a sumo wrestler in a crib watching Nick Jr. There's a guy in a bedroom at the end of the hall who opens the door and, while talking on the phone, directs us to sit on the couch near the sumo baby. He never reemerges. There's a woman who speaks little to no English and might be the little one's nanny, or mother, getting ready to feed her. Hilary and I exchange looks of combined confusion, horror, and amusement, and take our place on the couch. We're trying to carry on a normal conversation and not let our tones communicate what our eyes are so clearly shouting: *Where the hell are we?* For five minutes, we sit on the couch forcing small talk as we take in our surroundings. No one, save for the guy on the phone, has so much as acknowledged that we're here. If we left now, it would have been adventure enough.

While we're discussing Hilary's latest beau, the nanny-or-mother hands me the phone. I look at the woman, then at Hilary, and we both burst out laughing.

"Hello?"

"Yeah, you want to have your fortune told?" asks a voice on the other end.

"Yes, please."

"Okay, I'm about twenty to thirty minutes away. What kind of reading do you want?" I've decided that I want a tarot card reading, if that's an offering. Those have always looked intriguing.

"What are the options?"

"You can ask me two questions that I will answer for ten dollars. Or I do palm readings, tarot cards, crystals . . ." The tarot cards, she says, are forty dollars.

"We'd like to do the tarot cards, but forty dollars seems like a lot," I say.

"I can do it for thirty dollars if youse both going to do it." I can't place her accent. It's as if she's trying to make it sound Middle Eastern, but the "youse" sounds more Bronx.

"Okay, we'll both do that then. You'll be back in a half hour?" I refrain from asking why she didn't see our arrival in her future.

"How about you come back at six?" It's 4:15.

"We don't have time to wait that long," I say. "How about five?"

She agrees, and Hilary and I kill time at the local Starbucks before returning to what might be the oddest place of business I've ever encountered. This time, the fortune-teller answers the door. She has on no headdress, she carries no crystal ball. Such a disappointment. She's about 5'4" with reddish hair and a cigarette stench that's triggering my gag reflex. "Which of youse wants to go first?"

Hilary volunteers, so I take a seat on the couch. The obese, but actually quite adorable, baby is still in her crib, still watching Nickelodeon. I take a book out of my purse, grateful that I make it a rule never to travel without reading material. I discover the fortune that recently came with Matt's Chinese food stuck in between two pages. When I was little, I thought that maybe my life was a movie—I'd tuck my shirt into my Charlie Brown–themed boxer shorts so I looked okay even in my sleep, wondering if the kids at school were watching me when I'd write in my diary late at night. I grew out of that, but there are still times when my life feels scripted. This is one of those moments. I look around for the cameras, as if I'm on *The Truman Show* and someone has orchestrated this craziness. But there are no cameras, only the fortune. "You will soon find a kindred spirit for lasting friendship." Matt ate the fortune cookie, of course, but saved the inside for me—"You need it more than I do" was the message—but I'd forgotten it was in my book until just now. It's a fortune kind of day.

After about twenty minutes, Hilary comes out and I'm led into the fortune-reading "room," which is actually just the washer-dryer closet.

"Do you want me to tell you whatever I see, whether it is good or bad?"

"Yes, please." My voice is shaky in the same way it gets when I'm in job interviews. I have no idea why I'm nervous.

She tells me to think of two wishes. I should tell her one of them and keep the other to myself.

"Okay, tell me your wish."

"Um, I'd like to have two healthy children."

I tell her the healthy kids line because I figured it's generic, and I don't want to give away too much. This is a test. She's going to need to prove her psychic abilities with as little help from me as possible. The other wish was to succeed in my friend-quest, but she doesn't need to know about that. Unless she sees it, of course.

After the first round of cards, she begins her assessment. "I see long and healthy life for you. You have good, kind heart. Good person." Yeah, yeah. Get to the good stuff.

"But, I see . . . When did you have your loss of relationship?"

"Like, any relationship?" Damn, that was a giveaway.

"Yes."

"Well, my dad died close to four years ago." Rationally, I know that everyone's had some loss of relationship in her life, but still, it seems kind of freaky.

"Yes, I see inner turmoil for you. Something you have not made peace with yet. But you will this year. You must. You must let the past go."

She flips the next round of cards.

"I see three children."

"Three?"

"Yes. And I see a financial investment in the next, oh, five to seven years. This will be a good year for you, though. You will make peace with the demons inside you that are keeping you from being totally happy. You need to work on your self-confidence, because it is your inner demons, not any outer ones, that are keeping you from having success even sooner." What are my inner demons? Insecurity? BFFlessness? As much as I want to call BS on everything she's saying, I do need to work on my self-confidence. Fear of appearing needy and annoying is the single biggest obstacle I face in this year of friending. I wonder about the internal monsters that are keeping me from total happiness. She very well might use that line on all her clients, but could she be onto something? The inner demons keeping me from pure happiness are probably loneliness. Is this some sort of "become best friends with yourself and best friends will appear" law of attraction nonsense? I'm not so much into the New Age movement, but it's something to think about.

"Your inner demons can be worked out," she says. "Also, I

see that you could really benefit from my three-pronged read-ing next time—palm, tarot, and crystals. It is sixty-five dol-lars." Sure it is.

Hilary and I did some real bonding at the fortune-teller's, but she's not the only one who's extended an invitation recently. Jen hosted Alison and me for a TV night. Hannah asked me to dinner. Ellen followed up and we got pizza a week after we met. Margot and I ate sushi. Lacey sent me an Evite to her girlfriend's house-warming party. I feel like reciprocity is finally kicking in and my boatload of acquaintances are turning into friends. It's only May, and I'm on track to becoming the most popular girl in the Midwest.

FRIEND-DATE 19. Last month, a cousin sent me an article from the Jewish United Fund newspaper. The story was called "A Different Kind of Exodus," about the writer's best friend who had recently moved. The author, Pam, said she wished she could "recruit for a new best friend in town." Sounds familiar.

I'd been so encouraged by the response to my own essay that I decided to send this Pam a note. "I really liked your article and have been going through the same thing myself. I was wondering if you might want to grab a drink sometime?"

Pam replied, asking if she could publish my email in the let-ters to the editor. No response to the request for plans.

I tried again. "I was serious about grabbing a drink . . . I couldn't fill Jessica's size eleven shoe, but I love Cubs games and *This Is It*." The baseball team and Michael Jackson documentary were both on the short list of Pam's best friend requirements.

This time, she responded to the matter at hand. "I have a tough time getting asked out by guys but I'm happy that at least a girl asked me out. ☺

We're meeting at Orange, a brunch spot popular for its frushi—fruit sushi. Or, really, fruit wrapped in sweet rice. I think it's kind of gross but most Chicagoans love it. I'm interested in seeing if Pam and I hit it off. Her article also called for someone who will join her at Friday Night Shabbat services, which is to say, not me.

I've always classified myself as culturally Jewish. Gathering the family for the Passover Seder is important to me, though actually attending temple—even for the high holidays—is not. I had a bat mitzvah and got married under a chuppah. I went to a private high school in New York City and summer camp in Maine, both Meccas for teenage Jews. My sorority was considered "the Jewish one" though we had no actual religious affiliation. I grew up surrounded by Jews, so, until this year, they're who I flocked to. I didn't seek them out, but we usually bonded over a common upbringing.

That said, I don't think I could be less religious. I'd argue that Matt, my atheist husband, is more religious than I—at least he's interested in it. He reads about religion and ponders over it. He meets with religious leaders and thinkers to debate about God. But not me. I treat my Judaism like the pile of clothes in the back of my closet that needs to be hand-washed. I know it's there, but I don't deal with it. I'd rather just push it aside and forget for a while. I pull it out at Passover when the family comes in town for Seder, or when I'm invited to a Yom Kippur break fast (I don't actually do the fasting part, or even go to temple, so for me it's more about bringing wine and getting kugel and bagels for dinner). I imagine when it's time to have kids Matt and I will have to sit down and have a conversation about bar mitzvahs and temple, but we've got some time.

No matter how little my interest in religion, however, I

can't ignore it as it relates to my current quest. One of the most popular suggestions I hear from people when I mention my best friend search is to join a religious group. A friend of my mother-in-law told me she made all her closest friends when she first moved to Boston by joining a temple. My co-worker Ashley said her Chicago BFFs are the ones she met in Bible study after college graduation. Commenters on my online essay said women's church groups were their go-to meeting spot.

Harvard psychiatrist George Vaillant once gave a speech in which he discussed the duration of different organizations. "Today, the average lifespan of a Fortune 500 company is forty years," he said. "There are very few dynasties, and actually very few nations, that are more than three hundred years old. All of the world's greatest religions share two things in common: They've all endured for at least fourteen hundred years and, unlike dynasties and corporations, they're all based on love and compassion." Of course, this is only one way to look at religion. Because while, yes, it has been the most enduring uniter in human history, some would argue it's also been the greatest divider.

While religion isn't going anywhere, there are an increasing number of young people who, like me, aren't so into it. A 2007 survey of Protestants aged 18–30 found that 25 percent of them had dropped out of the church entirely. Another survey found that respondents cite places like bars and Starbucks as better meeting places than church. I'm confident that I'd get to know people if I joined a women's or young adult group at a nearby temple, but I feel like it would be under false pretenses. I'd be implying that I have certain values that I don't, which feels a bit sneaky.

I figure I can feel it out at lunch. Pam's the managing editor of the *JUF News,* so she's probably pretty knowledgeable about the local community.

When I arrive, Pam is already seated. She has wavy, shoulder-length reddish-brown hair, silver dangly earrings, and is flipping through a self-help book.

"I'm on a self-improvement kick," she says immediately, as if to make excuses for the reading material.

After talk about work and Northwestern (she graduated four years ahead of me), Pam mentions that if I'm really eager to meet new people, the JUF has lots of social events for young Jews in the city.

"There's a program called LEADS, where groups in different neighborhoods get together once a week to discuss Jewish issues. Then you all meet at a bar afterward for happy hour."

"I'm not really that religious, though. Do you think that would be weird? I wouldn't have much to discuss in the way of Jewishness."

"Oh, that's fine. Most people are there for the happy hour," she says. I'm still a bit skeptical—there are plenty of happy hours they could attend without having to do the discussion group first, or pay the sixty dollars, but I'll probably try it out. If one of the ultimate goals of religion is to bring people together, and my whole year is dedicated to connecting, I have to at least give it a whirl. LEADS doesn't start until October, so I have some time to get used to the idea.

Pam's a real sweetheart. She's a nurturer, I can tell, and is extremely interested in suggesting the perfect place for me to meet my new best friend, if not so interested in becoming the BFF herself. I think her essay was more an ode to Jessica than it was actually an attempt to find her replacement.

■ ■ ■

As my dates continue to rack up, it's getting increasingly difficult to plan follow-ups less than two weeks out. At the end of our dinner a few weeks ago, Lacey and I sat with our calendars trying to figure out a night for our two couples to try the new pasta place in my neighborhood. We came up empty. It wasn't just my schedule that was difficult—her girlfriend works for the Cubs and has to attend all of the night games—but it was a good reminder that it's going to be hard to turn these women into my best friends if they think I'm as hard to make plans with as I thought Hilary was. Part of the problem is that I'm doing all the follow-ups one-on-one. It's time to make this more efficient. Why not invite a few new friends over for a dinner party? Or take some ladies out for girls' night drinks? The women who responded to my essay are all looking to meet people, so they'd probably be interested. And I've definitely had moments on these dates where I've envisioned friend set-ups. *I bet Kaitlin would really like Amanda. Lacey and Ellen would be a great fit.* I could be the connector, rather than the connectee.

The tables are turning.

CHAPTER 7

I'm up against the first test of my search's success. It's Friday night and Matt is in Boston for the weekend helping his mother move. When all this started, I said I was looking for a friend to call on a weekend when I'm alone and want a partner in crime. Well, it's the weekend, I'm alone, and I surely need a Thelma to my Louise. I scroll through my mental rolodex of new friends. Hilary. Hannah. Alison. Margot. Kim. Jillian. I get out my phone and dial.

"Hello?"

"Hi. Can I come over tonight? I need someone to hang out with, Matt's away."

My mother is thrilled. She loves nothing more than to eat dinner and watch TV with me. "I have *Survivor* and *Private Practice* on the DVR," she assures me.

"Awesome. Nothing like raging on a Friday night with mom." I'm feeling sorry for myself—wallowing in the self-pity of someone who's been on nearly twenty girl-dates with apparently nothing to show for it—but my mother doesn't offend easily.

"Why don't you call one of your new friends? See what they're doing?"

"I just don't think I'm there yet with any of them."

"Hilary?"

"She's out of town."

"Hannah?"

"She has so many friends, I'm sure she has plans. We don't do last-minute calls. And I have lunch plans with Jillian tomorrow, so it would be a bit aggressive to call her tonight, too. I've got a million supposed new friends, and still no one to call." Then it hits me. "I don't even have their numbers!"

It's almost entirely true. Hilary's number is in my phone, and I could probably track down Hannah's because she has texted me about book club a few times (I keep forgetting to store her number, so instead I just remember that it's the only unidentified Boston area code that sends me texts), but that's it. The communication with my other dates thus far has been by email—we write to set up a dinner, and then again to say "I had a great time" and "we should do it again" and "when are you free?" We haven't even graduated to texting, so even if I wanted to call them tonight, I couldn't.

My mom is shocked. "You don't have their numbers?"

"Our relationships are email and Facebook only, so far." This is largely my fault, of course. If I were bolder I'd track down someone's number—Ellen maybe, or Jen—and text "Hey, what are you up to?" But I'm still cautious about asking for too much too soon.

One of my earliest memories of friendship with Callie is when she approached me in our ninth-grade hallway, a month or two into freshman year, and said "I'm going to call you tonight." And she did. We talked about who-knows-what for hours, and thus began a lifetime of phone calls. If only one of my new friends had made such a pronouncement.

Even if we were still teenyboppers, that interaction would never happen today. Evenings spent spiraling the phone cord around your wrist while gossiping for hours are so twentieth century. Now communication is in snippets. One hundred forty characters of Tweetiness or abbreviated words via text. My old-school phone call with Callie would today be a text message: "Did u c what Caroline wuz wearing? OMG. Heinous." According to one study, the majority of teens are more likely to use their cellphones to text than talk, and while 54 percent of teenagers say they text their friends at least once a day, only 33 percent talk to their friends in person that often.

The research may be about teenagers—and I'm a good decade older than the 12–17 range that entails—but the ways of the future usually start with the kiddies and trickle up to the rest of us. The text-only lifestyle has certainly found its way into adult friendships. These days, I only talk on the phone with my out-of-town friends. When the Chicagoans whose numbers I do have pop up on my ringing phone, I immediately wonder what's wrong.

John Cacioppo told me face-to-face is better than phone, phone is better than email, email is better than Facebook, and so on. It's unfortunate that phone calls are a thing of the past, but it's reality. No matter how close I get with any of my new friends, I think the "what are you doing tonight?" will always start with a text message. Phone calls feel like impositions of the neighborly pop-in variety. I picture my potential friends making dinner or working or watching TV, and I don't want to be the name on the caller ID that prompts a "why is *she* calling me?"

This might be a fundamental flaw in my search. I'm looking for an old-school friendship in a modern technology world. How am I supposed to find a call-on-a-Friday-night pal when I'm hesitant to call anyone, period? Maybe I need to revise my wish list to text-at-the-last-minute friend. Those phone calls with Callie elevated us to BFF status pretty quickly, and texts probably won't foster that same sense of closeness, but they're still something. Sure, a phone call comes with give and take, voice and intonation, an opportunity for understanding and empathy, but a good "saw a cute dress in the window of Banana—it's so you!" text will go a long way. If nothing else, it says, "I'm thinking of you." Always a nice thing to hear. But first things first, need to get me some digits.

The next morning I drive the twenty minutes to meet Jillian near her Andersonville apartment for brunch and a pedicure (a date set up by email, of course). First order of business: We exchange phone numbers. And then, over matching fontina quiches . . .

"Okay, so I have two presents for you."

"Presents? For me?" I probably sound like one of her twins, but I'm in shock. I love presents! (At 28 years old I'd still search the apartment in the weeks leading up to my birthday if Matt didn't know better and stash all gifts in his office.) I want to throw my arms around her and tell her I love her and that we should be bestest friends forever and ever. And I don't even know what the gift is.

"Well, I was in my favorite used-book store, and I saw this and remembered you said you loved *Little Women,* so I had to get it for you." She pulls out what looks like a wall calendar, but is actually a book of antique-looking watercolor paper dolls of the March family. Upon inspection, I see that the collection is from 1981, part of a series that includes "Dolls of the '30s" and "The Antique Dolls Go to a Paper Doll Wedding." It's perfect. The book is the type of gift that usually comes from the closest of friends—someone who knows that while you have no real use for paper dolls and no place to keep them, they'll make you smile. And they buy it for you, just because. Needless to say, I'm girl-crushing something fierce.

There are very few times in my life that I've not known what to say—or haven't just said the wrong thing anyway—but I'm stumped. All the professions of gratitude that come to mind would probably seem creepy and overly adoring for a friend I'm meeting for only the second time.

"Thank you," I say. "This is amazing."

"I couldn't *not* get it for you. When we saw it I told Paul, I've got to buy this for my new friend."

She called me her new friend! She told Paul about me! Matt's mom tells the story of the day he met his best friend of twenty-four years. Five-year-old Matt arrived home from day camp and proudly declared, "I made a new friend. His name is Noah Benjamin." And that was that.

Jillian could be my Noah Benjamin.

"The second gift is really just a loan," she says. "I ordered this on Amazon.uk." She hands me the third in Stieg Larsson's *Millennium* trilogy, which isn't due out in the United States for a few weeks. I hug it tight.

"I promise to take good care of it," I tell her. "Is it great?"

"Yeah, I couldn't put it down." There's something about how well we can relate to each other's nerdy love affair with books that just makes us work.

When we first met, I thought the similarities between Jillian and me were a sign we were meant to be. But I've been reading up on social connections, and apparently it's more science than fate at work here. There's more to my immediate connection with Jillian than just our shared passion for reading. Brothers and coauthors Ori and Rom Brafman, who examine the science behind these magic moments in their book *Click: The Magic of Instant Connections,* name similarity as one of the five "click accelerators" (the others are proximity, vulnerability, resonance, and a safe place). No matter how trivial and out of our control the likenesses may be—like the simple fact that Jillian and I both have brothers named Alex and fathers named William—they lead to greater likability. That's why I always remember the girl in grade school who shared my birthday, or why Matt might easily warm up to a fellow Red Sox fan. I put stock into random coincidences, but it turns out I'm just favoring what's called the "in-group." Jillian and I are both from the East Coast, lived in New York City after college, have family members with the same names, and adore reading and TV-watching above all other activities. Plus she has twins and I want twins. Take these similarities, and couple them with gifts? This is serious.

(Of course, my new friend Margot—the home-schooled bridal consultant with seven siblings—is pretty much my opposite when it comes to our backgrounds and I adore her, too, so there is also some validity to "opposites attract." But when it comes to those I'm immediately drawn to? Let's just say if I met a curly-haired Diet Coke–toting *Friends*-quoting bibliophile who had an inappropriate and inexplicable crush on Jeff Probst, I'd whisk her away on a girl-date before she knew what hit her.)

As if lavishing me with presents isn't enough, Jillian seems to put the same emphasis on friendship that I do, which is endearing her to me even more. She's got two kids, a full-time job *in Indiana,* and yet she still makes time to have brunch or dinner with me.

"I need adult conversation and some time to myself. Otherwise I'd go crazy," Jillian says. "But next time you need to meet the boys." Yes, please.

One quiche, three sodas, and ten purple-painted toenails later, I head to my car with book and paper dolls in hand, a new number in my phone, and the pitter-patter of friend-love in my heart.

FRIEND-DATE 20. When I arrive at Gibsons, a classic Chicago steakhouse, I elbow my way to the bar. Though Wendy and I didn't specify if this would be dinner or just drinks—so many of the setup emails begin with "I'd love to grab a bite or glass of wine sometime" and end with only "Great! Let's do Wednesday at 7"—this restaurant is expensive enough that I assume we can't be eating. I drop my gym bag on a barstool and head to the restroom before settling in to wait for my latest potential BFF. On the way back I notice a girl sitting alone, napkin in her lap, with what looks like a chocolate martini. Her back is to me so I can't see her face. Not that a visual would be that helpful. Wendy and I have only spoken online, and her description of herself as "a brunette on the short side" covers about 90 percent of the girls I know, myself included. Dinner here would be a pretty fancy date, but I figure I better ask. "Are you Wendy?"

"Hello."

It's a normal greeting, but something about the way she says it—sort of like Meryl Streep in *The Devil Wears Prada*—gives me the creeps.

I guess we're eating dinner after all. I grab my stuff from the bar and take the seat across from my new date. Facing Wendy, I can immediately see we're plenty different. I'm as casual and sporty as she is prim and proper.

"So, were you nervous about tonight?" she asks matter-of-factly, and I can't tell from her tone if this means she was anxious herself.

"No, not at all." It's true. I've become totally at ease with these friend-dates. In the early days, my response would have been different. There was a nervous excitement when I first met Hannah—Should we hug? What'll we talk about? Will she want to be my best friend forever?—but almost six months in, dates are just part of the routine. I know, look at me all blasé. *Me? Nervous? Never! I could friend-date you under the table.* I take a note for my mental growth chart: Nerves have left the building.

Wendy, who found me via LinkedIn.com after reading my online plea, tells me she reads my blog.

"I really like it. You are funny."

"Oh, thanks so much. I try," I say. "So you moved here from New York, too?"

"Yes, but let us talk more about you. I want to know: How did you become a writer?"

"How? Oh, well I went to school for it, and then got a job at a magazine out of college. I don't know, really. I've just always loved writing so when I moved out here I pitched stories and started freelancing. I had to stop for a while when I got my full-time job, so I'm happy to be blogging. It helps me maintain some creativity. What do you do?"

"I work in accounting. But back to you, tell me about your time in New York."

The conversation is teetering on the edge of uncomfortable. At least for me. Wendy is not particularly interested in telling me about herself. You never realize just how important the give and take of a conversation is until it's missing. This feels more like an interview than a friend-date. And there's something really distracting about her speech pattern.

"I loved New York. I obviously miss all my friends there, but my husband was in Philly and we wanted to be together after dating long distance for three years. You moved here to be with your fiancé, right? Tell me about you . . ."

Ever heard a painfully forced conversation? Welcome.

"I am just not that interesting. I am always fascinated by people who follow their dreams like you have. I was raised to go the safe money-making route, so I think you are really interesting. You are very funny." Yes. Thank you. You said that already. "I am so pleased for you."

Oh, wow. She doesn't use contractions. That's the mystery speech tic. Talking with someone who never utters a contraction—no "let's" or "can't" or "didn't"—is surprisingly jarring.

After a bit of prying, I get Wendy to tell me about herself. She's engaged and has lived in Chicago for four years. She's in a book club but usually doesn't like the books. Most recently, she couldn't finish *Let the Great World Spin,* which I'm in the middle of and loving.

"Cheating makes me uncomfortable," she says.

"Is there a lot of cheating in the book?"

"There are prostitutes." Hmmm. Okay then. She does, however, really enjoy the *Real Housewives* series. "Except fictional fighting makes me anxious." I don't even mention that the Housewives are, at least in theory, nonfiction. "So tell me more about you. I think you are so funny."

The third time it's creepy. Granted, I love being told I'm funny. It's a great compliment. But there's something about the way Wendy keeps repeating herself that makes me nervous. She's like a combination of a superfan and *The Cable Guy*.

I spend a large chunk of the evening praying for it to be over. Considering I've been doing this for over four months, and this is only my second truly bad date (the first being the two-on-one dinner with Heidi and Michelle), I've had a pretty good run. I finally understand that gouge-my-eyes-out bad-date pain my single friends regularly endure. It's the same anxiety I get during long and seemingly pointless office meetings. The . . . seconds . . . pass . . . so . . . slowly.

Eventually, our check comes. My half—for the single glass of wine and broiled salmon—is fifty dollars.

Financially, this search hasn't been easy. Pinot grigio and spicy tuna rolls don't come cheap. When the where-to-go suggestion falls to me, I usually throw out my go-to date spots, both of which are nice enough but not fancy, allow for sharing, and have cheap appetizer options that can take the place of an entrée. But I'd rather deflect the decision to my date. I try to be easygoing, and a simple "I'll eat anything, do you have a place you like?" helps establish me as a low-maintenance pal. It's a first impression I strive for in friendship. Don't want to be too difficult too early. Plus, I still feel like I'm in the discovery phase with this city, so I'm happy to explore new options. But deferring the decision-making comes with some risk. I may end up paying fifty dollars for salmon when I'd rather drop ten dollars for a shared hummus platter.

I wonder if romantic-daters have this problem. My friends on Match.com go in phases where they seem to date for a living. It's a multiple-times-a-week affair. But because they are women, the cost of first dates probably doesn't fall to them. In the friend-dating world, we're almost always splitting the bill. Which means I probably have it easier than some guys—the entire meal isn't on me—but fifty-two friend-dates over the course of the year adds up.

A quick email to my single guy-friends garners some thoughtful input. "Simply put, there is nothing else I would rather spend my money on than dating women while being single," one serial-dater tells me. "Every guy thinks about the cost of dating in a business context. It may sound crazy but it's all about the Return on Investment: What did I spend and what did I get out of it? It's not just about sexual ROI but also emotional ROI." The email reeks of the male brain, but he's got a point. Let's say my friend-dates cost, on average, twenty-five dollars. That means by the end of this year I'll have spent thirteen hundred dollars on friendship. Let's round up to twenty-five hundred dollars for all the follow-up dates, plus the classes and events (yoga, book club) I've tried, and those I still hope to take on, to help me meet people. That's a huge chunk of change. But if I come out of this year with a handful of new close friends, I'll be significantly happier and healthier. A number of studies have shown that having strong friendships is more likely to make a person happy than is having money. Is my health and happiness worth twenty-five hundred dollars? I'd say yes. It's cheaper than the costs that accompany the health risks of loneliness, that's for sure.

This whole year is an investment—of both cash and time—in my future. I recently read that having more friends when you're young translates to more money later on. Each high school student in a study (all of whom were male) was asked to name his three best friends from his senior class. Those people whose names were listed the most were considered the ones with the most friends. Per the study, "One additional friendship nomination in high school is associated with a 2 percent higher wage thirty-five years later." Granted I'm not in high school, but it'll have a similar effect eventually, right? *Right?*

I put my half of the hundred-dollar bill on my credit card, and Wendy and I head to the exit. There is no hug. Her formality doesn't lend itself to touchy-feeliness, so I follow her lead. She gives me her card, and I give my ticket to the parking valet. Another ten dollars down. Wendy and I part ways with no suggestions of "let's do this again" or "I'll call you." It's better this way. There's no concern of how to get out of a next date and it's clear she didn't have a great time, either. Knowing it was mutual makes me feel better. Sometimes you just don't have that spark.

"Do you have another friend-date on Friday?" Matt asks me when I get home from the date gone wrong. I've collapsed on the couch in front of his SportsCenter, exhausted from the mental energy required to keep a dying conversation alive for ninety minutes.

"Not as of now."

"Want to go on a husband date?"

"I'd love to!"

I may not be keen on reigniting the spark with Wendy, but the one with my husband? That one I'd like to afford some attention. Dating other women some six nights a week doesn't leave all that much time for romance. And we're still in our first year of wedded bliss. All those oh-so-hilarious jokes about marriage being the end of your sex life are great and all, but I'm not interested in becoming another punch line.

As men go, Matt's a romantic. He's never forgotten to get me flowers on Valentine's Day, and he even sometimes buys me jewelry *just because.* (I know! And no, you cannot have him.) But I'm the planner in the house, especially these days. That he is initiating a date night is all the romance I need. Well, almost all.

"I was thinking we could go to that new restaurant Gilt Bar." He's even thought of a restaurant. In advance.

Friends, shmends. I've got a hot date.

On Friday at 11 A.M., I get an email from Hilary. "You want to grab dinner tonight? I know it's last minute—I actually have a friend's b-day party but do not want to go out at 10 P.M. I'm too old for this nonsense. Plus, I have so much to do tomorrow. Say yes!"

My initial reaction? Annoyance. My internal thought process goes something like this: "You can't just ask me at the last minute! People have lives, we need to plan!" As much as I'd love to see Hilary, Matt's already made our reservation. He'd probably be fine if I canceled in the name of friendship—I have a one-year-only pass—but I'm looking forward to this dinner probably more than he is. Why can't she ever make plans in advance?

And then suddenly I feel like one of those cartoon characters, getting bonked in the face at the same time the light-bulb appears over my head. Isn't this what I said I wanted? I launched a search for a BFF with the definition of "someone I can call for a pedicure in thirty minutes." So why, when a new friend emails me for last-minute plans, is my first reaction one of frustration?

Probably because, if I'm really being honest with myself, I'm not an especially spontaneous person. I was once. Maybe in fourth grade. Back when I had no responsibilities or commitments and could call Katie, the BFF of the day, and say, "I have nothing to do. Want to go to the mall?" But now there's always something to do. Work. Exercise. Matt.

An inherent problem in this search might be that I'm looking for the types of friendships I made when I was a kid, but I'm 28. Childhood friendships aren't available to me now. Bummer, perhaps, but true, and no amount of "Can Lucy come out and play?" is going to change that.

I like having plans. I like keeping them. Even if said plan is to spend an uninterrupted hour watching *Friday Night Lights*. If I pass the day excited about solo time on the couch with a glass of wine, pad thai, and Tim Riggins, it's hard to shift gears and muster up enthusiasm for an invitation when it comes my way. That's changing of course. If I want my new friends to continue inviting me out, I need to say yes as often as I can, enthusiasm or not. If Matt and I weren't having date night I'd surely accept Hilary's invitation. But spontaneity isn't my natural state, and friendship goes two ways. I can't require a BFF to always be available in thirty minutes, and then get miffed if she reaches out in the morning for dinner seven hours later. And I can't strive for a spontaneous friendship when impulsiveness isn't really my thing.

The reality is that I don't need someone who's perpetually available for a spur-of-the-moment road trip—does that person even exist?—just someone I feel comfortable inviting if I decide to embark on such a journey. It's like I said about Jillian. With two kids and a full-time job she probably can't be a last-minute friend—she may even cancel more than others—but if I'm okay to call and invite myself over, then I'll have reached a pretty good place.

I write Hilary a simple "I'd love to, but Matt and I have dinner reservations. We need to get together soon! Rain check?"

in response to her message. We've scheduled a walk for tomorrow, but the email exchange has me rethinking my definition of BFF. Maybe it's not necessarily someone I call for brunch on Sunday morning. That's only one type of friend. Hilary's obviously good for last-minute plans, and I'm at a place where I would call her for an afternoon movie, but that alone doesn't make her my best friend. I wouldn't yet go to her with my problems or ask her to dinner with my mom. If I had to find a wedding dress today, I wouldn't invite her along for the shopping trip.

Maybe it's more of a comfort-level thing. My new BFF will be someone I'm totally myself with. No need to be "on." No stress during lunch dates, wondering what to say next to keep the conversation flowing. The last-minute phone call is really just a manifestation of comfort, anyway. Does it feel natural to invite her to drinks in an hour? Am I at ease hanging at her house, watching TV in silence? Would I be okay crying to her if something went really wrong?

I distinctly recall hanging out at Sara's house as a kid, running around singing at the top of my lungs and dancing like a maniac, just being silly, and actually noting that her apartment was the only place other than home that I behaved like this. I once even told her as much. "I only act this goofy at your house!" Little did I know when I was 12 that I had discovered the secret of friendship. When I found myself behaving the same way with my closest high school friends years later, I knew they were keepers, too. Even the men in my life have been measured by this standard. Do I sing at the top of my lungs in his car? Must be love.

On the way home from Gilt Bar, Matt drives as I belt it with Lea Michele and Idina Menzel to the *Glee* rendition of "Poker Face." If he doesn't enjoy my vocal stylings, I'm too lost in song to notice. Earlier tonight, when I mentioned I turned down plans with Hilary to keep our date, Matt said I didn't need to, but we're both happy I did. Mushroom truffle pasta, Hawaiian snapper, and a few glasses of wine do a couple good.

"I love you," he says as he reaches for my hand.

"I love you, too." Whoever says you can't balance rich friendships and a hot marriage clearly hasn't tried.

■ ■ ■

Remember Kim? The girl I met at cooking class last year? The one who called the prospect of hanging out with me, a new friend, "refreshing"? I've been trying to schedule a follow-up since our very successful—or so I thought—first date, but have been struggling to get something on the books. She says she's swamped with work, so it's been two months since we've seen each other. Not the best start for our BFFship. Or maybe no one told her we're supposed to be best friends?

For our second date I suggested Kim and I try out another cooking class. Apparently we weren't the only Chicagoans with this idea, because I've now been wait-listed twice. *Top Chef* has really done wonders for culinary education.

Since the nearby cooking school's Wine & Dine Girls' Night didn't pan out, Kim has invited me to a friend's birthday party. I feel a little uncomfortable crashing a celebratory dinner for someone I don't know, but Kim insists it's fine so here I am, standing on the sidewalk in front of De Cero, a Mexican restaurant, waiting for my girl-date. When she arrives and escorts me to our table, I see that this isn't a party in the invite-everyone-you-know-please-split-the-check-twenty-ways sense. There are only five of us. I've infiltrated a *Sex and the City*–style girls' night.

The first thing I notice: I'm the only white girl. It's a first for me. Kim, Laura, and Alicia, the birthday girl, are African American. Shilpa is Indian. It's anecdotal proof of research I read when I started this search, which found that minorities are more open to friends outside their race than white people are. I don't like it, but the truth is I infrequently end up at dinners with more than two races represented. Which is just embarrassing. Needless to say I'm pleased, as I'm hoping this dinner will be an opportunity to change that.

The second thing I notice: Laura doesn't want me here. "So, how did you get here again?"

"Oh, Kim and I had tentative plans to take a cooking class tonight, but we were wait-listed so she invited me here instead."

"Huh."

The frosty breeze coming from her direction makes clear she doesn't understand why a new girl is at her friend's birthday dinner. I can't say I totally blame her. I'd probably find it odd, too. You know, if the stranger wasn't me.

But Alicia, the birthday girl, seems perfectly pleased to have me. She and Shilpa are hilarious and the evening is full, mostly, of sex talk. There's much discussion of a gentleman who wanted, as Shilpa so eloquently put it, to "do it in the rear." Kim tells us she's dating a white guy for the first time. There are a lot of margaritas, laughter, and toasts.

While the other ladies are discussing work matters, I ask Kim how she's been.

"Good. Busy," she says. "I've been going home to St. Louis a lot to see my father. He's ill so I try to get back there when I can." She mentioned when we first met that he was sick, but only in passing. At the time she didn't seem like she wanted to discuss it so I didn't pry.

"I'm sorry to hear he's not doing well."

"Thanks. He has a blood cancer, he was okay for a while but lately has been having a hard time."

"What kind of cancer is it?" I'm not sure if this qualifies as prying, but I have to ask.

"It's called multiple myeloma, it's a cancer of the blood cells, it—"

"That's what my dad had." I don't know where to go from here. I don't want to scare her with the news of my father's death, but I can't not tell her. And it's too strange a coincidence. Myeloma—a cancer of the plasma cells—has an incidence of only 4 in 100,000. Even if it's just a similarity, not a sign, it's a surprising one.

"Really? That's so weird," she says. "I've never even met anyone who knew what it was."

"I know, me neither really." I'm still unsure of what to say. Just because my father died doesn't mean hers will, and I don't want to be a downer. But it's going to come up—I can't pretend he survived, that would just be weird. I'm hoping that from my use of past tense—"what my dad *had*"—she'll get the picture.

"So what happened with your father?"

"Well, he died almost four years ago, but he lived with it for seven years." I emphasize the second half—the good news.

"That's encouraging. My dad was diagnosed about three years ago and they said that might be all the time he had."

It's pretty heavy conversation for a margarita-and-nachos birthday dinner, but it's one of the first true heart-to-hearts I've had with any of my new friends. That we've both been unlucky enough to deal with this will link us forever, I'm sure. It's the same survivor bond I shared with Alison after her father died a few months ago, even though Kim's father is still alive. Social identity support and all. I recently read a *Psychology Today* article about breast cancer survivors similarly connecting. "Though the women no longer have breast cancer and have continued with family and careers, their social identity as survivors often remains so powerful that their primary bonds of friendship are with other survivors, the only people who can understand what they've been through and grasp their perspective on life." This is how I felt with Alison after her father died, and now with Kim. I tell her that if she ever wants to talk, I'm around, and offer my mother's services as a walking multiple myeloma encyclopedia. She's become an expert on just about every medication and treatment option out there.

The next day I reiterate as much in an email. Three days later, Kim writes me back. "It is pretty remarkable that we share similar experiences with something so rare. I'm really still wrapping my mind around that. I feel as if we were destined to meet, it's so crazy how this has all come about! I don't know if I mentioned it, but I'm planning for my dad to visit in a few weeks. He's not been up to Chicago to visit and it would be a great getaway for him. If he continues to feel up for the trip, I would love for you to meet him, if you're in town."

Aside from being a touching email—finding Kim was destiny!—it's a huge step in my friend-dating career. Meeting the parents is one of the most significant dating milestones on record. It's usually a ten-to-fifteen-dates-in move, and we've only been out twice.

In college especially, the "which friends should I invite to dinner with my visiting parents" question was a big one. They would offer a dorm-food reprieve and treat the chosen few to dinner at a nice restaurant. Plus, they'd get a sampling of the most important people in my life. That Kim wants me to meet her father is flattering. Clearly we're on the same page.

I read Matt the email and he immediately adopts his announcer voice. "And Kim's pulling ahead! Watch out Jillian . . ."

■ ■ ■

Warm weather, one might think, should lend itself to making friends. After eight months of hibernating, Chicagoans are out in full force. A walk along the lake might find me clearing the path for a unicycler, dodging cops on Segways, playing Frogger with countless runners and shying away from no less than a dozen dogs. (I'm determined to get over my thorny relationship with canines, as they are perhaps the best wingmen. The pet-owners in my life have promised that a single trip to the dog park could produce at least a few BFF prospects.) The streets are teeming with ladies just waiting for me to make my move, and they'll be so drunk on sunlight they may not even get creeped out. Yet it's only the end of May and I can see the upcoming summer season will pose some problems.

In our house, summer is synonymous with travel. Too much time away is going to cramp my friend-making style, but I don't have much choice in the matter. Over the next few months we're scheduled for two out-of-town weddings, a family trip to Vegas, a long weekend in Cape Cod, and, to cap it all off, our one-year-postponed honeymoon. Croatia here we come.

First up is a friendship throwback of the highest order. My ten-year high school reunion.

Matt's opted out of this trip, and no amount of guilting

could get him to change his mind. It's my own fault, really, because I initially told him I didn't care if he came. And I really didn't. I wasn't even playing that "I'll say I don't care but really I do so this is a test to make sure you love me enough" game. Until I found out my friends' husbands and fiancés would be in attendance. Then I cared, and asked Matt to come, but he made some good arguments—"I'm traveling the next two weekends"—and some questionable ones—"I'm a lawyer, Rachel, I need to be available." In the end I'm at O'Hare solo, getting ready to board a flight to LaGuardia, where Callie and Nate will be waiting.

"Hey, Rachel. Made any friends lately?" I'm surprised to see Ben, a former classmate of mine who I haven't spoken to since, oh, sophomore year, standing beside me at the gate. He's about thirty pounds lighter than I remember, but otherwise looks exactly the same. Eighteen to 28 must not be prime getting-fat-and-bald years.

"Oh! Ben! Uh, hi. Yeah, um, I've made some friends."

"I read your blog."

"Clearly. Thanks." This is without question the longest conversation we've ever had. "How's your biking?"

Facebook has basically made high school reunions obsolete. Ben and I, who are online friends but have never actually seen each other in the three years we've overlapped in the Midwest, know the big-picture themes of each other's lives because they pop up in our newsfeeds. He's always posting stuff about cycling that I don't totally understand—I think he's a racer?—and I only add status updates when I link to my blog.

Two hours later, Ben and I walk the halls of LaGuardia together. His parents' car is right behind Callie and Nate's, and Cal gets out to greet him.

"Ben! Happy reunion!" She gives him a hug. Callie loves

seeing people she was never really friends with and acting as if they've always been lifelong BFFs.

"I just learned more about him than I ever knew in high school," I tell her once we're on the road.

"Ben and I were actually kind of friends because of Spanish class," she says. This is what I mean. They were never friends.

"Well, I'm definitely in reunion mode now," I say.

When we get back to Callie's, all three of us get comfortable in front of the nationally televised Spelling Bee. This is our favorite night of the year. That it's taking place the night before our reunion, and thus Callie and I get to watch awkward adolescents go for the gold together while having a slumber party, is some sort of cosmic gift. Aside from the very controversial decision to give a girl "gnocchi" in the second-to-last round—any pasta-loving kid could nail that word—it's a rather boring bee.

Once Nate goes to sleep, Callie and I stay up past our bedtimes looking at the Facebook pages of random former classmates.

"What's that girl's name who always had a broken leg?" I ask her.

"Elizabeth! How can you not remember that?"

"I just pray that Evan will be there. Do you think he still talks with a fake British accent? Let's check his page."

This is why lifelong friends are so hard to supplement. The shared history is what makes our sleepover so entertaining. Whose Facebook page can I gawk at with a newbie?

Facebook-stalking could be the theme of the weekend. Since everyone has seen everyone else's profiles, there are no big surprises. Nerdy John's become something of a pimp? Yeah, I saw his latest photo updates. Socialite Samantha's hosting a fund-raiser? Got the Facebook invitation. The real shocker is not how much people have changed but how much they haven't. On a tour of the new gym (my high school upgraded athletic facilities immediately after I graduated. There is now an actual yoga room, complete with a Buddha statue.) I follow our faculty guide down the steps and we pass the crowd that would have been deemed "the druggies" if my life were a John Hughes movie. They're sitting on the rocks drinking beers as I'm taking instructions from a teacher. The same frustrations and insecurities and jealousies I felt ten years ago are bubbling up. Apparently I've traveled back in time.

After a few hours at my old high school, and another few at a bar with my former classmates, it's clear that while I may want to relive my high school friendships, I don't want to re-live high school.

"I can't believe no one has changed," my friend Emily says as we watch two very drunk classmates embrace.

"Seriously. It's kind of creepy and amazing at the same time. All the cliques are still the same," I say. "I mean, it says a lot about the relationships that they're still intact, but isn't it weird that so many people still hang out exclusively with high school friends?"

"Yeah, there's something to be said for growth," she says.

When I board my flight back to Chicago the next day, I'm full from a weekend with my dearest friends. It's a deep sense of satisfaction, like the pure contentment of eating a home-cooked meal. But now I'm ready to venture out into new cuisine. Now it's time for growth.

FRIEND-DATES 21, 22, 23, 24, 25. Brynn, Jackie, Dana, Mia, Morgan.

Nice, nice, bitchy, nice, nice.

Or more specifically: Nice, cool and kind of sarcastic, unfriendly, fun, hilarious. All five emailed me from my essay. Brynn and Jackie are fellow East Coasters (Brynn is from Boston, Jackie is from Westchester County, where I grew up) who recently relocated to Chicago with their men. The same is true of Dana, who moved from Manhattan within the year. I originally thought we'd be a great match. Her email was cute and witty, with references to the New York restaurants she missed and the Chicago haunts she's adopted. "I've always made friends through work or school, but it's much harder this time, especially with no children or dogs. I feel too old to friend some of the hipsters in my neighborhood, but too young to friend the fogeys at my office."

Upon meeting, though, it's clear it's not just that she misses her friends, she misses New York. And it's not just that she misses New York, she really doesn't like Chicago. She's got that New York edge only an outsider would notice, which tells me one thing: I'm not a New Yorker anymore. While our conversation reminds me that I have some Big Apple nostalgia—"I *loved* the Shake Shack!"—I don't wish I lived there. Dana does.

"I'm just kind of a mean person," she says, not at all jokingly. "My boss in New York used to tell me that he loved that I was mean, and I was like 'Great, I'm about to move to the friendliest place in the world.'"

I used to say this kind of thing all the time. "Yeah, I'm kind of a bitch, I'm a New Yorker! That's what makes me lovable." The last time I remember making such a comment was to my coworker Joan. "I was nervous that my New York sarcasm was rubbing everyone the wrong way," I told her once, before realizing that the constant references to my previous Manhattan life weren't interesting to anyone but myself. In fact, they were kind of obnoxious. Dana has that similar "New York is the center of the world attitude" which I don't begrudge her, but I do know she won't be all that happy in Chicago until she shakes it.

Mia lives around the corner from me. She's smart, likes travel and exercise, seems like a great activity partner, and gets huge points for living in the neighborhood. The perfect pedicure friend. Morgan's from L.A. and has bright red hair that's short and teased in a way that reminds me of a 1980s Molly Ringwald. I love it. In telling me about some of her mommy issues, she mentions she was an actress when she was young.

"Like, an actress actress? Would I have seen you in anything?"

"Have you heard of the show *Sisters*?" Um, clearly. I only watched it every single Saturday night of my preteen I'm-too-young-to-go-out-on-a-Saturday-night life. "I was on it for seven years."

I'm having my own superfan moment here. She also had bit parts on *Roseanne* and, later in her career, *Buffy the Vampire Slayer*. When I mention something of my love for Alyson Hannigan, she calls her "Aly." It's all I can do to not grab her phone to see what other celebrities are in her contact list.

It's in these moments that I love my search even more than I love the people I've met. When you force yourself to go out with fifty-two new potential best friends, you're going to get all sorts of characters sitting across the dinner table. A child actress, a pastor's daughter, a mom of twins, a southern Yalie, an aspiring Olympian. I'm starting to feel like the most connected girl in Chicago, and with my hand in so many different circles of the city it can be hard to keep them all straight. When I run errands now, I'm constantly on the lookout for familiar faces, and nothing makes me feel more local than bumping into someone I know. If at the end of the year I emerge with no BFF, I'll certainly have plenty of acquaintances. I could network you all over town. Need a wedding dress? I've got just the girl! Want to pursue Jewish studies? I'll hook you up.

In *The Tipping Point,* author Malcolm Gladwell talks about what he calls Connectors, "people with a special gift for bringing the world together . . . They are the kinds of people who know everyone." I remember the first time I read that chapter, in 2003, and thought about the people I knew who so obviously fit the bill. Reading it again I see that I'm getting there. "Connectors are people whom all of us can reach in only a few steps because, for one reason or another, they manage to occupy many different worlds and subcultures and niches. . . . Acquaintances, in short, represent a source of social power, and the more acquaintances you have the more powerful you are." Every time I read that sentence I'm filled with inexplicable images of Underdog, as if knowing a lot of people makes you some sort of social (and cuddly) superhero. I've gone from feeling socially isolated to socially powerful in six short months.

■ ■ ■

It's hard to believe that the search is almost half over. When I take stock of how far I've come, I think I'm on the right track. In the last two months I've loaded my social calendar with follow-up dates. Jillian, the front-runner, has been in heavy rotation. She brought her husband, Paul, and the twins along for a Sunday brunch and this time I didn't arrive empty-handed. All it takes to endear yourself to a friend's twin boys is Elmo, and I am not above buying a little adoration. I brought Matt along to their second birthday party—a significant step for the friendship, and not a bad form of birth control, either. Being in charge of the boys while Jillian and Paul cut fruit was certainly entertaining for the thirty minutes we were on duty, but by the time Matt and I got back home we were more than certain that the only baby in our immediate future (read: two years if you're asking me, more like four years if it's up to Matt) would be our nephew, Gavin.

Hannah and I took a trip to Printer's Row Litfest, a book fair downtown. Seeing each other once a month for book club is a good friendship booster, too. And, I swear, she has the best laugh of anyone I've ever met. Yes, I'm aware it sounds like I'm actually trying to date her, but have you ever thought about how vital laughter is to friendship? When I recall all the dates that went less-than-swimmingly—Heidi and Michelle, Jodie, Wendy, Dana—lack of laughter is the common denominator. If I look back at my friendships that work—Callie and Sara, my college friends, my work clique—sitting around in hysterics is the image that immediately comes to mind.

In her quest to boost her overall happiness with only small changes, Gretchen Rubin, author of *The Happiness Project,* jacked up the number of times she laughed in a day. "It's a source of social bonding," she wrote of the best medicine. "It helps to reduce conflicts and cushion social stress within relationships—at work, in marriage, among strangers. When people laugh together, they tend to talk and touch more and to make eye contact more frequently." If I had to pick a single indicator of whether a friendship will take off after the first date, how many times I laughed in a given meeting would be it. It separates the front-runners from the they-were-nice-maybe-we'll-have-dinner-agains. Just because the majority of my dates fall under the large and not-always-flattering category of "nice" doesn't mean they're all going to be BFFs. Shared laughter tips the scales.

Hannah and I laugh together a lot. And hers is a hearty, gulping, almost cartoonish laugh. Her laugh makes me laugh, which just makes me want to make her laugh all the time. I know, sounds like love, right?

Speaking of people who've made me pee myself with hysterics, my coworkers are still probably my closest friends in town. Aside from our daily lunches and link sharing (I get some combination of Neil Patrick Harris, *Glee*, and Justin Bieber videos hourly), Kari, Ashley, Lynn, Joan, and I have been making a concerted effort to meet for out-of-office gatherings. I hosted a *How I Met Your Mother* screening not so long ago, and on a recent Thursday we did drinks and tapas. I'm starting to hear talk of other jobs, but I'm feeling more confident that the friendships will exist—no, thrive—outside our corporate walls. My record at my old job was two for three—of the trio of work BFFs I was sure would be around forever, two were at my wedding two years later. But with this crowd, I'm optimistic. If we all go our separate ways, I'm rooting for a perfect score.

Margot the bridal consultant and I have had more dinners that lasted for hours. I met Amanda, the one who blogged about me, for Thai food and got an after-work pedicure with Mia, the essay responder who lives around the corner. Jen and Alison, my old NU classmates, met me for brunch, where Alison announced she got into business school (exciting!) . . . in D.C. (less so). My first fallen friend. Hilary and I went for that long Saturday afternoon walk, later I went to her birthday dinner, and once she even called me on the phone *just to say hi*. I was at the office and had to silence the call since cellphone talkers are shunned in the open-air cubicle environment. But I checked the voice mail immediately, obviously. "Hey, Rach, it's Hil!" (She's called me Rach since the first time we met. No one calls me Rach. It's cute.) "Just wanted to say hi, see how everything's going. Want to make plans to hang out soon, so call me! Okay, love you!"

Really? You love me? We've hung out, like, four times. Here's where I'm glad friending isn't dating. No "talk" necessary, no drama. Just a sign that Hilary probably says I love you to all her friends, which doesn't entirely surprise me. Not something I'd say quite so early, but harmless.

I've even had dinner with Jodie twice more. You know Jodie, the 40-something mother of two adolescents? The one I saw no future with? Right, her. I didn't pursue any more dates after our first lunch, but she emailed a few times inviting me out to dinner, and I didn't know how to say no. When it comes to friend breakups, I'm clueless. Women actually find it harder and feel more guilt when breaking up with a friend than a lover, and I'm certainly in that camp. It's not like I can only have one friend as long as we both shall live, not as if I can't see other people. To reject friendship, or at the very least dinner plans, with Jodie would be to say, "I don't like you." And that, well that's just mean. And not true. I don't dislike her. I just don't imagine we'll be best friends. So I met her for dinner, twice, and my verdict still stands. Jodie is a really nice woman who would make a wonderful friend. To someone else. We're just not best-friend compatible.

So here we are. One date shy of the halfway mark. I can no longer whine with any conviction about having no friends—not even on my most dramatic days. I tell stories about my new pals that start "My friend Kim said . . ." or "I was at a bar with my friend Ellen . . ." I've started making a more concerted effort to gather phone numbers, and on a lonely Friday night I might even use them.

The definition of BFF is definitely evolving with my search. In a pinch, I have some ladies I'd call for a pedicure. But if

Matt and I had a huge fight? One that involved tears? I still wouldn't bother any of these new friends with that. If I had a medical emergency and needed some friends to cheer me up? I'd probably call in the long-distance lifers. Hell, I'm not sure I'd ask any of these new ladies for a ride to the airport if it came down to it. So there's a ways to go.

Even so, I try to recall the girl who started this quest. It's as if I'm playing a movie reel in my head. I can picture her lying on the couch on a Friday night, clicker in hand. I see the morning I went for my wedding dress fitting, almost in tears because there was no one in town to come along for moral support. I can picture the "I need a friend to have lunch with" conversations with Matt—me at the kitchen table staring at my phone, him fixing a sandwich—when he was heading to play basketball for the day. I feel sorry for her. Almost embarrassed. But mostly just distant, as if she were my silly younger sister, not my former self.

SUMMER:

"IF YOU CAN'T MEET 'EM, JOIN 'EM": CLUBS, CLASSES, AND ONLINE FRIENDING

CHAPTER **8**

It's time to start the dirty work. As many people as I've met this year, my behavior over the last six months hasn't been all that different from the last three years. Instead of proactively seeking out potential friends, I've waited for them to come to me. Sure, I put some feelers out—asked friends to set me up and advertised my needs more broadly—but while declaring friendlessness might have been embarrassing, it was easy. I did it from my living room, no "You look nice, will you be my friend?" required. But I can't rely on mutual acquaintances and want ads forever. First of all, I'd like more control over who I friend-date. The online essay was great, but once I put myself out there it was in a reader's court to decide if we'd be a good match. I said yes to anyone who would have me, to mixed results. Now I want the power to pursue the ladies I think have BFF potential.

Secondly, one thing I've learned thus far is that meeting people is a valuable skill, one that I'm not naturally blessed with. My friend Jenna is the best people-meeter I know. She once met a guy while crossing the street. I kid you not. He was headed to Banana Republic and she had a Friends & Family discount coupon. She offered it to him. Turns out he was a tourist and invited her to accompany him on his shopping trip. Cut to one month later and she's visiting him in his hometown of Toronto. (It didn't progress much from there, but you've got to admit, that's a pretty impressive pickup.)

Jenna's remarkable ability to befriend has always served her well—socially, academically, and now in her law career. Though I can get along with almost anybody once I've met them, it's the introducing myself part that's hard. People who know me don't believe I could get nervous around new people—"I wouldn't exactly describe you as shy" a partner in Matt's law firm said after I filled his ear with tales of my search—but approaching strangers is intimidating. I've always hated it.

I need to work on this. Networking is one of the keys to success, and maybe if I had a better handle on it I wouldn't have found myself three years deep in a new city without a nearby best friend to speak of.

The first step toward choosing which friends to pursue is to meet all the candidates. I've signed up for some friend-dating websites (who knew?) and plan to attend every meet-and-greet event I can find. Social scientists say the quickest way to make new friends is to join a group or sign up for a class. Participate in something you're interested in and you'll find people with similar values. Plus, research shows that being a part of a group that meets just once a month will give you the same increase in happiness as doubling your salary. I've already got the book clubs, but perhaps I can quadruple my emotional income?

On the suggestion of that same partner at Matt's office, I've enrolled in an improv class, which pretty much makes me want to crawl into a hole. You know what's more awkward than meeting new people? Mock-raking leaves, feistily, while speaking only in gibberish. But Mr. Partner swears it will present me with a class full of new friend prospects and train me to think on my feet when would-be pals cross my path.

After all this *doing*, I'll weed through the new prospects and ask out the ones I think could be a match. That will at least ensure the part about me liking them. Whether they like me is a separate question.

There's one problem with taking on all this work. I'm tired. Like, really, almost unbearably, worn out. I want to stamp my feet, plant myself on the ground with arms crossed, and whine like a five-year-old. "I don't waaannaaa!"

Besides navigating a summer full of travel plans, I'm juggling almost two-dozen budding friendships. The only way to see everyone as often as I'd like is to double book. I'm working girl-date two-a-days—lunch *and* dinner—and while it's exhilarating at times, mostly it's exhausting. I enjoy my new pals, but they're still fresh enough that I have to be "on" during our dates. Relaxing it's not.

"I can't do it anymore," I tell Matt from bed one morning. "What?"

"Make friends. I hate friends." I hear myself, but I can't help it. Fatigue will do that to you.

"Perk up, babe!" he shouts in his best pep talk voice. "It's the year of the friend, can't stop now."

"I'm tiiiiiired." I bury my head farther into my pillow.

"You wanted to do this. Think about Jillian!"

He's right. I asked for this and it's working, so there's nothing to complain about. But there are days when I honestly feel like if I meet one more person I might break down and sabotage the whole project. Would it be too soon to burst into tears on a first date?

Take last weekend, the only one in June when I stayed in

town: I went to happy hour with Ellen on Thursday, book club Friday, and dance class with my coworkers Saturday morning. I was scheduled to meet Hilary for a street fest in the afternoon (she spaced and forgot to call. A blessing, really), and spent the evening at Matt's friend's barbecue. Sunday brought brunch with Hannah, a pedicure with Brynn, and dinner with Jillian. It's a far cry from where I once was, but there are moments—like this morning—when I want to cry uncle. The glass-half-full perspective is that while this year is about connecting and being social, it's simultaneously giving me a new appreciation for alone time. In the pre-search days, too much bonding with myself was boring at best, desperately lonely at worst. Now I covet quiet time. But I'm not feeling especially optimistic today, so instead of taking an "appreciate the new appreciation for solitude" approach, I'm hiding under the covers.

Getting out of bed would also require getting dressed. This brings us to the other downside of friend-dating, which has been spilling out of my jeans. I've gained ten pounds since I started this quest. Thanks so much, wine and sushi. I didn't even know a person could expand that much in six months, though Matt claims he put on similar weight during the weekend he spent in Amsterdam junior year of college. But I've eaten no space cakes. I can't blame the munchies.

The average American gains two pounds per year, and that seemingly small amount has sounded some serious alarms. Those annual additions are why the words "obesity epidemic" are as familiar as "Big Mac and fries." If I keep going like this, I'm looking at twenty pounds. Ten times the national average. Such an overachiever. I'll see your typical American, and raise her eighteen big ones.

I'm determined to stop the upward creep in its tracks but

eating out every night doesn't make it easy. I used to think that people ate more when they were alone. It's a lot less embarrassing to inhale a plateful of fries when you're huddled late-night in a dark corner of your kitchen than in front of a potential lifer. But eating with others is actually one of the prime determinants of how much people consume. Food psychologist Brian Wansink, author of *Mindless Eating: Why We Eat More Than We Think,* studies how external factors affect eating habits. Did you know that people drink more from a short wide glass than from a tall one? Counterintuitive, but true.

According to Wansink, when you eat with one other person, you take in about 35 percent more than you would alone. A table of four increases your intake by 75 percent, while a table for seven translates to 96 percent more. I guess the new bulge around my midsection is no big surprise. I've become a statistic.

So, basically, I'm tired and fat. Or, at least, fatter. Not the best way to go into another six months of meeting people.

There's not much I can do about it now but down a Diet Coke, slip on my loosest dress (or so it was once), and head to work.

Five hours later I'm sitting in my cubicle, staring blankly at my computer, when Ashley and Kari appear in my doorway. (It's more like a slight opening in the box where I spend my weekdays, but "doorway" sounds so much more dignified. Almost as if I have actual personal space.)

"We're going with Lynn to see She & Him play at Millennium Park tonight, want to come?"

This is just the kind of thing I should be saying yes to. It's a free concert, it will continue to build the out-of-office relationship with my coworkers, and might even be a prime spot for meeting new Chicagoans.

"Um, I do but . . ." I can't bring myself to commit. After months of yessing, the lure of a quiet evening at home is too strong.

"We're going to have a picnic," Kari tells me. "Come! It'll be fun."

"I think I just need a low-key night with my couch," I tell her. Just hearing the words come out of my mouth is embarrassing. Passing on a girls' night out in favor of television goes against everything I've come to believe in.

"Say Yes" is my cardinal rule of friendship. Accepting random invitations is the best way of organically meeting new people. For the first time, I'm breaking my own commandment. I wish I could say it feels good to be bad just one time. To take a mini-break from all these friendly people. But it doesn't. It's the familiar shame of deciding to pass on the gym "just this once" for no real reason other than a USA airing of *You've Got Mail*. Again.

I know I'd feel better—energized, satisfied—if I went, but I don't want to feel better. I want to nap.

Two hours later, watching three of my best work friends leave the office with a beach bag full of towels, red wine, and Stacey's Chips, I attempt to ignore the mix of guilt and jealousy settling into my chest.

There might be another reason for my momentary listlessness. This week marks the four-year anniversary of my father's death. In my family, we commemorate the day with a night out. I wouldn't call it a celebration, but rather than sit around and grieve we go to dinner, eat good food, and tell stories. My mom is in New York with my brother, so this year it's just Matt and me. On Wednesday, we go to a small Mexican BYOB that was recently named one of the best new restau-

rants by *Chicago Magazine*. Not surprisingly, the memories
that are top-of-mind during the meal all relate to my father
and friendship. He didn't consider himself especially popular,
but his funeral was standing room only. A maintenance man at
the temple said he'd only ever seen it that full in the days after
September 11.

I grew up in Westchester County while all my high school
friends lived in New York City. On Friday or Saturday nights,
I'd make my sweetest, most irresistible Daddy's-girl face and
ask my father, often at the last minute, often around 9 P.M., to
drive me the thirty to forty-five minutes into Manhattan. He
always said yes.

I wish I could say those rides were filled with heart-to-hearts.
Usually they weren't. They mostly consisted of whatever song
the top 40 station had in rotation and me jabbering on about
my rude history teacher, and then saying "Dad? Dad, are you
even listening?!?" But there were moments. Like when he'd
bust a move to the latest pop sensation, or pretend to barrel
though the EZPass barrier at full speed just to hear me scream,
or recite absurd jokes he'd heard from his middle schoolers.
(Why couldn't the Dairy Queen get pregnant? She was married to Mister Softee!) And there was the time I called home
after an ill-fated trip to visit my one-year-older boyfriend,
then a college freshman, and asked my parents to get me
the morning-after pill. The condom had broken, the student
health center wouldn't help a non-student, and I was terrified.
Later that week, during one of our drives, Dad brought up the
incident for the first time.

"I'm really glad you called us," he said. "I can't believe my
little girl is doing such grown-up things—I wish you weren't—
but I hope you'll always call if you need help. I'm proud of
you."

I responded like a typical 17-year-old. "Daaaaad, stop. Fine. Whatever."

But still, I remember.

It's hard to know if my parents influenced my strong interest in friendship. Maybe if my father had thought it absurd to chauffeur his daughter into Manhattan every week, instead of unfailingly agreeing to it, I'd care less about seeing friends on a consistent basis. Perhaps I'd be okay with fewer social connections. For their book *Connected: The Surprising Power of Our Social Networks and How They Shape Our Lives,* Nicholas Christakis and James Fowler studied more than eleven hundred sets of twins, the ideal subjects for the perpetual nature-versus-nurture debate, and found that genetics were a key factor in popularity. "On average, a person with, say, five friends has a different genetic makeup than a person with one friend," they write. Biology might also be responsible for whether you are the queen bee or a quiet follower in your group of friends, the authors say. Your mother and father, their mothers and fathers and the generations of mothers and fathers before them could be directly responsible for your level of trust and trustworthiness, cooperation and loneliness. Christakis and Fowler claim that the "diversity of feelings about being connected and sharing with others"—i.e., the fact that some of us want so much to be connected that we focus an entire year around that need—is inherited, so while my desire for sociability is probably due to my parents, so is the significant void I felt when my local connections didn't meet my intimacy standards.

Matt and I sit in the crowded basement restaurant inhaling our dessert of peanut butter empanadas with fruit compote and chocolate dipping sauce. I'll lose the weight soon, I swear.

"It's almost July," I remind him. "I'm halfway done."

"And?"

"And it's working. I definitely have new friends," I say. "Do you?" I want the fruits of this quest to rub off on Matt. He has good buddies in Chicago, but only a few. He doesn't seem to especially want any more, but I've become a friend pusher. Plus, I've started to feel bad leaving him alone so often, ditching my husband for another night of girl talk. Not bad enough to stop doing it, but I'd feel better if he was spending a night with the guys. Sara recently asked what dear husband does while I'm out every evening, and I had no idea. Watch ESPN maybe? Read the paper?

"No new friends for me," he says. "But you're happier, which means I'm happier."

"Aw, look at you. You're like a real live husband."

"You used to complain all the time about how you had no friends. It got pretty old. Especially because we *had* friends. They just weren't the kind of friends you wanted."

It's true that before this search we had a decent number of invitees for birthday outings, but I never thought of them as *my* friends. They were Matt's friends, or our friends, or my cousin's friends. They were friends of friends I'd seen once or twice, but to whom I didn't feel a personal connection. It's a deeper satisfaction to have friends that are completely my own.

"It wasn't all the time," I say.

"Yeah, okay," he responds, deciding not to argue the semantics. "Either way, you have more friends. I don't have to hear you complain. It's better for everybody."

■ ■ ■

On a Sunday night—or, actually, Monday morning—a few months back, I went on my first sign-up binge. I'd recently learned about MeetUp.com, a website that bills itself as the world's largest network of social groups. Their mission is to "revitalize local community and help people around the world self-organize." Basically, you register (for free), sign up for groups that interest you, and attend meetings as you see fit. With about eighty thousand local meetups, you're pretty much guaranteed to find something appealing no matter how offbeat your passion. A quick search of my neighborhood turned up a gathering of tantra lovers; a group dedicated to raising awareness of hula hoopers, fire performers, and poi (consider them a success: I am now aware that poi is a performance art out of New Zealand, which consists of swinging a cord with balls on either end of it, sort of like nunchucks); a golf club; and a collection of Chicago webmasters. In a matter of minutes I signed up for five groups: 20 and 30 Somethings Chicago, The Chicago Children's Literature Meetup Group, Chicago Cooking Chicks, The Chicago Cooking Lite Supper Club, and Read the Classics—The 1001 Books Challenge.

This enrollment rampage took place at 1 A.M., high time for my most ambitious—or ill-advised—decisions. (Many an overemotional email—or worse still, crazy-girl phone call—has been sent in the middle of the night. There's something about lack of sleep that once made me think it was okay to show up late-night at Matt's dorm and wake him up so we could "have a talk about where we are." My sanity has returned in the time since that sophomore year debacle, but I'd still do well to be cut off from the world after midnight.) The next morning, with the clear head of a decent night's sleep, it was obvious that the reading groups weren't my most brilliant idea. As much as I'd love to devour all 1001 books to read before I die, doing so on top of the two book clubs I'm already committed to might just kill me sooner. The 20 and 30 Somethings, which apparently had almost fifteen hundred members and entailed mostly happy hours, seemed a little broad and unfocused. If I wanted to gather with a mass of perfect strangers at a bar, I'd just go to a bar. Better to focus my energy on the cooking groups. Food—making it, not eating it—is a personal interest not currently serviced by this quest. From a strictly self-serving standpoint, it makes the best sense.

The Cooking Chicks' upcoming meeting worked with my schedule and I loved that it was a brand-new group. The meeting to which I RSVP'd was the inaugural gathering, so I wouldn't be walking into a bunch of already-established friendships and inside jokes about feeling fried or salad toss-ing. From the online profile photos, the Chicks looked like a younger crowd, while the Supper Club women seemed pri-marily in their forties. Chicks it would be.

A few weeks later, Matt dropped me off at Kenmore Live Studio, a kitchen-meets-social-media space that hosts and broadcasts cooking demos. According to messages from Vanessa, the supremo Chick, our first gathering was going to be filmed and streamed live on the Kenmore Facebook Page. A real twenty-first-century cooking extravaganza.

When I entered the stark studio there were about ten women circled around Vanessa. She was giving the lowdown on the space and why she started the group—presumably to find fel-low food-lovers, but also as a résumé builder—and I was over-come with jitters. Whenever I feel like I've started to conquer this quest, my inner wallflower comes out. Meeting someone with whom I'd already emailed was one thing, but I was start-ing at square one with these ladies. I couldn't fall back on a witty essay or a mutual friend. Hovering outside the circle, I was momentarily paralyzed. Don't let anyone tell you meeting new people is like riding a bike. It doesn't come flooding back. Introductions are more of a use-it-or-lose-it skill. A muscle to be exercised, not a reflex to rely on. Should I finagle my way into the circle or hang back and take it all in? Ultimately I went the name-tag route, sneaking through the crowd to sign in and get my sticky identification. Hello, my name is Rachel.

As the circle broke off into smaller conversations, I stood aside, trying to purposefully gaze around the room. The pointed stare is my classic I'm-standing-by-myself-but-I'm-fine-with-it move. I like to think it says "I'm not alone because no one will talk to me, I'm just really fascinated with this crown molding."

Eventually another seemingly solo girl settled in next to me, looking equally uncomfortable.

"Did you come alone, too?" I asked her.

"Yeah." Thin, tall, blond, and wearing heels, Erica struck me as exactly the type of girl who'd have an inseparable clique of her own and wouldn't need a meetup group to make friends. What was she doing here?

"Are you a big cook?"

"I used to have potlucks with some coworkers, but a few of them moved away and the dinners kind of petered out, so I thought I'd try this."

Erica was pleasant enough. She's from Wisconsin, works in PR, and lives in an apartment she can't stand in Uptown. "I've moved every year since I came to Chicago five years ago," she told me. "This is the worst apartment yet."

As we talked, another two girls wandered in our direction.

"We came here together but swore we wouldn't only talk to each other," a girl in a long flowy black skirt and a gray cleavage-y T-shirt said. "We thought we'd introduce ourselves."

Karen, in the skirt, and Abby, wearing jeans, sneakers, and one of those extra-thin cozy American Apparel T-shirts, recently moved to Chicago. They both graduated from the University of Indiana last year. Abby was looking for a job in real estate, while Karen was biding her time nannying for her niece before moving to Japan to teach English. When we were finally called over to the cooking demo the four of us took the last row, like high schoolers clamoring for the back of the bus. I sat next to Abby, and we chatted and laughed throughout the presentation—mainly about how it was becoming apparent we weren't going to do any cooking ourselves. Or eating, for that matter.

"Maybe we could swipe that entire pot of gnocchi," Abby suggested.

"It smells delicious, and I'm hungry enough I might eat my own arm," I said. "How can a cooking event scheduled from six to eight not have food? I'm so confused."

"Also confusing? The mime. And creepy."

A fine point. The Kenmore Studio mascot is named Kenny Moore. He's a mime, painted face and all, and between demos he juggled milk cartons and balanced a chair on his nose. He's a strange choice for a cooking space. If it were up to me, no member of the clown species would be allowed in my kitchen—face paint away from the food, please. But Kenny was a great conversation topic, if simply for his sheer bizarreness.

At the end of the night, as the Chicks got ready to leave, I knew I had to ask Abby for her contact info. We had great banter, after all, and if laughter really is the best friendship detector, we had serious potential. But should I just casually say, "Hey, what's your number?" Would that sound desperate? In the time it took me to gather these thoughts, Abby and Karen had already started heading for the door.

If I went home without even trying, I knew I'd kick myself. Not to mention the fact that cheerleader Matt wouldn't let me hear the end of it. "You gotta do it, babe!" I could hear him in my ear.

My mom had been pushing the business card approach for some time. If I offer mine, the natural reaction would be for people to reciprocate. Or so goes her argument.

I caught up with the college buddies. "I'm just going to give you guys my card, because . . ." There was no natural way to finish the sentence. Because I think you're supercool? Because I think you could be my BFF? Because I really really want you to call me?

"Um, okay . . ." Karen looked confused, as if this was her first business card offering. Considering her only job since college was working as a nanny, it might well have been. But then—

"We're going to grab a bite, do you want to come?"

How easy was that? "I'd love to," I said.

And we all held hands and skipped off into the sunset.

Or, Karen invited Erica, who declined, and the three of us found a nearby Thai restaurant and inhaled plates of Pad See Ew over talk of college days and foreign travels and out-of-context silent performers. There was a lot of laughter.

"Call us!" Karen yelled as I got into the cab. This time I'd been sure to get their numbers. "We go out all the time—we're so much fun!"

FRIEND-DATE 26. It took a couple of months for me to contact them but tonight I'm finally meeting Abby for our long-overdue date. Karen has family in town, but considering she's moving in September, I'm more interested in her friend. Coldhearted, but true. I have to be practical.

Our sushi dinner is delicious, but the stellar chemistry from our cooking escapade has simmered. I can't tell if it's due to the lack of a mime to mock or because Karen isn't here or what. Certainly too much time has passed. The momentum from the meetup has fizzled, so it feels as if we're starting all over again. Further proof that I need to follow up on promising dates right away. Our age—or life-stage—difference is another culprit. It's the same story of my date with Rebecca the intern some months ago. (Maybe I should introduce them?) Abby has just graduated college. She still uses "party" as a verb. When she hears I'm 28, six years her senior, she says "But you don't seem old," which makes me want to pop in a hearing aid and show her my dentures.

■ ■ ■

"They should make a Match.com, but for friends."

About 50 percent of the people I've told about my search have pitched me this idea. The good news for me, less so for their entrepreneurial spirit, is that something similar already exists. GirlFriendCircles.com is a website for women looking to expand their friendship base. Before signing up—this would be my first pay-for-play in the friendship world and buying BFFs still seems iffy—I get on the phone with Shasta Nelson, the company's founder and CEO.

Nelson came up with the concept for GirlFriendCircles while she was working as a life coach in San Francisco. "I had three clients who hired me for very different reasons, but when it came down to it, what they were all lacking was people nearby to support them," she says. "They could go online to find jobs and romance and homes, but when I tried to find something to help them fill the friendship void there was no resource." So Nelson created one herself: an online community that brings women together offline. The presentation is a bit touchy-feely for me—the website has a lot of pink, I generally hate the word "girlfriend" when it doesn't refer to a romantic relationship, and the "Introducing women. Inspiring friendship" slogan reminds me of Jack Handy—but the concept makes sense. Once you sign up, you get access to calendars of local events, classifieds, profiles of all members and invitations to ConnectingCircles. This last option is the most popular. ConnectingCircles are gatherings of about six women at a restaurant or coffee shop within twenty miles of your home. It's the easiest way to meet new people since the event is set up for you.

"All you have to do is show up," Nelson says. "The average member attends three ConnectingCircles. That's about how long it takes to find the right match."

Nelson, who has an infectious passion for self-help and uses life-coach jargon like "we need to give each other permission to talk about this," is a big proponent of group friendships. "It's easier to find friends in groups because you don't have to have the 'we didn't click' conversation," she says. "And the others don't have to be just like you for it to be incredibly meaningful. If they weren't part of the same group do you think Miranda and Charlotte would have been friends?"

But what about the payment aspect? Am I really such a social leper that I need to purchase my relationships? "People often say 'I can't believe you expect me to pay for friends, this is so low. Friendship should be free,'" Nelson tells me. "My response to that is, 'If you don't want to pay, then don't. If you can do it without my service, go for it.' But my question, if I were life-coaching them, would be, 'Then why don't you have what you're looking for already? Obviously you were on my site, so you have a need.' You can exercise for free and if you can go jogging, do it. But some of us need to belong to a gym."

I have access to free treadmills both at work and in my apartment building, and I still pay a health club for the classes and nicer machines. I get it.

"People who invest in something value it more, and I really want to keep a high quality of women on the site. I don't want to open it to anyone who's in the mood one night to start a profile and then not have active members. Who cares if there are ten thousand profiles if only seven are really on board?"

Fair enough. I assure Nelson I'll sign up.

Afterward, something she said sticks with me as I think back on my year thus far: "I've found that most of us need to meet with somebody twice a month for three months before we will consider them a friend."

I love this. If there's anything I wanted when launching my search, it was a friending formula. In retrospect, I think I've adhered to this schedule pretty well with the top prospects. I see Hannah and Jillian once a month at book club and we usually have a separate one-on-one (or one-on-one-on-twins) date during that thirty-day period. Margot and I have lunch fairly often, usually twice a month. Hilary is one of those either-three-times-a-week-or-once-in-two-months friends. A second batch of ladies—Mia, Amanda, Lacey, Brynn, Jackie, Ellen—haven't necessarily met Nelson's quota, but they're gaining ground. A meet-and-greet dinner party is already in the works.

Then there's Kim. After our myeloma connection and the invitation to meet her dad, I thought we were getting serious. And then, nothing. Three of my emails went unreturned, in-cluding one about her father's visit.

"Maybe something happened with her dad and she doesn't have time for new friends," my mom says. "Or maybe your association with myeloma was too much for her."

Maybe, but it seems far-fetched considering her last email. Everything was going so well.

"Sometimes guys just disappear into thin air," Sara tells me on the phone one night. "Maybe with friends it's the same."

I want there to be a reason: Is it her dad? Did she read my blog and get turned off? Did she get overexcited at the Lincoln Park Zoo sea otters and hit her head on the glass, get a concussion, and suffer a horrible case of amnesia? As much as I want to create excuses for her, to give our budding friendship the benefit of the doubt, there's only one explanation that makes any sense: She's just not that into me.

I've been dumped. For a second time.

■ ■ ■

Matt and I are spending the Fourth of July weekend at his mother's house in Cape Cod. En route to an annual barbecue, I notice I'm wearing a red jacket, white shorts, and a blue tank top. What can I say? I'm proud to be an American.

"Is that what you wear on your friend dates?" Zach, a childhood friend of Matt's, gets a real kick out of himself.

"Every time."

Zach's sister-in-law Colby and her sister Carly sit beside us at the kids' table ("kids" being a generous term for the 20- and 30-somethings at this multigenerational affair). "Do the girls you go out with know about your search?" Colby asks.

"Do they think it's so weird?" echoes Carly.

These are the questions people ask most when I tell them about my quest. I know Matt's family friends are just curious—

and excited—about this project, but this weekend the inquiries feel more like an onslaught. I answer the first as I always do: "They definitely know I'm looking for new friends. I don't think they know I'm going on fifty-two dates . . ."

But as I respond to Carly's question, I realize my answer has changed. At the beginning, when people asked if my potential BFFs think I'm strange, I'd say, "I don't know. I hope not." But with twenty-six under my belt, I'm quite confident in my new response.

"No, they really don't," I tell her. "I thought they would. I was nervous everyone would think I was either really pathetic or really annoying, but so far they're mostly flattered. People want friends, they're just embarrassed to ask for them."

Carly gives me the crazy eyes. She's not convinced.

My coworker Kari once told me that after she graduated college, whenever she and her now-husband Tony would go to dinner, he'd spot potential friend prospects and encourage her to introduce herself.

"I'm not just going to walk up to them and say 'Hi, I'm Kari,'" she'd say. "That's so weird."

"But if someone had introduced herself to me? I would have been so excited," she told me, eight years later.

Most women I've met are similar. We all think we're living in a world of grouches, so we're too self-conscious to be the overtly friendly one. A 2009 survey found that 75 percent of adults say Americans are becoming ruder and less civilized. I was part of that three-quarters of the population when I moved to Chicago. I thought overtures of friendship would be received with suspicion rather than appreciation, so I hung back for fear of being the weirdo. Now I think I was wrong. It's not that people are less civilized, it's just that we *think* they are, and so we act accordingly. We don't reach out unsolicited for fear of being rejected. We don't talk to new people because we assume they don't want to be bothered. But as I continue to pursue friendships, I'm constantly surprised at how receptive people are.

Toward the end of the evening, as if just to prove my point, I hear the ping of a text message. It's from Jillian.

"Hi! I went book-hunting at the thrift store and they had two copies of the British edition of *Harry Potter and the Chamber of Secrets.* Clearly, I got them both, and one is for you. Hope you are enjoying Cape Cod!"

I smile, adrenaline coursing strong at this evidence of real friendship. It's not the gift, really. It's that Jillian thought of me. I could hardly be the only person she knows who reads *Harry Potter.*

Shasta Nelson told me the biggest problem with making friends is that there's no easy way to talk about it. "We can't hammer the importance of these relationships when there's not even a vocabulary in place," she said. "There are no platonic words for courting or flirting or hitting on a potential friend."

Right now that would be helpful. I'd have a language to explain the honeymoon phase of this friendship, full of thoughtful gestures and innocent excitement at a simple text message. I'm all giddy, as if the captain of the football team just asked me to the homecoming dance.

FRIEND-DATE 27. When I first started my blog back in March, I figured it would be a solitary endeavor. A means of chronicling my search for a BFF, but certainly not a way of finding her.

I'd learned from coworkers that the way to make your mark

in the cybercommunity is to comment on other people's blogs with links back to your own. As blogger etiquette goes, people whose sites you comment on will do the same for you. It's the unwritten rule of reciprocation. So I started leaving notes at the end of interesting blogs, and, sure enough, the authors started commenting on my posts in return. Which often lead to email exchanges, and even the occasional "If only we lived closer!"

I'd read about blogger Meetups and Tweetups, blog carnivals (when a group of bloggers write on the same topic), and becoming IRL (webspeak for "in real life") friends. Hiding behind a computer screen seemed an illogical friend-making method, but the more blogs I read the clearer it became that the online community was fiercely loyal. When I posted about this surprise discovery one day, other bloggers virtually nodded in agreement in my comment section. One wrote, "Sometimes I feel like my bloggy friends understand me better than my real ones."

Maybe blogging is the modern-day version of pen pals. We can read each other's daily posts—entries that range from a mundane to-do list to a biting "here's who I hate today" rant to a Dear Diary entry of innermost secrets—and suddenly understand a perfect stranger's thought process. You know each other in isolation, separate from any context that might lend itself to prejudgment. But it's a slippery slope. Enlisting the blogosphere as a way of connecting is great, but, as I've been warned, using it as a replacement for face time can be dangerous. So when a fellow blogger—one whose work I admire—commented that she was local, I asked her out. In real life.

As I wait outside Piece, a pizza place in Wicker Park, I search the street for someone with kinky curls that dominate her face. That's Maggie's defining feature according to the tiny profile picture on her blog. All I know about her is what she's written online. She has three kids. She looks like she's in her early thirties. She likes to draw and make sarcastic notes in the margins. I especially enjoyed a recent sketch of some El commuters who were playing their music too loud. A personal pet peeve.

When she arrives, Maggie's hair is in braids. My vision of a curly comrade is shattered.

After half an hour, so too are my dreams of our IRL relationship.

We don't laugh together. Not once in ninety minutes. Our commonalities start and end with blogging, which can only sustain a conversation for so long. And while it's something we both do, it doesn't say much about who we both are.

From what I've read of her, Maggie is really funny. In person, I'm not seeing it. She would likely say the same about me. I saw a greeting card the other day that said "I'm much more interesting on my blog." It might have been created for this very date. Our enjoyment of each other's online personas isn't translating to the real world.

Maybe these communities are online for a reason.

Toward the end of the meal I excuse myself to the restroom, where I text Matt an SOS. Unfortunately we haven't set up a rescue plan, and feigning some "Hello? What? There's an emergency? I'll be there right away!" is so sitcom it would never work.

I have no idea how to fill the long silences. Maggie already told me about her kids and her ex-husband and her job. I told her about Matt and our move to Chicago. And then, nothing. She doesn't have time to watch TV or read, she tells me, which rules out my go-to conversation filler. In the movie version of our date, here is where the birds start chirping.

"Care for some dessert?" Our waitress is shoving the menu toward us.

Please say no. Please say no. I give Maggie my best "it's your call" expression.

"I think we're all set," she says. "Just the check, please."

We walk together toward the train and my car. As we part ways, I'm reminded of that *Friends* episode where Chandler says "We should do it again sometime!" at the end of every date, even the awful ones. As Maggie and I stand on the corner, trying to gracefully part ways, I hear the Mr. Bing reflex going off in my head.

"Well, we should definitely get together again," I tell her.

"Totally," she says.

What? Why? It's that uncontrollable urge to leave on pleasant terms and avoid an even slightly uncomfortable encounter.

"I don't think this worked out so well but have a great life" just doesn't have the same ring.

■ ■ ■

"Um, I'm here with GirlFriendCircles?" It's not really a question, but my voice hikes up an octave as I tell the hostess at Frasca, the pizza-and-wine-bar locale of my very first ConnectingCircle, why I'm here.

She stares at me blankly.

"Is there a reservation?" I ask.

"I don't see one."

"Okay, I'll just go check if anyone's seated yet." In my hand is the official "Table Tent," a place card to identify myself if I'm the first one here. A quick walk-through tells me that I am, but when the hostess asks if I want to be seated I politely refuse.

The Table Tent has a drawing of two female stick figures who seem to be holding hands, or maybe dancing, in a swirl of bright orange, green, and pink polka dots. Next to the image, in bold letters and similar colors, is an announcement: "We're meeting new girl friends tonight."

I'll broadcast my search online, I'll hand out my business card to strangers, I'll even pay $29.95 for a six-month membership to a friend-matching website. But I will not sit alone in a crowded restaurant wearing a sign that might as well say "I have no friends."

At the beginning of this year I wondered if there was anything I wouldn't do in service of my quest. This is it. The line has been drawn.

I wait by the door until I see Jane, whose red hair and glasses I recognize from the photos of the other RSVPs. We exchange a timid hello and show ourselves to a corner table. We never put up the Table Tent.

My group is made up of Jane, Melissa, Rose, Logan, and me. Jane and Melissa don't talk much. Rose tells us she signed up for the service because a book she's reading encouraged her to try activities outside her comfort zone. I pull my second Chandler Bing in a single week and take it upon myself to fill every silence with a lame joke.

"Sure I'll have a second glass of wine, maybe we can make this GirlFriendCircle *really* interesting!" Ugh. What is wrong with me?

The other ladies laugh. Whether out of nerves or pity I can't tell.

Logan is a 4'11" spitfire. She shares her life story—her move from California to Chicago, her recent transition to self-employment—without taking a breath. She's dating a guy long distance at the moment ("though Skype helps!"), and is planning the solo trip to Paris and India she's always dreamed of. "I thought of it long before the whole *Eat, Pray, Love* thing," she insists.

I've set a goal to ask out at least one potential BFF from each mixer I attend or group I join. Logan should expect to hear from me soon.

■ ■ ■

After all this blind connecting, I'm excited to spend a night with people I already know. My kitchen is stocked with pizza dough, a vat of tomato sauce, and eight girls in search of new BFFs. In a mere twenty-four hours I've gone from connectee to connector. Brynn, Lacey, and Ellen are laughing like old friends in the living room; Mia and Amanda are discovering their common California roots; Jackie, Kari, and I are sporting aprons and rolling out pizza dough, and Margot's surveying our progress, red wine in hand.

It's the evening after my GirlFriendCircles adventure, and I'm playing host at my first ever dinner party. I invited mostly the new friends who I don't see as often as I'd like and who reached out to me after reading my online essay. They all admitted to feeling similarly disconnected, with a shortage of local friends for whatever reason, so we can use one another's company. I added Margot to the list because while we have lunch decently often, I think she'd get along with this crowd. And Kari, my coworker, was recruited as a buffer. She has a knack for friendly chatter, so having her on deck to help guide conversation eases my nerves. After all, the rest of us have openly admitted to having trouble making new friends. There might be a reason for that.

Tonight's gathering is a make-your-own-pizza-and-cupcakes

affair. At yesterday's ConnectingCircle, we had "sharing questions"—What's your favorite book? Where would you like to vacation and why?—to keep conversation going should there be a lull. At this shindig, I ward off collective boredom and anxiety by putting my guests to work.

On my kitchen counter are three pizza stations: Margherita; Pepperoni and Shallot; and White Pizza with Sun-dried Tomato and Scallion. Aside from the ice-breakerness of cooking together, the make-your-own aspect takes some pressure off me and my cooking skills.

I said I was interested, I never said I was good.

"I read it's better to roll out the dough by hand than with a rolling pin," Jackie says.

"Go for it." I give her the rectangular baking sheet that will double as a pizza pan for tonight. She's wearing one of my four cooking aprons—remnants of two kitchen-themed bridal showers—and seems to have an idea of what she's doing.

Kari and I choose the rolling-pin route, and soon we're all gathered around my couch, talking weddings and job offers in between bites.

"Where's Matt tonight?" Mia asks me.

"At my mom's. I sent him there to watch LeBron." I'd warned Matt about the ladies' night a while ago, offering our bedroom as a private refuge, but he wanted to steer clear. My mother loves hosting her son-in-law, so she's made him a dinner of pasta—his carby favorite I try to keep out of our kitchen—and relinquished her couch and flat-screen. The entirety of America, minus some nine pizza-loving ladies, is tuned in to an ESPN circus, watching LeBron James announce that he will be leaving Cleveland to take his talents to South Beach. A quick refresh of my *USA Today* app tells me the news,

I share it with my guests who nod in semi-interest, and we get back to girl talk.

I've eaten three slices of pizza and one cupcake before I notice the clock. It's 10:45. Nearing my bedtime and long past Matt's. I never imagined my 7 P.M. call time would keep a group of strangers here so late. It's the sign of women who have been seriously craving some female bonding. As pleased as I am that the evening is a hit, I'm wondering if there is a polite way to kick them out. It's a school night, people! But Jackie is deep in conversation with Margot about what wedding dresses would work for her body. She's getting married next May, on the same day as Amanda, who's grilling Brynn with questions of health benefits. Amanda is waiting on a job offer from a small consulting firm, and Brynn is in HR at a mammoth company. She has lots of insights—on timing, retroactive coverage, and similarly titillating topics—all of which Amanda is eating up.

I close the door behind my last guest at 11:30 and check my phone, knowing Matt must be itching to get home, if he's even awake. There's a text from my mom. "Please call as soon as they leave. Matt is sound asleep." I call and give her the all clear. Ten minutes later Matt sleepwalks into the kitchen, eats a slice of homemade pizza, and crashes.

The next morning there's an email to the group from Mia. "I'd be happy to host the next one. Sushi night?"

And a bona fide cooking club, maybe even a new group of friends, is born.

CHAPTER 9

"Okay, you're a priest and a nun. Go."

Andy runs up to me, flailing his arms. "Father, Father, I don't know what to do!" He's using his best girly voice, and I immediately take on the role of priest.

"What's wrong, my child?" My hands are hooked together and raised chest-level like the Von Trapp Family Singers. I don't know why, but since I've never actually interacted with a priest, this is how I imagine they stand when on the clock. Maybe because Maria was a nun.

"I'm having these strange feelings . . . for a woman of the convent."

"Please, take a seat," I say.

"Have you ever encountered this problem before?"

"Well, there was this one other sister . . ."

"And by sister, do you mean a nun or an African American woman?"

"Both, actually," I say. "She went by the name of Sister Mary Clarence."

"Oh yes, I think I remember her," Andy's high-pitched alter-ego says. "As portrayed by Whoopi Goldberg?"

"And . . . scene!" Kimmi, our teacher, cuts us off on a high note.

It's week four of my improv class at Second City, a school that boasts alumni including Tina Fey, Steve Carell, and Chris Farley. This is the first scene I've done that hasn't made me want to run away. It's also one of the only where I was allowed to speak. Our inaugural class was made up entirely of getting-to-know-you games, the second was silent scenes, and the third was gibberish. That was a nightmare. "You're raking leaves and you're feisty," my teacher told me. You know the song "Nothing" from *A Chorus Line*? The one where Diana Morales can't bring herself to "be a table, be a sports car, ice cream cone"? That's how I felt. I proceeded to make my best raking motions while simultaneously shaking my head and growling. Is that even what feisty looks like? Unclear.

Despite the fact that I'm most certainly not going to be the next Liz Lemon, I am actually starting to enjoy these classes, if not so much for the activity as for the company. There are some definite potential friends here, and because we have class every week I can get to know them before bringing the relationships to the friend-date level. Consistency is one of the tenets of friendship, and the fact that I can count on three hours with these people every Tuesday night is helping to solidify relationships.

There's also the fact that we keep making asses of ourselves in front of each other. I mentioned earlier the "click accelerators" that Rom and Ori Brafman pinpoint in their book *Click*. Improv is the perfect place to put the vulnerability accelerator to the test. I may not be revealing my greatest fears or weak-

nesses, but standing up in front of a crowd and acting a fool—
and having them actually laugh *with* not *at* me—is a fast track
to trust.

Kimmi demonstrated this very truth in our second class.
First, everyone in the room had to stand in front of the group
and tell a funny story. (Mine involved my 6-year-old self
driving around with my mother, who would yell "Move, Jerk!"
or "Nice turning signal, Jerk!" or "Learn to drive, Jerk!" until
I asked her how it happened that we were always behind the
same person.) For the second round, we told embarrassing
stories. (Me, twenty years old, too many shots of Beefeater
Gin, vomit. Tale as old as time.)

"You might have laughed at the funny story," Kimmi told
us afterward. "But you probably felt a moment of connection
with the embarrassing one. You felt humiliated for him, or
you flinched or covered your eyes. You *felt* for him. And that's
what you want the audience to do for you." Apparently winning over a crowd isn't all that different from wooing a BFF.

I didn't know this going in, but improv is a male-dominated
art form. In my class of twenty-two, we have seventeen boys
and five girls. I was disappointed at first—No ladies? No
friends? No, thank you!—but being in the minority has
bonded us women. And I'm not necessarily averse to making
male friends. Andy's great, and there's Eddie, who's gay and
hilarious and a BFF waiting to happen.

As for the women, Jenny is an itty-bitty thing who gives
the impression of a porcelain doll until she opens her mouth
and always, every single time, goes for the dirty. If she's not
sitting on a toilet, she's getting a bikini wax. Or getting it on.
It's so unexpected out of her small frame that it always gets a
laugh. In real life, Jenny is a producer at a local news station.
We've discussed the possibility of getting together with our

husbands—hers is a Matt, too—but nothing has come to frui-
tion yet.

Right now the most promising prospect is Rachel. She's 22
and just graduated from the University of Iowa. On paper,
she's another mini-me. Aside from the first name, her middle
name is Levin while my married name is Levine. This much
we figured out in the first week. During the following week
we discovered that our moms are in the same quilting group.
Then that we were in the same sorority. She lives in Evanston, where I went to college, and loves all the same TV I do.
Though I haven't had good luck with dates in her age group
thus far, Rachel seems like a winner. Having weekly class in
common gives us a solid context in which to anchor our relationship.

The fact that Rachel comes equipped with a pal for my mom
gives her a leg up on my other potential BFFs. I've joked about
mother-daughter double dating before, but Rachel and I have
already discussed it as a real possibility. Our moms are friendly
in their quilting group, and Rachel lives at home. It only makes
sense that my mother and I would head out to Evanston for a
ladies brunch.

My mom has been continuing her own BFF search alongside mine, though she wouldn't explicitly call it that. She
befriended Shelly, the fellow widow with whom she said she
could go on cruises back when I was friendless and totally jealous of her. Then she secured a seat at the lunch table with a
group of quilters. (Even quilters have cliques! I can't stop picturing Regina George, fifty years later, instructing her minions
that "On Wednesdays, we wear pink.") She belongs to some
three different quilt guilds. It appeared she was having it easy
until I started to notice the loneliness in her voice from time
to time. There are threads of my own story in my mother's,

and I want to encourage her to buck up and go for it when she gets invitations to parties where she doesn't know anyone. Still, her hesitance is about more than the difficulty of meeting new people.

Mom hates being "the token widow" and I can't blame her. (When my father first died, I dreaded being "the one with the dead dad" in my group of friends. I don't know why this concern took such hold of me, but in the haze of grief we latch on to irrational fears.) Take a few weeks ago, when she went to her best friend's son's wedding.

"The hardest part was not having someone to zip up my dress," she said.

What can I say to that?

If you look past the résumés, Rachel is actually much funnier and more outgoing than I. She's supergoofy, in a self-deprecating and endearing way. She's constantly tripping herself up in scenes and then trailing off with some collection of unrelated words. "I. We. Yeah. Lunch. Fail." Even her gibberish, which sounds like a poor attempt at German—"Flargen bargen fargen"—makes me laugh. And she's just enough younger than me that she has no difficulties with friend-making. She's proof of what I've come to call the Second City Factor.

The gist of my Second City theory (which is completely unrelated from the improv school) is that it's in your second city after college when friend-making gets tough. When young 20-somethings arrive in their first post-grad home, they're surrounded by other real-world freshmen in the same boat. Everyone's a novice in the workforce, unfettered by college classes or midterm papers, looking for buddies to drink, gossip, and go to the movies with. Making new friends is easy—everyone is more or less looking for the same thing.

The decision to move to the second post-college city (or suburb, or town), however, is usually made independent of friends. No matter if you do it for love, career, family, or school, the second move is on your own terms. And given that you've probably got a few post-grad years under your belt, you're not guaranteed a sea of new-in-town friend prospects this time around. Plenty of the companions you're looking for have lived in your new city for years and have already filled their BFF quota. Suddenly, you're floundering in the search for that certain someone, despite having been surrounded by plenty of perfect someones all your life. The trick is to find other second-city dwellers or slowly infiltrate the established ranks. That's when making friends becomes the tricky dating dance: Am I coming on too strong? When can I call her again? Did she like me, or did she like like me?

I'm currently grappling with my second city, while Rachel—and most of our improv classmates—are in their first.

That's the other thing. I'm one of the oldest students in the class. From what I can tell, Beginning Improv is a course that people sign up for when they still live at home and are trying to figure out what they want to be when they grow up. My class is mostly filled with aspiring actors/comedians/writers who have day jobs (sometimes) but not careers. Being a 28-year-old professional with no dreams of the stage seems to be the exception rather than the rule.

During our mid-class break, Rachel and I have been taking shopping trips to the Walgreens across the street, where she'll tell me about her most recent text exchange with Bill or pre-class dinner with Josh.

"You and Bill text?" I'll ask, baffled by the ease with which she socializes with our fellow improvisers during the off hours.

"Sure," she'll say.

"When did that start?"

"I don't know, I got his number sometime. Probably at drinks after class. We don't say anything interesting."

"Did you just text him randomly one day? Or did he contact you? Was it weird?" Each week I grill her for the specific logistics of how she has already turned our entire class into a band of BFFs. It comes easy to her, not like something that needs to be overanalyzed, and I'm starting to realize that I sound both insecure and generally socially inept. So, after four weeks, I decide to curb the inquisition and make a move of my own.

The next day, via email, I ask my younger self out. We put a pre-class dinner date on the books.

■ ■ ■

The further I get into this year, the clearer the necessity of regularity becomes. It's like Shasta Nelson's formula: Twice a month for three months makes a friend. A few of my semi-successful girl-dates—Muffy, Pam, Morgan—haven't evolved into real relationships because we have nothing that reliably brings us together. If it were important enough to both of us, we'd make plans to ensure some consistency, but that has to be a two-way street. There aren't enough days in a month for me to schedule bi-weekly dates with everyone—at least not if I ever want to enjoy a quiet night with Matt, or yoga, or *30 Rock*—so I've focused mostly on the ladies who I absolutely adore (Jillian) and those who reciprocate my interest in our friendship (Hilary, Margot). The other contenders at the front of the pack are those who I already see regularly (Hannah at book club, my co-workers in the office). And hopefully my new cooking club will manufacture some regularity with that promising crowd.

The difference between the monthly consistency of book club versus the weekly nature of improv is that it takes four times as long to get to the same place. So while I've belonged to two book clubs since January, I'm just now establishing independent relationships with some of the members. In New York, my fellow book clubbers became some of my favorite people. They came to my wedding, they've visited me since my move. We had such girl-crushes on our nerdy little gang that we'd plan mid-month nonbook gatherings, just so we'd get more time to love each other.

Aside from Hannah and Jillian, I've still never seen any of my Chicago book club friends outside of our meetings. Though I have started emailing with one of my fellow readers whenever there's something important to say about *Modern Family* or *Friday Night Lights,* and with another when I notice her updates on Goodreads.com. And Natalie and I exchange messages about yoga.

You may recall that Natalie is Matt's coworker, the one who brought me along to her friend's cookie party earlier this year. We've been friendly since then, but two book clubs ago we bonded over her newfound love of yoga—she had started only a month earlier and was already doing a thirty-day challenge—and the fact that I got engaged at an Anusara retreat gave me yogi street cred in her eyes.

(It's true. Almost two years ago, I booked a trip to Tulum, Mexico, for a week of beachside downward dogs. I'd begged Matt to join me, but since he couldn't take the days off I decided to test my tolerance for solo travel. There would be like-minded people, I figured. New friends! On the first night, after class but before dinner, I waited, naked and in the dark— we only had electricity late at night—for my shower to heat up. Suddenly a shadow of a man slipped into my hut. I was about to get raped by a local vagabond. *Why had they told me I didn't need to lock my room?* After screaming, jumping some five feet in the air and simultaneously trying to cover my lady parts, I saw that the Mexican hobo rapist was in fact Matthew, who'd booked the trip in secret. Nothing like mistaking your fiancé-to-be for a sexual predator. That's romance.)

It's been about six weeks since Natalie and I first bonded over yoga. But the magic moment when our friendship really took flight was at our last meeting, on a Friday two weeks back. We'd read, or reread, *The Great Gatsby,* and one of our fellow members was hosting us on her family's boat. Ten ladies, F. Scott Fitzgerald, and Lake Michigan.

As with most of our meetings, discussion about the actual book lasted about thirty minutes. At which point Natalie and I decided to play with our host's new iPad. She subscribed to *Us Weekly* on that thing! Brilliant.

"I think I want a romper," I mentioned as we admired Alicia Keys adorably sporting her baby bump in a khaki number.

"You're kidding." Natalie looked horrified. "They're awful!"

"I think they're cute. If you can rock it, which I'm not sure I can. But they'd be perfect vacationwear. Nice and comfy, no waistband . . ."

"Right. Wear a dress."

"I do, but rompers are a good alternative. No thigh chafing!"

"Rachel. Rompers are for infants. They are onesies. A grown woman should not wear one in public."

The debate continued with no resolution. Until Saturday afternoon when I had lunch with my brother and his girlfriend, who was wearing a glorious Armani Exchange thin-strapped, gray-and-white graphic-print romper.

Gotta love modern technology. Within minutes I'd texted Natalie a photo of Jaime with a note. "See! Cute!"

It has become our Great Romper Debate. Whenever I spot a woman wearing one well, I send Natalie the photographic evidence. Whenever Jessica Simpson wears one, Natalie sends the resulting tabloid attacks my way. This happens more than it should. Some bodies do nothing for my cause.

The romper has become our inside joke. Our friendship tipping point.

FRIEND-DATE 28. Two weeks after the inaugural dispute, Natalie and I are at the Cubs game. With our men. It's a perfect double date because there is baseball for the guys, rampant rompering for us, and Matt actually knows these people.

If there's anything to complain about, it's that yoga and rompers play such starring roles in our fledgling friendship that I can't think of much else to say. Romper this and yoga that. Whatever. I'll take it.

◼◼◼

Matt and I are going to Croatia next Friday. It's our honeymoon, almost one year after the fact. We took a two-week Mediterranean cruise about seven weeks before our wedding, so taking another week off after the nuptials wasn't in the cards. As it turned out, had we booked a big trip we would have canceled, given how sick Matt's dad was by the time of the wedding. We couldn't have known that then, we just lucked out. Well, really lucking out would have been having our fathers walk us down the aisle, but given the circumstances, we took what we could get.

Going to Europe for a full seven days means I'll have no

choice but to double up on girl-dates this week. It shouldn't be too hard, as follow-ups have been tough to come by this month. The majority of my new friends are on the wedding circuit and traveling a ton. I've been out of town six out of the last nine weekends. People talk about fair-weather friends, but from my experience, the warmer it gets the harder it is to pin people down. I may get my Chicago residency revoked, but I'm just going to say it: I can't wait for summer to end.

If I really wanted to maintain my once-a-week policy, I could shoot for an impromptu Croatian jaunt with a fellow airline passenger, but that might be pushing it, even for me. Girl-dates are probably not the best addition to a honeymoon agenda.

FRIEND-DATE 29. Logan, my GirlFriendCircles connection, is not on speed (I don't think) but she could be. She's like a tornado, a mini–Tasmanian devil. Given that she's less than five feet tall, it almost feels as if her tiny size can't contain her big personality.

I'm a talker, too, so I don't mind, but it's exhausting just listening to her. The intense energy she expends telling story after story—and the lack of breaks for, you know, breath—has me on edge. It's as if she might pass out at any minute and needs to get it all in now. Sort of like Six in *Blossom* or the Micro Machines guy.

"And you should totally come to the trunk show! It's at my apartment and there are tons of girls, and gorgeous earrings, bracelets, necklaces." Logan pulls a catalog from her purse. "And wine, of course! It's so fun! Rachel, you'll love it!"

There's real pep here. She's genuinely excited to tell me stories of jewelry sales and networking events. It's no wonder she works in PR. There are few women who could pull off this kind of enthusiasm without appearing totally fake. She's constantly hosting Tweetups, she says, and is an active member of the Step Up Women's Network.

"You should come to our event next week! It's going to be fab."

I can't make it—the whole Croatia thing—but I shouldn't worry. "I'll keep sending you invitations. You'll get sick of hearing from me!"

I might, but I appreciate the enthusiasm. She even seems to be the first grown woman in history to love dating. The single ladies I've met who are over the age of 25 all harp on the misery of the singles scene. I can't dispute them, as my most recent experience on the circuit—aside from with my husband—was eight years ago. I went out with a guy I met at a bar in San Francisco my junior year of college. I was interning at *San Francisco Magazine* for three months and had given my number to said gentleman when we met in the Marina neighborhood, around the corner from the room I was renting. A week later, we were to meet at the same spot. I drank an entire cranberry and vodka before he even arrived, let him make out with me on my stoop, and avoided his phone calls ever after. So no, I'm not an expert. But Logan's lack of woe-is-me attitude is refreshing.

"I told him, 'Ross, you've got a perfect girl here. If you want to see me, you need to book a ticket to Chicago. I'm not traveling to Seattle. Don't F this up.'" Logan's been talking to a guy who lives across the country. A different one than the South Carolinian she'd been pursuing last month.

"But, you know, I love dating. You never know what you're going to get!" At 35, I'd think she was being sarcastic, except I'm not sure she knows how.

I nod and smile. It's unnecessary to interject.

* * *

FRIEND-DATE 30. Rachel and I meet for the early-bird special, a 5:45 stir-fry dinner before improv. We're basically eating with our grandparents.

"I think Kimmi hates me," she tells me.

"Me too! But I have a girl-crush on her anyway," I say.

"Yeah. She's way too cool for us."

Rachel's speaking my language.

She has an interview to be an intern at a casting agency and needs advice on what to wear. I give her my best how-to-nail-an-interview tips. Afterward, we get vanilla ice cream cones from McDonald's and agree to make this a weekly date, as soon as I get back from Europe.

■ ■ ■

I wonder if a honeymoon has ever led to a divorce. Not that mine will. No siree. But I could see how one could. People always describe their honeymoons as "romantic," "magical," "blissful." But traveling for a week with one other person, spending twenty-four hours a day with him and no one else, is sure to lead to a few spats. No one ever admits this, probably for fear of confessing that the honeymoon was over before the actual honeymoon was over.

Our week in Croatia is romantic, blissful, and magical, except for when it is hostile, frustrating, and bitter. Ours is a stupid argument, of the we'll-laugh-about-this-later variety, but without any friends around for refuge, a little nothing feels like a huge something.

It comes four days into our trip. We are in Korcula, a charming little island off the Dalmatian coast. Actually, we've taken a morning escape from Korcula to Stupe, a tiny beach island with only one structure—a seafood restaurant. There are no sand beaches in Croatia. It's all rock. I actually prefer it this way, as I'm not a fan of dumping sand out of my bathing suit bottom after a long day in the sun. Still, given the terrain, it probably wasn't my best idea to scale the entire island in only a pair of black flip-flops. But I'm not unlike a child who fancies herself an explorer, so I run ahead of Matt—in his sensible sneakers—in search of the perfect flat rock to set up shop.

We quickly learn what it seems all the other island visitors already know. Other than the bit of beach directly in front of the restaurant, there is no perfect space to set up shop. It seems we are the only people to have had the bright idea to trek the perimeter of the entire island, and the last bit of rock, which we need to traverse in order to get back to the dock and restaurant, is the most jagged yet. There's only one solution.

"Take my flip-flops," I tell Matt. "I'm going to swim it."

"Okay, be careful," he says.

It's only a short distance and the person who needs to be wary is Matt, who's maneuvering the slippery rocks while wearing his huge backpack and his beloved camera around his neck. We make it with no problem.

Until.

"Matt, there's a weird pain in my foot and there are these strange black dots on the back of my heel that I can't get out."

"It's probably just rubber fibers from your flip-flops," he says.

"I don't know what that means. These shoes don't even touch the back of my heel. And when I try to get them out it starts to bleed."

"I'm sure you're fine," he says. "You did all that rock climbing with your flip-flops on, they probably rubbed off on your foot. I wouldn't worry."

Despite having never heard of flip-flop fibers embedding themselves in someone's skin, I choose to trust my husband. Until ten minutes later when I hear a group of British children in the water yelling, "Watch out for sea urchins!" Except "urchin" sounds more like "uhhchin" and I wish I could infuse such an accent into my would-be offspring.

"I see a sea uhhchin!"

"Don't touch the sea uhhchin!"

I have no idea what a sea urchin is—they're in sushi, yes?—but it appears these kids and their parents are all wearing aqua socks, while I chose to swim barefoot.

"What is a sea urchin, exactly?" I ask their mother, with whom I'd started up a friendly conversation in an effort to get this very information.

"They're the black spiny things in the water," she says. "You can spot them if you keep an eye out, but if you step on one the tentacles can get stuck in your foot like a splinter."

"Do you think that's what this is?" I shove my heel in her direction.

"I don't really know. I've never seen what the sting looks like, actually."

I'm still of the belief that moms know everything. Not just my own mother. Anyone who's ever borne children. "You're a mom, does this rash look funny? Who should I call to fix my washing machine? What's the square root of 6,629?"

A quick referral to my Lonely Planet Croatia guide tells me that sea urchins are everywhere on the floor of the Adriatic and that swimmers should wear aqua socks to protect themselves. If you do get the spiny needles stuck in your foot, olive oil can help remove them. If you do not get them out, they could become infected, the book says.

It would have been a good idea to read this earlier.

"This is definitely a sea urchin," I tell Matt. "What were you even talking about, rubber fiber? Is that even a thing? The Croatians are going to cut off my foot, I know it."

I'm not usually much of a hypochondriac, but the fear of having an infected heel in a foreign land has visions of amputations dancing in my head.

"Rachel, you need to calm down," Matt says. "It's going to be fine. We'll go to the pharmacy when we get back, don't let it ruin our day."

Too late for that. "Not ruin our day? There are tentacles. In my foot. What if they're poisonous?"

"Then the book would probably have mentioned that. I think we would have heard about it if there were deadly animals all over the ocean floor."

I want these things out pronto. I can't think about much else. We eat our lunch in silence, except for when I request a bottle of olive oil to douse my foot with. (They don't have any.) I'm frustrated that Matt clearly doesn't appreciate the severity of the situation, he's annoyed that I'm acting crazy.

When we get back to Korcula we head straight to the pharmacy, where, after a questionable exchange in broken English, they give me some antibacterial ointment and Band-Aids. At the hotel, I ask the concierge, a stronger English speaker, what she thinks.

"Does it hurt?"

"Yes, kind of."

"Huh. Well, I think it's fine. I've had one in my leg for three years." There's a distinct hint of pride in her voice.

I'm still not convinced, so I do what any rational self-diagnoser would. I consult the Internet.

Well, that's it. These Croatians don't know what they're talking about. According to WebMD I should be shaving off the top layer of my skin and then digging out these needles.

"I need to go back to the pharmacy," I tell Matt. "Got to buy some tweezers and operate."

"Don't you think *that* is what will infect your foot? Shouldn't you trust the pharmacists instead of the Internet?"

It's 4 P.M. The rest of the day continues along this path of me overreacting and Matt not overreacting nearly enough. He's furious at me for blowing this out of proportion, while I'm enraged that he's not freaking out right alongside me.

What we need is a break from each other. Not a Ross-and-Rachel-style break, just an hour or so to each come back to neutral. Matt should watch a game with some guys and grunt about how I'm unreasonable, and I could use a friend to give me the face-to-face emotional support I need, which in this case means figuring out a better solution than "if it's still really hurting in a few days we'll go back to the pharmacy, even though it will already be too late."

The sea-urchin-shaped cloud dissipates throughout the next day and disappears entirely after we arrive on the island of Hvar, where I find a pharmacist with a magic ointment that extracts the needles. "Put it on your foot every day and they should come out on their own in less than a week," she tells me. It's a pitch-black cream that smells like tar, but it has solved my current marital problems. I refrain from enveloping her in a bear hug.

It was a blemish on an otherwise perfect trip. Nothing a little breathing room couldn't have quickly squashed. But our fight was emblematic of what is happening in plenty of marriages these days, when couples are so determined to keep the honeymoon alive that they try to maintain their vacation-from-the-world attitude long after the suitcases are unpacked.

Recall the 2004 General Social Survey, the one that reported social isolation in America is increasing. It found that the average American reports feeling close to two people, down from three in 1985, and that a whopping 25 percent of the survey respondents reported feeling close to no one at all. The only good news to come out of the study was that the percentage of people who include a spouse in their circle of closest confidants increased by 8 percent—from thirty to thirty-eight. This speaks well for the future of marriage. Long and happy relationships are made of trust. But while it's great that more people can confide in their spouses, the number of people who reported that they can confide in *only* their spouses increased by almost half.

Confiding in your spouse: good. Confiding in no one *but* your spouse: bad. What if something happens to your hubby? Or if he's the very person you want to vent about? Then who do you turn to?

This is where things get tricky. Alongside the increase in communication among spouses has come a tendency for couples to isolate themselves from the rest of their social network. A 2010 study found that when the average person couples off, she drops two friends. A pair of researchers who studied U.S. national data from 1994 to 2004 found that married couples had fewer familial ties and were less likely than single folk to socialize with neighbors or friends. "Once people get married, they seem to feel relieved of social obligations toward family and friends," write Jacqueline Olds and Richard Schwartz in *The Lonely American*. "Cocooning is the couples version of social isolation. It does increase closeness in marriages. It also increases the fragility of marriage, the burdens placed upon marriage and, over time, it increases the likelihood of both divorce and loneliness."

Our European vacation can't exactly be qualified as social isolation. It was a welcome and necessary getaway, complete with wine tours and yoga, banana boat rides and massages, people-watching and the best seafood I've ever eaten. We spent significantly more time laughing, talking, and being all, you know, romantic than we did squabbling. But it can't be a co-incidence that our first big fight since early in this friend-quest came just as we were a thousand miles away from the rest of our social network.

We land in Chicago on a Sunday night with gifts, some three thousand photographs, an empty tube of SPF 85 sun-block, and one bandaged heel. Good old Mom picks us up at the airport. I am not particularly thrilled to be home—would you be? After a week of island-hopping on the Adriatic Sea?—but I'm not sad to return to the new women in my life. Much worse, after all, would be returning to no one.

CHAPTER 10

Summer may be tough for girl-dating, but it's prime time for catching up with old friends. I guess that's what my new pals are doing, too. Everyone is taking advantage of the nice weather, using it as an incentive to persuade lifelong friends to visit—Chicago winters scare off potential guests ten months of the year—or to take those unused vacation days for trips of their own. I've already done the high-school-ten-years-later thing, and next week my summer camp is hosting five hundred alumni for a one-hundred-year anniversary weekend in Maine. And despite having gotten home from Croatia just yesterday, this week Matt and I are playing host to friends who are in town for Lollapalooza, Chicago's annual summer music festival.

Our first guest, Sam, is a buddy from the college days. He's part of Matt's close-knit group of guys—men who maintain their ties six years after graduation by way of fantasy football—but he and I actually connected long before either of us knew my husband. We became friends in the first few weeks of freshman year because we lived in the same dorm (the only prerequisite for friendship in the early college days) and he went to high school with Sara. She'd been singing his praises since we both got accepted, so I had my eye on him from day one. (Platonically, that is. He came to NU with his high school girlfriend, who is another close friend of mine.) Now Sam is staying with us for a week, exploring the city while Matt and I work.

One of Sam's most endearing qualities is how awkward he purports to be, when in fact he's one of my most accomplished friends. He graduated from Northwestern undergrad and Georgetown Law School. He taught English in Japan, worked on immigration law in Geneva, and monitored human rights in the Congo. He's hardly an underachiever. Yet to hear him tell it he's a bumbling fool, so he's genuinely in awe of the concept of friend-dating.

"I went out to dinner with this guy in Geneva once. We were introduced through a coworker," he tells Matt and me over dinner. "It was a total man-date. Very intense. And uncomfortable."

"A bromance in the making?" I ask.

"Hardly. It was painful. I had no idea how to behave." I'm willing to bet Sam's behavior was perfectly appropriate, but his discomfort wasn't unusual. An intimate dinner for two is not the male bonding method of choice. It goes back to the face-to-face versus side-to-side friendship theory. Men prefer the latter—watching sports or movies, playing golf or poker or video games, going fishing or drinking or camping. Author Jeffrey Zaslow, whose book *The Girls from Ames* recounts the forty-year friendship between eleven girls in Iowa, tells a story about how he's played poker with the same guys for eighteen years but none of them knows his children's names. I've always found it hard to believe—by the time I leave a girl-date I can usually recite my new friend's entire family tree, not to mention her offsprings' names and ages. I was so skeptical of Zaslow's story that I recently grilled my uncle George about his own poker game.

"You play with them every week, do you know the names of their kids?"

George thought for a moment. "I'm not even sure which of them has kids," he said.

That's not to say that male friendships are less vital to their health or happiness. One study of Swedish men found lack of social support to be one of the two leading risk factors for heart attacks and death from coronary heart disease. The other factor was smoking.

The trouble for men comes as they grow older and disengage from the activities they once enjoyed. According to the research, when men get married and have families, the pressure to balance wives and kids and jobs doesn't leave time for the office softball team or weekly card game. They reluctantly cut back on time with friends, seeing the existing ones less and abstaining from activities that help them make new ones. By the time they realize what they've lost, they feel like it's too late. And unless he's Paul Rudd in *I Love You, Man,* no guy is going to set out on a friend-dating quest.

Sam is not married and doesn't have kids, so he isn't at this family-or-friends crossroads just yet. One botched Genevan man-date is no big deal. He has recently returned to New York City for good, his first permanent residency stateside since he graduated law school. Considering he was born and raised in Manhattan and all his BFFs are still there, I think he'll be just fine.

■ ■ ■

The girl on the yoga mat next to mine looks incredibly familiar, but I can't figure out how I know her. I do a mental scan of my personal rolodex. Was she a girl-date? No. Phew. I have a perpetual fear of running into one of my lady-dates and drawing a blank. It wouldn't happen with one of my new friends, but what about someone I've only met once? Five or six months ago? Definite possibility.

Then, mid–triangle pose, I place her. She taught an exercise class I took at a different studio last year. The old me would silently register this coincidence and go on my way. But a consequence of this year has been that I talk to everyone now. As it turns out, shopping is more interesting when you know the saleslady's life story, meals are more delicious when you dissect each dish with the waiter before ordering. I'll chat with the woman in line behind me at the movie theater, the guys next to me at the sports bar, anyone. It makes life more fun.

Well, more fun for me. Not everyone in my life loves my newfound everyone's-a-potential-BFF attitude. My mother recently treated our whole family to dinner at celebrity chef Graham Elliot's restaurant, and I didn't want to botch the ordering. After some discussion with the waiter—who was quite friendly and seemed to appreciate having his culinary knowledge put to use, I might add—I went with the suckling pig.

"You get everything you needed?" my brother, Alex, asks. He looks mortified.

"Yup. Why?"

"You talked to him for fifteen minutes."

"I didn't know what to get! Now you're all going to be jealous of my meal." And it was three minutes, tops.

"It was a little ridiculous," Alex says. My brother's not unfriendly, but he is perpetually concerned with how others perceive him and he embarrasses easily when people don't behave "appropriately" in public. To him, appropriately means using proper etiquette and being polite, but also not inconveniencing people. And talking to a waiter—making too many special requests or asking too many questions—is, by his standards, an inconvenience. He's of the "don't bother the waiter or he'll spit in your food" mind-set, just as I was earlier this year.

"How do you eat with her?" my brother asks Matt.

"Oh, I just tune it out."

Nice guys. I used to be on their team though. I was annoyed when strangers talked to me—*I'm trying to get things done here, people, not have a pow-wow*—and even more frustrated when the people I was with chatted up everyone in sight—*Um, hello! I'm right here. Pay attention to me!* I'd stand off to the side with a half smile, not knowing when to jump in or how to cut the conversation short.

Now I'm the talker. Not the kind that can't read social cues and overstays her welcome (although I'm sure that's what they all say), but the kind who gets pleasure from a few bits of friendly banter. And you know what? I like life better this way.

"Don't you teach at The Daily Method?" I ask the yoga girl after class.

"I do."

"I thought so. I took a class with you last summer." She looks guilty, as if I've caught her in bed with the enemy.

"I'm cheating on them!" she says with a laugh. "But actually a lot of the teachers take yoga as a complement." I want to tell her she doesn't need to justify herself to me.

"Aren't you getting married this summer?"

"Wow, that's some memory."

I've always had eerily good recall. I remember this tidbit

because when we met she told me she did The Daily Method in hopes of getting arms like Jessica Biel's for her wedding. I wanted the same thing.

"It's actually in three weeks," she says.

"Congratulations! That's so exciting." We talk about her nuptials as we roll up our mats and head out. I'm not even toying with the idea of asking her out. She's getting married in less than a month. I know how busy and exhausting the lead-up can be, and I can hear the stress in her voice. I have no interest in adding to her anxiety.

A year ago I wouldn't have talked to her at all. Six months ago I might have, but only to get a girl-date. Maybe now I'm just friendly, no strings attached.

When I tell Matt and Sam about the encounter, which isn't much on its own but is a nice model of my growth, they seem impressed.

"You've become quite the friendship expert," Sam says.

"Ha! Maybe you missed the part about how this whole year started because I had no friends?"

I *have* started to feel like something of a self-made friendship scholar though, if only because relationship behavior is the framework through which I now see the world. Got a beef with your boyfriend? Maybe you're cocooning. Sending a text? What a modern-day communicator! Even going to brunch is like that restaurant scene in *Being John Malkovich*, where the actor's face is everywhere and all anyone can say is "Malkovich Malkovich Malkovich." Except in my world it's tables of friends everywhere I turn, taunting me with their air kisses and giggly BFFness.

Even when Sam and I go to the zoo later in the week, all I can think of is how friendless the lone polar bear must feel.

* * *

FRIEND-DATE 31. I've wanted to get together with Dianne since she started working with me a year ago. We have some mutual friends so we'd both been given the heads-up about the other when she was hired. We've talked about getting after-work drinks, but the few times we've tried, work got nutty and Dianne had to cancel. She's on the tech side of things while I'm just a words person, so she is called on at the eleventh hour to fix problems way above my paygrade.

Dianne sent me an email while I was out of town about a new social dining website in Chicago. Grubwithus is similar to OpenTable, the online restaurant reservations site, but instead of reserving a table, you secure only a seat or two at a party of eight. "Being recent transplants to Chicago, we wanted to meet new people but didn't want to hang out at the bars and clubs every night," the founders say on their website. "We thought it'd be much more fun to bond at the best restaurants in Chicago for a discounted price."

Basically, they're me, but they launched their search over family-style dining rather than girl-dates.

It's a brilliant idea. A real why-didn't-I-think-of-that in our Groupon-hoarding *Top Chef*-obsessed culture. Meals cost anywhere from fifteen to twenty-five dollars, and even though the company is brand-new, they've already set up partnerships with some trendy Chicago restaurants. From a friend-making standpoint, it makes perfect sense. Nothing brings people together like food, except maybe drink, and these meals promise to be rife with both.

I am definitely intrigued.

The problem is that since the site is still in its infancy, you have to be invited to join and I haven't been issued such an honor. So when Dianne tells me she's thinking of going to the inaugural meal—she was granted access for being a prolific Chicago restaurant Tweeter—I jump on my chance. I know each diner is allowed to bring a friend.

"I'd love to try it out," I tell her, completely inviting myself along. When you're on a determined quest you must be willing to be assertive and this is too good an opportunity to pass up. It could be both a friend-date with Dianne *and* a chance to meet future date prospects.

I'm not entirely clear on the ethics of picking up a potential friend while I'm already out with one. Perhaps the most egregious romantic-date transgression is the wandering eye. Checking out other prospective mates—no matter how cute they are, or how horrifically inept/obnoxious/meatheaded your date is—is not okay. Does the same hold true in the world of friend-dating?

I wouldn't want Dianne to feel like I'm only half paying attention to her. But friendship is not romance, no matter how similar girl-dating and the romantic kind are. There is no exclusivity. We don't have to have The Talk. ("What *are* we?" "Why do we have to give it a label?" "But do you like me? Or do you like like me?" "I just want to be friends! Not best friends. It's too much too soon.") And adding a third to the mix doesn't bring up any porn imagery.

At dinner, it quickly becomes clear that this concern is a nonissue. Dianne is as interested as I am in new methods of socializing, and she spends more of her time talking with our fellow diners than she does with me.

Our group is seated at a long rectangular table, not the ideal scenario for group dining. I'm at the end, which means I have three people within speaking distance—Dianne, who's seated next to me, the girl across from her, and the girl across from me. If I shout I can talk to one of the company's founders, who is sitting on Dianne's other side, but she has his ear. Early in the meal she mentioned that she'd found some flaws in their website, so they're debriefing operating systems or coding problems or some other such techspeak.

"How are things going in the office?" I ask her during a break in their conversation.

"Fine. Crazy. You know. I'd love to get home before eight some night soon," she says before turning back to Daishin, the founder.

Luckily the girls across from me are talking books and I jump in as the conversation turns to *Harry Potter*. Sonia, a nurse practitioner, is an überfan. We talk shop—the theme park, the real-life Nicholas Flamel (I had no idea he was an actual guy!)—and our conversation takes off from there. As if single-handedly advancing child literacy weren't enough, J. K. Rowling has now been the guiding force behind two of my friend connections. It's a bit overachieving.

I don't gel with Dianne nearly as much as I expect to, but I do find Sonia. And I sample three appetizers, a sushi roll, three entrées, and dessert for eighteen dollars. Overall, I'd call it a win.

■ ■ ■

When it comes to sleepaway camp, there are two, er, camps: Those who get it, and those who don't. Even today, twelve years after my last summer, I find myself struggling to articulate to noncampers why my nine seasons at Tripp Lake (plus one as a counselor) were so life altering. It's a losing battle.

"I don't get you people and your camp obsession," my coworker Kari said recently, after I told her I was going to Maine to sleep in old bunks and shower in what can only be described as a moth-filled plastic box.

"If you didn't go you'll never get it," I said. "It sounds a bit ridiculous in the retelling."

"I went to tennis camp for two weeks," Ashley offered.

"Not the same!" She looked offended. "I don't know what it was, specifically. We sang a lot, played a ton of sports, made pottery. We basically played all day long. What could be better?"

I was lucky to get to spend the summers of my youth in a corner of Southwest Maine rather than having to work. My noncamp friends had jobs or family reunions or swim team, while I played soccer and beaded bracelets and learned to water-ski. All in the same day. Even then I knew how good I had it. I was eight years old my first summer at Tripp Lake, and it didn't take long for me to develop a "cult-like mystical connection" to my seasonal home, as *This American Life* host Ira Glass once perfectly described it. I became *that girl*, memorizing lyrics to old songs, keeping scraps from every occasion, having the camp logo spray-painted onto my tennis racket strings. During the school year I counted down the days until I could go back, and during the summer I counted the days I had left. Sara and I would have long talks about how much we "worshipped" life at "The Promised Land." It was all fairly melodramatic.

But more important than the activities or the songs or the amenities was how easy it was to be a camper. You didn't have to be good at anything specific, you just had to have a good attitude. The Spirit of Tripp Lake Award was the most coveted honor each summer, and to win it you just had to be an easygoing, happy, excited kid.

The school year took work—balancing school and dance class and basketball and friends. When you're a type-A child with perfectionist tendencies, the stress of those demands can take a toll. At camp the pressure was off. We wore uniforms. There were no boys or schoolwork. Our greatest worry was having last-choice activity sign-ups. It was a two-month-long slumber party.

If I had to pinpoint one experience from my childhood that is responsible for my perhaps unreasonably high expectations of friendship, camp would be it. If you live in a bunk with six other girls for all that time, they become like sisters. Of course, there were fights—this was a summer camp not a commune— but there was a level of intimacy not rivaled by school or sports teams.

Which is why I have no qualms about boarding a plane to New York City less than two weeks after my return from Europe and driving six hours up to Maine with Sara and two other ex-campers for Tripp Lake's one-hundred-year alumni reunion.

"I made a special camp mix for our road trip," Sara says when I arrive. "I also went digging in my parents' apartment and found my old uniforms and our yearbook videos." She's as camp-crazy as I am. Maybe more.

We pop the tapes in the VCR (our camp days were pre-DVD, but it's completely characteristic of Sara to still have a VCR) at 11 P.M. Three hours later we're still up watching old movies. This one is from our final summer. 1998. Flashes of other campers bring up obscure memories I didn't even know I had. Remember when 8-year-old Micah woke us up every morning singing from *Joseph and the Amazing Technicolor Dreamcoat*? Remember the year Bruce the rock-climbing counselor hit his head on a barbell and the hippie counselors sang that war chant in the talent show? We're in the midst of a serious this-isn't-that-funny-but-I-can't-stop-laughing fit when Lizzie, Sara's roommate, emerges half-asleep from her room.

"Are you guys actually watching this?" We can't pull it together long enough to respond. She rolls her eyes and heads to the bathroom.

That night Sara and I share her bed for our sleepover, hoping to doze for all of three hours before we hit the road.

This isn't the kind of friendship I'm looking for this year. My relationship with Sara is eighteen years in the making. Nothing I find in twelve months can come close to our intimate understanding of who the other is and who she once was, and I don't need it to. But it's certainly an aspirational model of what, with a little time, a friendship can become.

"Can you guys keep it down? My daughter is trying to sleep."

On top of being an alumni weekend, this reunion is also a mother-daughter affair. The bunk next door is home to a group of 7-year-olds and their moms for the weekend, and we're keeping them up.

My bunk consists of thirteen women, all of whom were in my age group or the one above me while we were campers. Each of us has slipped back into our roles from those years ago—the class clown, the nurturing mom, the up-for-anything, let's-just-have-a-party girl. I haven't spoken to some of these people in ten years, but if a stranger walked in right now she'd think we've all been best friends since birth.

"Bertsche, remember when your hair looked like a boy?"

No one calls me Rachel here, and no one will ever forget the bowl cut my mom forced on me my first summer. She was scared I wouldn't brush it and would come home with a rat's nest for a head. She was probably right.

(My mother met one of her best friends on the train to their Wisconsin summer camp when she 9 years old. Joy took one look at Mom's short hair and said, "What are you doing here? This is a camp for girls!" I guess it's a rite of passage.)

"Yeah yeah," I answer Tara, whose bed is next to mine. "Remember when you lip-synched to 'Chantilly Lace' for the talent show when you were nine?"

The night continues like this, everyone shouting out memories, laughing as if the incidents happened yesterday. Sociologist Ray Pahl, author of *On Friendship,* calls these kinds of friends—the ones that you may not see for years but with whom you can always pick up where you left off—"fossil friends." It's a rare breed of pal, usually one with whom you've shared a significant life experience, but we all have them.

Here, the effortlessness of our reconnection has a lot to do with environment. Back when I lived in Manhattan I ran into some of these women on the street or at bars, and while we had nice chats it wasn't the seamless time travel that is this weekend. Now that we've returned to where the relationships were born, we ease back in like we would a comfy pair of footie pajamas.

On Sunday our caravan packs up the car to road trip home. I'm wearing the necklace I made in enameling yesterday, the same day I went sailing, played field hockey, and climbed the rock wall. In my real life I'd feel exceptionally accomplished having done just one of those things. Where did we find the energy?

"How was your weekend, camper?" Matt asks me. I tell him about conquering the rock wall and attempting to steer a sailboat, but there's no use trying to explain the social dynamics of my bunkmates, most of whom he's never even heard of. That's another thing about fossil friends. The relationships are so intricately woven into your personal history that to try to isolate just one and relay it to an outsider misses the point. It has no meaning without the full tapestry.

"We had fun," I say of my cabin, and leave it at that.

■ ■ ■

It's quite impressive how many meet-and-greet mixer options are out there for someone who's looking. Since I've amped up my participation, my schedule can hardly keep up with the different activities geared toward friend-making. Tonight I am going to a Mac 'n Cheese Mingler, an event hosted by local connector Saya Hillman. By day she's a video producer and entrepreneur who runs her own digital media company, Mac 'n Cheese Productions (named for the comfort the dish inspires), but she's best known around Chicago for the "linking strangers to strangers" parties she's been throwing since 2007. Anyone can sign up to attend one of these getting-to-know-you gatherings, which are held in Hillman's apartment. The only rule is that you can't know anyone else in attendance. Apparently Hillman keeps extensive Excel spreadsheets to ensure that no two guests have prior connections. I'm not really sure how Excel would know such a thing, but it's been working for her for three years so who am I to question the method?

Matt gives me a ride to Hillman's house before heading to play poker for the evening. It feels a bit like when my dad used to drop me off at playdates. I even give Matt the it's-okay-I'm-at-the-door-now-you-can-drive-away wave.

When I enter Hillman's two-story loft, with its exposed

brick and garden patio, I'm struck by the art house vibe going on here. Low lights, indie music, an older woman wearing dangly parrot earrings. Someone should start reading beat poetry, stat. Instead, Hillman sticks a name tag on my back.

"There's a character written on this name tag. As you introduce yourself to people, have them give you clues to who you are," she says. "A fun little icebreaker before we get started." These are the games I will not miss when this year is over.

I wander over to Mr. Darcy and Chandler Bing.

"Oh! You're my favorite," I tell Chandler. So helpful.

"Am I a fictional character?"

"Yup. I like you, too, actually," I say to Darcy.

"I'm not actually even sure who you are," Chandler tells me. Darcy checks out my back and looks horrified at this admission.

We decide to move on to more typical small talk—the whole "Where do you live?" "What do you do?" babble. I have a good feeling about Mr. Darcy, a tall redhead whose name is actually Gretchen, but before we can get too deep into a conversation Hillman separates us into three groups. Gretchen and I are not together.

"I'm handing out a list of questions," our host says. "Everyone in the group should answer and then as a group you'll pick the most interesting response to share with the whole room."

I settle into my group of three other women and two men as Hillman hands me the list. It's long.

"Okay. Question one. Share one unusual fact about yourself," I say. We stare at each other blankly. "I'll start. I was the president of my high school gospel choir."

"I can talk really fast," Ruth, who is sitting across from me, says. "I was on *America's Funniest People* for speed-talking."

"Really? Can you show us?" I ask.

"You need to give me something to talk about."

"Cars," offers Darryl, the guy sitting next to me.

"WellIreallyneedanewcarbutIdon'tknowwhattobuycausemy oldcarhardlyruns. . . ."

Forget what I said about Logan. Ruth *is* the Micro Machines guy. She goes on about cars for probably thirty more seconds. It's a much better icebreaker than any guessing game.

"Question four. What is an off-the-beaten-path activity that you've discovered in Chicago?"

"Freezing," Darryl says. Five confused faces turn in his direction. "I'm a freezer."

"Excuse me?" Ruth asks.

"I freeze. It's performance art. At a designated time we all freeze for twenty minutes."

"Freeze as in stop moving?" I ask. When he said he was a freezer my mind first went to the dessert portion of my refrigerator, then to a David-Blaine-stuck-in-a-giant-ice-cube type of trick.

"Yes," he says, though it's clear what he wanted to say was, "*Duh.*"

Everyone is intrigued. We're firing questions at him. "Where do you do it?" "How many of you are there?" "Do people ever get mad?" "Do they throw things at you?" "Have you ever had to stop early?"

"Hard-core freezers could freeze in an avalanche," he says. He is so passionate about extolling the virtues of freezing that he doesn't even notice the pun. "I've only broken once. It was in front of DePaul University and the security guard of the dorm was not having it. He kept asking us what we were doing, but of course I couldn't tell him, and then he called the cops. So I had to explain that this was an artistic expression. It was devastating to have to call it early."

We're collectively mesmerized—if a bit amused—by his passion for standing still.

"You guys should try it. Such a phenomenal rush," he says. "It will seriously change your life."

I wonder if I sound like this when I talk about camp.

"Question six. What's the best or worst date you've ever been on?"

"I had a really horrible date with this one girl," Darryl chimes in. "You see, I'm not very good with small talk. I really like to get to the core of who a person is."

Yeah, so we've learned. If we've discovered anything in the last five questions it's that Darryl is, shall we say, intense.

"This one girl, I just couldn't get to her. I was trying and trying to break her, and she wouldn't open up. Eventually she mentioned that she really wanted to travel to Europe. So I asked her, 'If Europe were an animal, what animal would it be?'"

Silence. The entire group is once again staring at him, stunned.

"You actually said that?" I ask.

"Yeah."

"Do you think she thinks *you* were *her* worst date, because you asked her what animal Europe would be?"

Darryl shrugs.

Our evening started at 9, and by the time the question portion is over and the subsequent sharing with the group ends, it's midnight and I've hardly had a chance to talk to Gretchen.

"Everyone keeps telling me they don't know who my name-tag person is," I tell her as our groups finally split up. I'm one of the last remaining guests still wearing a name tag.

"Seriously?" She sounds disgusted. "It's Ira Glass." She has just enough sass for me to know I'm going to like her.

The next morning—because friending stops for nothing!—I donate my time to Chicago's City Farm by way of One Brick, a no-commitment volunteer organization. Plenty of people have suggested that volunteer work would be the perfect way to make friends, but most of the programs I'm interested in require a regular commitment or a rigorous orientation process, neither of which I have time for this year. One Brick staffs other nonprofits, so you can sign up for whichever projects sound fun and fit into your schedule. Plus, the organization encourages a "social atmosphere around volunteering" and invites volunteers to gather at a local restaurant after each event. You do good, you make friends—a win-win. (And if it's a BFF bust, at least you've changed the world and all that.)

My morning consists mostly of weeding, but for a brief moment I get to pick beets. We only need one hundred and I come late to the party, so I only actually pick three, but still. I am basically a farmer!

Lunch afterward is an eclectic crowd, and I'm bummed because Marvin, one of the guys I was weeding with, doesn't join us. I was hoping to make him my first platonic straight male friend. Of course, there's plenty of debate as to whether that's really possible.

I recently asked Matt what he thought about my taking on a man-friend.

"No," he said.

"No, what? No I can't be friends with a guy?"

"No you can't ask a straight guy out on a friend-date. It wouldn't work. He'd think you were hitting on him."

"Oh, I don't think so. If I were wearing my ring?"

"It's just hard to imagine you putting all this effort into a relationship with another man."

I'm not sure what I think. I do have male friends—guys like Sam who were there when Matt and I got together, and a few at the office who serve as my work husband (in an office full of women, it's imperative to have one drama-free man on your side). But it is hard to imagine how I could initiate a platonic male-female friendship out in the real world. It's great in theory and I'd like to believe it would be no problem—I'm not delusional enough to think every guy I meet would fall for me—and yet I've seen *When Harry Met Sally* approximately twenty times. It's branded into my brain.

It's a moot point because Marvin isn't at lunch. Instead I sidle up to Margarita, one of the group leaders, on the walk to the restaurant and secure the seat next to her at lunch. This is not my first rodeo.

FRIEND-DATES 32, 33, 34, 35. My participation this month has produced a good handful of friend prospects.

Sonia from Grubwithus meets me for dinner at a nearby Thai restaurant. Aside from our mutual love of *Harry Potter,* we share interests in *Self* magazine and peanut sauce. It's not a ton to go on, but at this point I can pretty much talk about anything.

I found Veronica, a recent Chicago transplant from North Carolina, in the comments section of Jezebel.com. I figure these big blogs call it "community" for a reason, so I emailed her through the site after reading her comment on an article about . . . drumroll . . . how to make friends. We meet at a wine bar and talk for three hours.

Mac 'n Cheese Mingler Gretchen and I go to lunch a week after we met. I'm into her. She's got a dry sense of humor that simultaneously intrigues and intimidates me. She's in the midst of all these self-improvement projects—a hundred-mile bike-ride challenge, a dabbling in the Mennonite church—that one might call a quarter-life crisis. I can relate. Some might— and do—say the same about my year.

One Brick Margarita invites me to go shopping in China-town. We peruse the stores and eat a quick lunch at Tasty Diner. That's actually what it's called, and it delivers. My egg drop soup is, in fact, quite tasty. When I board the El train back to Lincoln Park I've got new pashminas (two for ten dollars!), a pair of black Mary Jane flats (seven dollars instead of five because I opted for the fancy velvet), and a small framed canvas Andy Warhol print.

It was a good month for new friends. My parting with Sonia was of the noncommittal "we should do this again" variety, but I invited Veronica to join the cooking club—apparently she makes mean biscuits and grits—and she accepted. Gretchen and I discovered we know a couple in common, so we made tenta-tive triple-date plans. Margarita and I made a date to see the education documentary *Waiting for Superman* later this week.

I don't think it's a coincidence that my dates have gotten more successful now that I'm choosing them instead of letting them choose me. And yet, when I catch wind of a local friend match-maker, I'm pretty eager to hand over the reins.

Joe Drake prefers to be called a friend broker. He com-pares himself to a real estate agent, but instead of finding you a house, he'll set you up with a friend. I found out about his service, Meet Joe, through a recent article in *Time Out Chicago*. Like Saya Hillman, Drake is a connector. The 31-year-old entrepreneur has contacts all over town, and now, for only $29.95, he'll introduce me to a few of them.

I signed up for the service as soon as I read the *TOC* profile. If I were more narcissistic I'd think the local Chicago area was learning about my search and creating companies just for me. And while, yes, hiring a matchmaker goes against the concept of culling through the friend-options and picking the perfect fit myself, it might be even better. I'll meet with Drake, he'll get a sense of my winning personality, and find me my Princess Charming. No glass slipper necessary.

We meet at the local Argo Tea. In his email, Drake said I'd find him because he is "an Asian guy, which usually separates me from the crowd, and I'll have a little computer with me." I immediately spot him and would have without the description. He has an air of friendliness. While others are hunched over their computers, shut off to the world, Drake is sitting up, almost smiling at his laptop. Malcolm Gladwell writes in *The Tipping Point* that the defining characteristics of connectors is not only that they are embedded into many different subcultures, thus making acquaintances far and wide, but that "their ability to span many different worlds is a function of something intrinsic to their personality, some combination of curiosity, self-confidence, sociability, and energy." This is why, despite embedding myself in various social circles this year, I may never become a full-fledged connector. While I am becoming friendlier, it's still a conscious choice. I think to myself "I should talk to this girl in yoga instead of pretending I don't recognize her, that would be the nice friendly thing to do." It's not my natural instinct. With true connectors, it's a reflex.

Forging new connections is as innate to their personality as singing butchered show tunes is to mine. We can't help it.

The energy that Gladwell describes radiates from Drake. As soon as we start talking it's clear why he's so socially integrated. He's magnetic—not in an "I want to sleep with you" kind of way, but more of an "I want to hang out with you and soak up some of your positive vibe" sense. He's charmingly dorky, and strangely easy to talk to. Drake, like Hillman, seems to relish making new connections.

Five minutes into meeting I realize I'm telling him my entire life story, not that he asked.

"Sorry, you're supposed to be interviewing me, not listening to me ramble on," I say.

"No, this is good. I'm just trying to get a feel for who you are."

I feel like I'm in therapy.

"Tell me," he says, "what kind of friends are you looking for?"

"Um, nice ones?"

"Well, tell me about the local friends you have, or what's missing from your local network."

I give Drake the full history—that when I started this search I had some local friends who went to Northwestern with me. That while they were all best friends with one another, I was the "other" one. That we made dinner plans once a month, but I didn't have a local friend I could call just to say hi.

"Why didn't they make it over the hump do you think? What makes your best friends your best friends?"

This is the toughest interview I've ever had. I was prepared to tell him my favorite books and TV shows, but there's more self-reflection required than I anticipated.

"My best friends, well, they're all . . . fun. They love pop culture. They're easy to talk to. But we can sit around watching TV without talking, and that's fine, too. We laugh a lot. I always say I want friends like the girls in *The Babysitter's Club,* that kind of bond."

Drake nods, but I start to second-guess myself.

"I feel like I'm making myself out to be a real teenybopper. I swear there's more to me than my love for *Entertainment Weekly.*"

Thank God this isn't a job interview.

"Well, if your friends—ones who didn't know one another—were to explain you to me, what would be the thing they'd all say?"

It's a good question, and probably one I should have asked myself before I started this search. "You know what it is? I think they'd all say that I don't take myself too seriously."

For the second portion of our interview, Drake gives me a bunch of different scenarios. "Imagine your new friend calls and suggests these different activities for a Saturday," he says. "Then tell me how you would react."

"Okay."

"Go to the movies . . ."

"Sounds great."

"Take a trip to the casino."

"I'd say 'when can you be here?'" Drake is surprised. "I come from a long line of gamblers," I say. He's taking furious notes.

"Go to a standing-room-only concert of an up-and-coming indie band you've never heard of."

"I'd say okay because I try to make it a policy to say yes to everything, but it wouldn't be my first choice."

"Go to the newest, hottest club and get bottle service."

"Well that's just silly."

* * *

Drake and I say goodbye after ninety minutes of soul-searching. I'm almost sad to leave. Our meeting brought some unexpected clarity to what I'm looking for from this year and from friends in general. It was the first time I've really probed my own role in friendships, rather than focusing on what other people bring to the table. It's something I should have thought about months ago.

My thirty dollars bought me this meeting plus one setup, but Drake usually tries to wrangle a group of three or four for the first date. If after that I want to meet even more people, I'll have to fork over additional cash.

Given how thorough he was with his questions, I have a feeling he'll nail it on the first try.

I leave our meeting with a promise that I'll be matched within weeks, and lyrics from *Fiddler on the Roof* running through my head.

■ ■ ■

Last weekend, the day before girl-date 35, was my first wedding anniversary. I had originally planned a friend-free day. In the ongoing effort to balance marriage and friendship, the first anniversary was a no-brainer.

Until Matt forwarded me an email. The purpose of the forward was to clue me in on our friend Sergio, who lives in Mexico City and only checks in occasionally. I, being the normal curious wife that I am, figured it would only make sense to scroll from the bottom up and read the entire exchange between my husband and his friends. That's not violating privacy, right? He's never been a master when it comes to technology, but if there were any secrets he'd surely delete them.

It made for some interesting reading. The most fascinating part was the discussion of when they should hold their annual fantasy football draft. In a note from Matt to his pals are the words "My vote is anytime on the 29th." August 29th, of course, is our anniversary.

I drafted an email of my own. "You pushed for your draft *on* our anniversary? Do you not understand how anniversaries work? I know this is your first one, but let me explain: You spend them with your wife."

I wasn't mad so much as amused. It was pretty obvious that Matt had forgotten the date entirely. By the time I caught wind of his slipup, there was no fixing it. So when our special day rolled around, he camped out at his computer and I invited over some entertainment of my own. Jillian, Paul, and the twins.

The gang showed up just after 11. Luckily my mother still has the matchbox cars from my 31-year-old brother's childhood days, so the twins had something to play with. That is, when they weren't running around the track that is my apartment.

I never realized that my home's layout lends itself to running in circles—through the kitchen, through the hallway that wraps around the kitchen, and back through the kitchen again—because who runs circles around an apartment? Two-year-olds, that's who.

We feasted on bagels and cupcakes—I like to keep things nice and low-carb. It was a fun morning, but the highlight came at the end.

"What are you doing next weekend?" Jillian asked. Labor Day was coming up and I had nothing on the schedule.

"Not much. Living it up on a three-day weekend."

"My parents are coming and they've been dying to meet you. Want to come for brunch Monday?"

"That'd be great!" My first offer to meet the parents—from Kim a few months back—fizzled when she disappeared. This gave me a second shot at the friendship milestone.

A week later, I'm in Jillian's dining room, checking out her father's family photo calendar and giving her mom book recommendations. Jillian's mother, with her curly blond hair and tie-dyed T-shirt, would be the perfect best friend for my own, if only she didn't live in Connecticut.

We sit around the table eating cinnamon buns and granola, watching the boys play the drums with their sippy cups. It feels not unlike the Sunday mornings of my youth, those post-sleepover breakfasts with my BFF-of-the-moment's family. Besides the fact that this time around my friend has a husband. And diaper duty.

CHAPTER 11

This evening I'm going speed-friending. Yup, speed-friending. It's like speed-dating—where you meet a variety of potential partners for only two minutes each—except this here's an all-female affair. The event is hosted by GirlFriendCircles, the same organization with the ConnectingCircles and the Table Tent and Logan, the energetic whirlwind I went out with earlier this summer.

I hate to admit this, but I'm dreading the whole thing. I've worked hard to become more open-minded and not write off potential friends before we meet, and overall I've been fairly successful. But there are moments when I can't stop myself. Like tonight.

Before this year I never would have signed up to speed-friend. It would have seemed too desperate, too contrived, and too unlikely that I'd connect with anyone who could really be a BFF. But once I decided to dedicate this year of my life to forging friendships, I committed to doing everything I can— no matter how scary or pathetic or absurd it seems. You never know, right? And I can't conduct a complete search without following every lead. (Don't say all those *Law & Order* marathons never taught me anything.)

In keeping with my resolution, I eagerly signed up for speed-friending as soon as registration opened up. Now that it's tonight, there's a question repeating itself over and over in my head: *What kind of person signs up for speed-friending?* Well, me, for one. But why would someone who *isn't* deliberately test-driving every meet-and-greet method want to do it? I'd be lying if I said I'm not anticipating finding a bunch of weirdos.

I am the first to arrive. I'm about fifteen minutes early because I was worried about finding a parking spot, but also because I was excited to meet Shasta Nelson, the GirlFriendCircles founder, in the flesh.

Nelson is every bit the friendship enthusiast in person that she was on the phone. She has a dirty blond bob and is noticeably fit, wearing jeans and a neon pink GirlFriendCircles T-shirt. She immediately envelops me in a hug—we're like old friends by now—and I congratulate her on the company's spot on *The Early Show* this morning.

"It's a start," she says. "There's definitely a market of women out there just like you."

By the time we get going there are twenty women in attendance, two of whom were in my original ConnectingCircle. We're separated into groups, under 40 on one side of the room and over 40 at the other, and seated at tables of three people each.

"Each of you has been given a form to help keep track of who you meet," Nelson explains. "After each round, fill in something about the person—red sweater, loves to travel—that will jog your memory. Then, when you find out who you matched with in a few days, you'll remember who she is."

Nelson says she'll give us a different question every round, and we each need to answer for two minutes. During those two minutes no one else is allowed to talk.

"For some of us it can be hard to talk about ourselves for two full minutes, but you are all interesting people! You have lots to say!"

The questions are softballs: What do you love about where you live? What do you like most about your best friend? What's an activity you're interested in learning or wish you did more of? Who in your family do you most resemble? Personal enough to give others a sense of who you are, but not so hard-hitting that it feels like an inquisition.

As is almost always the case, the women I expected to be a group of misfits turn out to be perfectly interesting, nice, friendable people. I should have known better.

In fact, I'd like to meet at least four of the women again. Erin does lighting for a local dance company and loves to travel. Nicole works in finance and is an amateur photographer. Susan is dying to take trapeze lessons and is an aspiring cook. Keisha says she's here because her best friend in D.C. is her go-to phone call, and she'd love to have that relationship locally. No kidding.

These are not outcasts or misfits. These are women who, like me, are busy and work long days but want to invest time into genuine friendships.

Better even than the new potential friends are Nelson's short lectures throughout the evening. Actually, lectures is the wrong word. Those are the boring speeches philosophy professors give while hungover freshmen sleep in the back of the classroom. These are more like sermons. I want to stand up and shout "Amen!" after each talking point.

As it turns out, on top of being a life coach and entrepreneur, Nelson really is a pastor. She and her husband lead a spiritual group called Second Wind, "an inclusive and progressive church community in San Francisco," according to the website. She knows how to captivate a crowd. She's warm, funny, and inspiring. Ours is a rapt audience.

"Your friends probably thought it was weird that you were coming to do speed-friending, but do you know that what you are doing right now is actually one of the best things you can do for your physical, emotional, and mental health?" She recites to us some of the research on friendship, and for all the pink girliness of her website, her talk is very grounded. It's not about celebrating sisterhood and doesn't sound like one of those cheesy chain emails that moms always forward.

Nelson speaks specifically to the logistical difficulties of making friends and of scheduling that second date.

"We spend so much time emailing back and forth about our calendars, saying 'I can do this date, what about you?' or 'I can't do it then, how about the week after?' that by the time we meet again too much time has passed. The spark has died. If you're out with a friend and you want to see her again, suggest a date. Pull out your planner and figure it out right then."

Nelson expounds on the four components of female friendship, as determined by Paul Dobransky in his book *The Power of Female Friendship*. "Friendship is consistent, mutual, shared, positive emotion," she quotes.

"Consistent, because, let's face it, if you meet someone tonight and you never see her again or you only meet once more, that's not friendship. That's someone you've met," Nelson explains. "Mutual because it has to go both ways. If you are the only one doing the work, it's not a friendship. Shared because if you are the only one revealing things about yourself, well then this person is a therapist, not a friend. And positive emotion because nobody wants to spend time with Debbie Downer." These four traits are a variation of the friending tips I uncovered early in my search, but they're a welcome and necessary reminder.

Twenty women are feverishly taking notes. I'm getting a side of self-help with my speed-dating, and I'm feeling totally impassioned. If I lived in San Francisco, I'd be signing up for her church group.

Before the evening is over Nelson makes us each promise, out loud, that we will reach out to whomever we match with within two days. "This is friendship, there is no playing hard to get. There is no two-day rule before calling back. You are all here, you obviously want the same thing."

It's time for me to list the ladies I'd like to see again. I talked to a total of eleven women and I feel bad not writing down everyone's names. They all seemed to be worth at least another meeting, but Nelson was very clear that we should be ruthless in our choosing. We're not mean girls if we don't pick everyone, she said, and we need to be realistic about our time and not waste theirs. I list my top four choices—Erin, Susan, Nicole, and Keisha. One perfectly nice girl gets axed for living in the suburbs, another I'd already met, and the others just didn't seem like the right fit. If the women I choose list me in return, I'll get their contact info by the end of the weekend.

And if no one picks me? Nelson swears it's never happened. "Don't think about that," she says. "Won't be a problem."

Still, it's hard not to worry that there's a first time for everything.

In fourth grade I sent a friend to deliver a note to little

Tommy Braig after lunch. I was a precocious 9-year-old girl, determined to go after what I wanted. The full body of the message read: "I like you. Do you like me?" Waiting to hear back was killer. It was the longest recess *ever*.

The next few days will be the Tommy Braig incident all over again, even if this relationship is of the platonic variety. (Though, who are we kidding, it's not like Tommy Braig and I did anything more than say hi in the hallways, even when we did finally "go out.") It's enough to send me into a tailspin.

I check in with Nelson before I leave, and tell her how skeptical I'd been earlier.

"When I first launched this company I thought, 'Is it only going to be losers who sign up?'" Her words, not mine. "But I'm constantly amazed by my clientele. It's not lonely needy types, it's professional, beautiful, insightful women who have enough confidence to say, 'This matters to me.'" Professional, beautiful, and insightful? I accept.

FRIEND-DATE 36. Eddie is in my improv class and, from what I can tell, has been wanting to get a peek at my life since he found out I live in Lincoln Park. My neighborhood is, I'll admit, yuppie central. When Matt and I first decided to relocate to Chicago, Lincoln Park wasn't on our list. Not our style, we thought. Until we got a look at our current apartment and the tree-and-bakery-lined streets surrounding it and fell in love. Still, I remember thinking there must be something in the water when we first moved in, because everyone within a five-block radius seemed to be pregnant. It's a baby-and-dog haven, Lincoln Park. Neither of which we have.

Eddie lives in Pilsen, a South Side largely Mexican American neighborhood that's much hipper than our North Side home, and I know he finds my setup—the Lincoln Park writer married to a lawyer and living in a two-bedroom home—entertaining and intriguing in a look-at-the-animals-in-their-cages sort of way. It doesn't bother me, maybe because his attitude is more wonderment than condescension. Or maybe because I'm also often amazed at how my life has turned out. So when he texted me last weekend—"What's going on in Lincoln Park this week?"—I invited him to head my way for some wine and sushi.

Aside from being snarky and hysterical, Eddie is also gay. And I've always wanted a gay best friend. Who needs a Monica to my Rachel when I could have a Will to my Grace? The gay BFF has become something of a pop-culture token in recent years—*Sex and the City*'s Stanford, *Glee*'s Kurt, and the purple Teletubby are all fan favorites. Rickie Vasquez of *My So-Called Life* fame is my personal dream BFF. And while the media portrayal of the gay best friend often veers into one-dimensional territory—no friendship consists exclusively of fashion advice and scoping out men—there is something unique about the straight-woman gay-male friendship.

In their book *Girls Who Like Boys Who Like Boys,* Melissa de la Cruz and Tom Dolby call this relationship the "quintessential urban marriage." The anthology, which was turned into a reality TV series, celebrates the bond that exists between "gay men and their gals," and I won't deny it, I want to be a part of that.

The straight-girl gay-guy friendship doesn't involve the competition or jealousy that can turn a female friendship toxic, and there's no sexual tension. It's a win-win. As my friend Emily, a gay rights activist with an army of homosexual male best friends, says, "It's the purest relationship you can have without hidden complications. When I moved from New York to D.C., it was easier to make gay male friends because I could be myself and not worry about ulterior motives."

I know plenty of gay men. One of the most memorable nights of my life involved dancing my heart out with a gay pal to "Jenny from the Block" in the middle of a sports bar and then racing, on foot, to the nearest IHOP. But I've never had the intimate, tell-each-other-everything, completely open and honest relationship with a gay man that some women brag about. Perhaps Eddie will be the one.

"Hey, hey, here we are," he says when I pick him up from the El. Eddie is wearing his standard uniform of black skinny jeans, black Keds, and a V-neck T-shirt with a hoodie. We're eating at a BYOB sushi restaurant, so we're each armed with a bottle of white.

Discussion at dinner revolves mostly around our improv class, but halfway through Eddie mentions he's thinking of moving to L.A. Another potential BFF on the run.

"It would be a nice new start," he says. Eddie grew up in Michigan, so yes, I imagine L.A. would be a serious change of scenery. "But I'm all talk so who knows, don't start missing me yet."

After dinner I invite Eddie over for a nightcap and a peek at my yuppie home in all its glory, but he declines. "I'm going to go meet this guy who keeps texting me," he says. "I'm not sure about him, but I might as well give him a chance."

As long as he'll give me one, too, we're all good.

■■■

This Saturday is September 11. It's also Callie's wedding. People are generally taken aback when I tell them the date of my

best friend's wedding, and then ask if she got everything at discounted prices. I have no idea, but since she's getting married
in Massachusetts' Berkshires and not in Manhattan, I doubt it.
When Callie first told me her wedding date I suggested she include a disclaimer on the invitations: "If you're not having fun,
the terrorists have won." (I can't take credit for the slogan, I
borrowed it from a coworker.) She chuckled just enough to
make clear she didn't find it funny.

"It's just another day on the calendar!" Callie yells every
time someone asks her stance on her loaded anniversary date,
so I've stopped mentioning it. I want to be the supportive
friend, not another inquiring mind putting her on the defen-
sive.

Callie's wedding marks my first stint as a bridesmaid. The
whole ritual of naming a bridal party—and the subsequent
identical outfits—is undoubtedly bizarre. It's the only time in
adult life when it is completely acceptable, and totally expected,
to publicly declare our best friends. In elementary school my
friend Katie and I had all the BFF-4-EVER jewelry. We tagged
each other's binders and mix tapes with "BFF! LYLAS!" There
was no ambiguity there.

Katie and I outgrew the necklaces as surely as we eventually
outgrew each other (we lost touch when we went to separate
high schools). Never again could we so simply and uncon-
troversially proclaim who the *best* of our friends were, so we
didn't. Until weddings came along.

Choosing bridesmaids can be prickly. Once we're of marry-
ing age, saying "I feel closer to you than you," or even, "I like
you better than you," is sure to piss someone off. That's why
I chose not to do it. I knew I could ask Callie and Sara, my
two oldest friends, without ruffling any feathers, but I had to
draw the line there. Otherwise I'd end up excluding someone

or having eleven bridesmaids, and neither option sounded especially attractive.

Anyone who's been a bride—or a bridesmaid—knows that selecting the wedding party isn't always about whom you feel closest to, anyway. Sometimes it's about family. Or your husband-to-be's family. Or the random friend who asked you to be in her wedding so you feel you have no choice but to reciprocate even though you don't really like her.

Such drama was avoided with Callie's attendants. She has seven bridesmaids and each of us will be wearing a one-shoulder ruffle getup in periwinkle. The whole matching dresses tradition is the most curious aspect of the wedding-party custom. But any seemingly outdated, completely nonsensical practice had to start somewhere. A quick search of some wedding websites tells me that in early Roman times bridesmaids acted as a "protective shield . . . to intervene if any wayward thugs or vengeful suitors tried to hurt the bride or steal her dowry." The Western tradition, however, is said to stem from ancient Roman law requiring witnesses to wear outfits identical to that of the bride and groom. These marriage decoys would confuse any evil spirits or jealous suitors who might show up to ruin the wedding. Unfortunately there's no such tradition in place for warding off sloppy drunks intent on being the life of the party, a much more immediate concern in my experience.

If this reasoning holds up, Callie should probably get rid of her current party and find some ladies who look like her and could kick some wayward thug ass. Or who could at least throw an evil spirit for a loop. I fear her current batch of bridesmaids is more likely to run away at the sight of ghosts.

The modern-day bridal party phenomenon is really more about being surrounded by the people you love, and I'm excited to be one of those ladies for Callie. As for the dress thing? That's just about the photos really. And making sure no one standing near the bride is wearing anything heinous. (Or, some might say, making sure everyone standing near the bride *is* wearing something heinous, so as not to upstage her. But my best friend isn't like that.)

My mother, Matt, and I arrive in Albany at 9 A.M. and drive the hour to our Massachusetts hotel in a rented Hyundai Sonata. As soon as I can get Callie on the phone I ask for an assignment.

"What can I do for you? Do you need food? Does your mom need anything?"

My excessive desire to take on bridesmaid's duties and be of some help to my best friend comes from a place of kindness, for sure, but also largely from my own insecurity. Due to the distance between us, I missed many of Callie's pre-wedding festivities. I did fly to New York for her engagement party, but her shower was on a Thursday evening so I couldn't make it. Her bachelorette party, which took place while I was in Croatia, was scheduled after I'd already booked my ticket. (I did send a giant penis cake in my stead, which should count for something.) I know the other attendants have played a more active role in the pre-wedding celebrations and I feel like now is my chance to make up for my absences. This weekend I can establish myself as A Good Bridesmaid.

Aside from wanting to live up to my end of the bridal party bargain, I'm anxious to reaffirm my best friendship with Callie. Not that we've been growing apart, but I've been so unusually focused on making new friends and she's been so busy with work and wedding planning that lately we haven't talked as much as we used to. This is largely a product of living seven hundred miles away from each other—research shows that emotional closeness between friends declines by about 15 percent a year in the absence of face-to-face contact. My search is about complementing Callie and Sara locally, not replacing them. So while I stomp around pronouncing that Callie is my best friend forever, I need to do my part to ensure the "forever" part sticks.

I don't want to be forgotten.

"Callie wants a curry chicken sandwich and a Diet Pepsi," I announce to Matt and my mother after hanging up with the bride-to-be at lunchtime. "I told her we'd pick it up and bring it to her; she's getting her hair and nails done."

"Look how excited you are," Matt tells me. I'm literally bouncing out of my seat.

"She's my best friend!" I say. "She held my wedding dress when I peed. I just want to do the same."

When I was planning my wedding, plenty of people warned me that the weekend would be over as soon as it began. "Make sure you stay present and soak up every moment," they'd say. "You don't want to miss a second."

Maybe because I'd been put on such high alert, I was acutely aware of each memory as it was made. My wedding didn't fly by as I'd feared. I danced and laughed and lived it up, and I didn't let myself get bogged down by overlooked details (a missing tablecloth here, a misspelled name card there), or wardrobe malfunctions. (My mom stepped on my tulle gown before the ceremony even started. Awesome.)

Callie's wedding, though, feels like it doesn't even happen. By the time the ceremony starts—after the rehearsal dinner and speeches, the full day of primping and picture-taking—I'm so excited to catch up with my old friends in attendance that it's over before I can even share a dance with Matt.

The crowd of high school friends at Callie's wedding is largely the same as the group at Emily's Miami nuptials earlier this year. And while the bouts of frenvy—that specific brand of jealousy that hits when I'm with old friends and am reminded of the lives they share back in New York without me—do bubble up, they occur less frequently and with far less force. When Jill and Callie reference their crazy adventures in Brooklyn— "This is just like the time we went to that bar, remember? The one that had the thing? With the psycho girl?"—I feel on the outside of an inside joke, but it doesn't make me wish I lived in New York. Instead it makes me miss Chicago and the comfort I've found in my new groups of friends—my book and cooking clubs, my coworkers, Rachel and Eddie and the improv gang.

Visiting old friends used to make me feel like I was back on the mother ship. I felt like a stranger in a strange land in the Midwest. But there's been a welcome, if unexpected, reversal this year. Curling up with lifelong besties will always be the ultimate creature comfort, but my life—the one spiraling forward, picking up steam and determining my future—is in Chicago. With my no-longer-new husband, and my very new friends.

FRIEND-DATE 37. There's new compelling evidence that this quest is working. My girl-dates from earlier in the year are starting to introduce me to their friends. My social net is getting cast wider, extending as far as three degrees. I'm 50 percent Kevin Bacon.

Take tonight's date, Alexis. I was introduced to Alexis through Hannah, who I met through Sara. In January, Alexis and I were separated by three degrees. Now we're at only one.

This is triadic closure at work. Remember that theory? The one that says one's friends will find it easy to become friends with each other. Earlier this year I got sick of only meeting friends of friends. I wanted to establish my own relationships and create my own networks. I've finally achieved that. I've woven friendship webs, even more of them than I can sometimes keep track of.

I see the merits in both approaches to friending—expanding social networks or forging numerous independent relationships. The former allows you to be at the center of a cluster, having several tight relationships within a given group, while the latter puts you in the role of connector between different social webs.

According to *Connected* authors Christakis and Fowler's research, Americans are more likely to take the network expansion route. The probability that any two of our friends know each other, they found, is 52 percent.

Hannah, Alexis, and I now fall into that category. Alexis is planning an extended trip to Italy and wants to keep a blog while she's there. Hannah sent her my way for general blogging advice and because "you two will have a lot to chat about."

"My dream is to be a food personality—to teach and do cooking demos—rather than run a restaurant," she tells me. "So I'll be spending three months in Italy to cook and eat and drink. And eat. It's my specialty."

Alexis has Snow White coloring—pale skin and dark hair—and is long and lean, with perfectly sculpted arms that I covet. "How do you stay so thin doing all that eating?" I ask, gazing at the biceps I would like for myself.

"Are you checking out my arms?"

Caught. She totally just called me out. "I am. This is totally embarrassing. But I want mine to look like that."

"That was hilarious. You were just, like, literally talking to my arms."

I should be mortified. I'm not. I love calling people on their ridiculousness, so I can take it. If anything, the exchange makes us feel like old friends. We already have an inside joke.

After we down two glasses of wine and one volcano roll, Alexis tells me a story of skinny-dipping at a friend's and realizing that one of the girls there, a lesbian, was into her. "Later in the night she grabs me by the hand and drags me to the car to go get more beers with her, and I finally just said, 'I can tell that you like me, but I'm straight.' And then she kissed me. It was quite a night."

It's not the usual first girl-date conversation, but I think that's why the dinner is going so well. There's a difference between the potential friends who are "nice," and those I sense could become lifers. Alexis falls into the really-could-be-a-BFF category and I have a feeling that one day, when we have twenty years of friendship under our belts, we'll look back and pinpoint this story of the misplaced affections—and my blatant arm gazing—as the beginning of it all.

Rom and Ori Brafman, the authors of *Click*, are experts on those small euphoric moments that tell us a relationship is going to stick. As this year has progressed I've tried to incorporate their "click accelerators" into my everyday life—standing closer to someone I want to befriend (proximity), being fully present in each conversation (resonance), and joining defined communities that are conducive to forging bonds (safe place). But what if I already have a girl-date planned, and I really want it to go well? What if I think, "This girl is The One, I just need her to feel the same"? Is there a way to manufacture a click?

According to Rom Brafman, people tend to overlook one

particular weapon in the friendship arsenal. The power of story-telling.

"My guess is that if I recorded a conversation between you and your friends in New York, I'd hear each of you relating stories of things that happened to you. Whether it is funny or gossipy or newsy. 'You'll never guess what happened' type of stuff," he told me over the phone recently.

When we meet new people, he explained, we switch into interview mode. We think the person sitting across from us needs to know how long ago we graduated from college or what we majored in.

"It's factual, but it's not very interesting," he said.

He's right on point. A distinguishing feature of the few girl-dates that had me giddy, aside from laughter, was that we went beyond the boring exchange of information into more personal, story-driven territory. There are ways of obtaining the factual tidbits—the where-are-you-froms and what-do-you-dos—without grilling your girl-date, Brafman said. The details emerge through narratives.

A story of skinny-dipping and unexpected makeouts? Click click click.

The next day I send Alexis an email with a link to some popular food blogs we discussed at dinner. I include in the note a variation of my usual "we should get together again" spiel, as I like to get the plans for the second date moving quickly. In the spirit of network building, and also because I adore her, I suggest we invite Hannah next time, too.

Five days later (apparently she wasn't quite as smitten as I) Alexis writes me back. "You are totally raw and hilarious," she says. "My kind of personality."

When you spend the majority of your time setting up girl-dates, there comes a point where you have to think outside the wine-and-sushi box. Before this year started I was so comfortable in my personal bubble—one that consisted of the office, restaurants, movie theaters, and yoga studios—that I felt no need to stray. Now that I'm constantly entertaining the ladies, I've expanded my repertoire. I've brought dates to free workouts in the park, readings at independent bookstores, musical improv performances, and community running groups. I'm basically the Casanova, or The Situation, of girl-dating.

My new friends have expanded my Chicago in return. They've introduced me to fortune-tellers and community gardens and new neighborhoods—Margarita to Chinatown and Jillian to Little Vietnam where I had some pho that was to die for. (To Die Pho! What a brilliant name for a restaurant. A project for my next life.) It's the free-gift-with-purchase of this quest: Invest in new friends and rediscover your hometown at no extra charge.

Today I'm joining Mia—who I met through my online essay, is in my cooking club, and lives around the corner—and some of her friends for a day at a suburban winery. Until a week ago I had no idea that Illinois had wineries, but this thirty-year-old bed-and-breakfast, just a forty-five-minute drive outside the city, ships in grapes from California and makes vino on-site.

Mia won this wine tasting for ten people in an auction last year, so I was flattered when she told me to expect an invitation. In Matt's ongoing horserace, Mia has been inching her way toward the front of the pack. She's the up-for-anything type who actually follows through when we discuss fun outings. She's easygoing but interested, and loves a good session of girl talk, whether it's about her latest suitors or my most recent deadline horror story.

Since she lives so close—a three-minute walk from my apartment—we have become mani-pedi buddies. Mia is really good at pedicure maintenance, while I'm more of the "oh, my pinky toe looks like a stump, maybe I should paint it so you can tell there's a nail" type. I must say, since she came into my life my toes have never looked better.

Plenty of research has found that geography is one of the most influential factors in whether two people will become friends. Having similar addresses has been shown to matter more than having similar values or interests. Luckily, Mia and I share all three.

"How do you two know each other?" asks one of Mia's friends.

We look at each other with a grin. It always sounds odd when I tell people that a new friend responded to an article I wrote about wanting more friends.

"Mia read an essay I wrote online and she reached out to me," I say. "Turned out we live in the same neighborhood and we've been friends ever since."

"That's so great!" Mia's friend says. Once again, what I fear will appear desperate actually sounds pretty impressive.

"Yeah, isn't it?"

My nose is buried in my third glass of red wine when my phone rings. The caller ID shows it's my brother, Alex, but I hit the IGNORE button. I'll call him back later. New friends and new wines demand my undivided attention.

Sixteen hours later I'm hunched over the computer when

my brother calls a second time. I have assignments to finish up so I hit IGNORE. Again.

Modern technology makes it virtually impossible to disappear entirely—especially when my communication with co-workers is almost entirely over instant message—so within minutes an IM pops up on my screen.

"You avoid my calls now?" Alex asks.

I explain that I was wine tasting with one of my potential BFFs yesterday, and that today I'm swamped at work.

"I'll be available in ten minutes," I tell him.

"Okay, I'll call you then."

Something is very obviously up. Alex and I are as close as any siblings I know. We talk all the time. But his determination to get me on the phone ASAP is suspicious. He's proposing to Jaime, I bet.

Alex and Jaime have been dating for three years. They met when they were attendants in the same wedding and decided to brave the trials of long-distance romance. Selfishly, I'm glad they did. I love Jaime, and though we don't hang out without Alex often, she already feels like family. Plus, her Chicago residency means I get to see my brother a ton.

As cross-country relationships go, theirs seems manageable. Alex travels almost every weekend for work—he's a sports TV producer and is constantly on the road for games—so he tacks on a few days in Chicago whenever business brings him to the general Midwest region. But, as with friendship, a romantic relationship conducted across state lines isn't ideal. You can hold on to faraway friends while you make new ones nearby, but it's not so easy with dating. Alex can't exactly supplement his long-distance relationship with a local one.

My entire family awaits the news that someone is moving

somewhere. Who will do the relocating is the big question mark.

Staring at my phone, waiting for it to ring, I imagine Alex telling me that he's going to propose. Once they're engaged, I figure Jaime will probably move to New York.

"So?" I ask when I get the call. Alex knows that I suspect he has news to deliver.

"I just wanted to call and let you know that I am moving to Chicago in two weeks."

"What?!?" This I was not expecting. I'd certainly entertained the idea that Alex would move to Chicago—our family is here, and he and Jaime can certainly get more for their money than in Manhattan—but I figured I would get a bit more warning. I consult my big brother on every decision I make, so I forget sometimes that he's a guy—with all the disinterest in talking things to death that this entails.

The proposal I was hoping for is not to be. Yet. This move means they'll probably be engaged within six months, tops.

Alex's relocation adds a whole new element to my search. If the definition of BFF is someone you talk to almost every day, someone who understands you so well you never need to explain yourself, someone you can always call for last-minute plans, someone who laughs at all the same things you do and is there when you need advice, then my brother is it.

He is, as Jaime pointed out recently, the male version of me. She discovered this while commiserating with Matt over our common bad habits—nail biting (and not always cleaning up the scraps), technology addiction, getting worked up before bedtime as we recount our day—so I'm not sure she meant it as a compliment. But still.

Plenty of people consider family to be their best friends. The same General Social Survey that found that Americans are lonelier reported that the percentage of Americans who named at least one nonrelative as part of their core group went from 80 percent to 57 percent in twenty years. That means 43 percent of respondents said their only confidants were family members—be it spouse, parent, sibling, or child. Almost half of America has an inner circle made up entirely of relatives.

I subscribe to the separate-but-equal approach to relationships. I like to keep my marriage separate from my friendships separate from my family. The bonds of each have different tenets and different functions. "A best friend is that person who gives you the most delight, support, and comfort, often in those realms where family cannot help," Joseph Epstein writes in *Friendship: An Exposé*. "A best friend is perhaps the only person to whom you can complain about the difficulties presented by your family." In other words, family—for all their unconditional love and support—brings out the crazy in us. Friends ground us back to earth.

He may not qualify for BFF status, but I'm delighted my brother is going to be in town. And not just because he'll round out the full life I've established in my new city. I'm equally excited because he will be another friend for Matt.

For someone who's so supportive of my BFF search—his relentless cheerleading can get downright annoying—Matt is still perfectly content to play poker with a bunch of strangers on a Friday night. The last time he told me he'd be heading to the casino to play Texas Hold 'Em while I went out with new friends, I tried to put my foot down.

"Why don't you call Max? Or Ben? See what they're up to," I said. "Male friendships are important. You need to be social. It's really so much healthier than sitting silently at a casino table with a bunch of shady dudes. It'll help you live longer!"

"Don't you friendship me," Matt said. I've never heard

friendship used as a verb, but it works. And I will friendship him. This research he's been encouraging me to collect can now be used against him.

Wouldn't most husbands kill for their spouse to encourage a night out with the guys? I should win Wife of the Year.

■ ■ ■

Last week I got my first match from Joe Drake the friend broker. I'm supposed to meet Stacey and Maureen—women who, according to Joe, are different enough from me that I'll find them interesting, but similar enough to get along on a basic level—at a wine bar near my apartment. I'm not sure what to expect out of this setup, as the set-upper isn't a close friend but a paid service provider.

Joe sent us each some ground rules so I have a tentative road map for this first date, though they come pretty naturally by now. I always like specific instructions—Don't talk about the weather! Don't be late!—so I appreciate Drake's effort to facilitate a successful encounter. Part of me wishes I had hired him before my year of dating even started. His advice would have come in much more handy back then. Like this nugget, which I would pass on to anyone who might be inspired to do some girl-dating of her own: "Expectations . . . they can be a killer. At this point you may be hopeful that your upcoming meeting will yield you a new best friend (or friends), or fearful that it will be the most awkward thing you've ever done. It's a safe bet that neither extreme will unfold, so give yourself and each other a break, and enjoy one of the last nice evenings of the season out meeting new people. Ideally, you'll just come out of it saying, 'I'd like to see [her/them] again.' And then you will."

Managing expectations has been a learning process. In January I honestly thought that I would meet a girl at a restaurant and music would start playing and the stars would suddenly align and it would be as if we were both shot with Cupid's arrow. Or the arrow of Cupid's little sister, the Goddess of Girl-Crushes. I figured that we would start texting as soon as our first date ended, and that we'd assume the BFF roles in each other's lives as if we'd been besties since birth. We'd be like Oprah and Gayle, without all the lesbian rumors. (What is that about anyway? Why can't two famous women be best friends without everyone assuming they're getting it on? Theirs is the real-life tell-it-like-it-is do-anything-for-each-other crazy-adventure-seeking friendship I still hope will one day come out of this search, so I've never understood the in-the-closet speculation.)

When I was young, it really felt that simple. I'd meet a friend, or friends, and on rare occasions it would feel as though they were the final piece of the puzzle. They made me whole. It hasn't worked like that this year. Even if the first date goes well, the second can be equally hard—if not harder—to schedule. It's takes more than a simple click. It takes being proactive, and setting aside time despite hectic schedules on both sides. But if each potential BFF is excited about the prospect of a new friendship, they'll do the work. If *He's Just Not That Into You* taught us anything about relationships, it's that "if a (sane) guy really likes you, there ain't nothing that's going to get in his way." The same is true of a potential best friend.

I don't care anymore if I sound anxious. If I want to see a new friend again, I email in the next day or two. If a girl-date is just okay, I usually wait for them to contact me, or until my schedule quiets down a bit. Sometimes it never does, and those dates don't get a second chance. But with more than three dozen of these outings under my belt, I've realized if I really want to pursue a friendship, I will. My desire—or lack thereof—to reach out immediately is my internal barometer of just how taken I am with a potential relationship. If my girl-date invites me for a second get-together, I always say yes. Though more often than not, if I don't follow up, she doesn't, either. Women can judge dates (of any kind) pretty well. General feelings of there's-no-future-here usually go both ways.

I still hold out hope that I will meet my Gayle King or Christina Yang (in a recent episode of *Grey's Anatomy,* Meredith told Christina that "Derek's the love of my life, but you're my soul mate." I actually screamed at the TV. "Yes! Exactly!" That Shonda Rhimes just gets me), but I have learned to temper my expectations. One person can't make me whole, anyway. That's something I need to do for myself.

FRIEND-DATE 38. Stacey is sitting at the bar when I arrive. Dark hair pulled back, khaki jacket, jeans, and boots. All I know of her is what I've heard from Joe Drake. She's from Rogers Park, works in marketing, graduated from University of Illinois (undergrad and MBA), and she's single.

With two out of three present, we take a seat. This bar is pretty empty—that's what happens when you meet for drinks at 5 on a Sunday—so Maureen will find us.

Stacey is a wine connoisseur. This is a good trait in a potential BFF. Sometimes I wish I could staff my friends like I would an office—we'll need one social coordinator, one finance whiz to handle dividing group checks, a fashionista to approve outfits and track down the perfect pair of jeans, and a computer genius/Ms. Fix-It to help me repair stuff around the house. I call these my Friends with Benefits. (A different kind than Matt was before we started dating.)

Screw fantasy football leagues, how about a fantasy friend

league? A foodie with good wine knowledge could come in handy.

For half an hour, in between bouts of the usual small talk and divulging why we each decided to sign up with Meet Joe (many of Stacey's friends have coupled off and moved to the suburbs, so she's looking for more local buddies to hang out with), we keep our eyes peeled for Maureen. By 5:30 we accept the obvious: We've been stood up.

It doesn't ruin our good time, though. I enjoy a flight of pinot noir and Stacey gets two glasses of wines I've never heard of. She tells me about her love of volunteering and some culinary organizations she works with. I share some yogi insight into my favorite studios around town. By the end of the evening, we've discovered our shared love of Bravo's *The Rachel Zoe Project* and are spewing out "I die" and "It's so major." I have a slight buzz, which might be why I find this hilarious.

Drake gave us specific instructions not to exchange contact info. He promised he'll send it out with our permission after the date. If necessary, he'll be in charge of letting someone down easy.

It feels strange to leave without exchanging information, but Drake has done a good job so far (minus Maureen the no-show) so we defer to his rules.

"Hopefully we'll be in touch," Stacey says.

"Definitely."

The red wine is still coursing through my veins as I walk home. When I get to my computer I already have an email from Drake, checking in on our evening. He's like a fairy godmother.

FRIEND-DATE 39. One week later, on a cold and rainy Saturday, I meet Nicole and Erin—two speed-friending matches—

for brunch at the Art Institute of Chicago. When Shasta Nelson sent me my matches a few weeks back, I was relieved to get email addresses for all four of the women I'd hoped to meet again. Unfortunately, Keisha and Susan couldn't make this outing.

Erin, who does lighting for a local dance company, has dark hair with bold blond highlights. She seems slightly uncomfortable in this atmosphere, which surprises me because she is wearing plaid pants. The courage to wear plaid pants has, to me, always signified the sort of person who isn't uncomfortable anywhere.

Nicole, whose hair has a side part and is tied in a tight, low ponytail, is the financial analyst and amateur photographer. She organized this meeting, but she seems equally unsure of the protocol.

"What are you guys up to this weekend?" I ask as soon as the first silence takes hold.

And then . . .

"I love butternut squash soup. And it's so easy to make at home," I say later, as I finish my bowl.

Finally . . .

"I wonder what's on exhibit downstairs. Since I'm here I might as well look around," I offer toward the end of the meal.

I do most of the talking at this brunch. Whether it's because first girl-dates are second nature to me now or because I dread silence, I'm not sure.

Nicole and Erin are both perfectly nice. After lunch we walk together toward the loop before parting ways—them to different El stops, me to a nearby bookstore (I decided to pass on the museum exploration after all). We discuss abstract plans to "do this again sometime." While I like them both, I'm not sure we'll meet again. They seemed to hit it off with each other better than either of them did with me, so I don't know if I'll follow up, and I don't expect to hear from them, either. Some girl-dates—like this one—feel every bit the first-date. Others, like Alexis a few weeks ago, feel like you already know each other. I have to focus my energy on those.

Three-quarters of this search are now behind me. I've gone on thirty-nine girl-dates in nine months. If three months in I had acquaintances and after six I had friends, today I feel like I'm very much on the path to bestfriendom. Aside from Jillian's family visit, Labor Day weekend included a trip to the dog park with Margot (a true sign of how much I like her), show tunes night at a local gay bar with Kari and her husband, a movie with Hilary, and a yoga workshop with Natalie. I even had to pass on a night out with Hannah, as she texted me that she'd be in my neighborhood—a last-minute invite!—after Matt and I were already out on a date. My work BFFs—Ashley, Lynn, Joan, and Kari—are still my daily lunch mates and the people with whom I exchange about fifteen People.com "breaking news" links a day. We make off-campus plans infrequently, but five days a week of chatter can really bring people together. I finally have total faith that we'll remain friends even if we don't always share an office.

Over the past month I've seen Alexis again—she came over for help with her blog—and continued my weekly pre-improv dinners with Rachel. Eddie often joins us now, too. I even signed up for the second level of Second City classes. I never planned on advancing—I'll find a friend and run for the hills, I thought—but when Rachel and Eddie both said, "You have to do it!" they made the decision for me. The sound of new friends imploring you to stick around is a beautiful and powerful thing. Like the call of the Sirens. Plus, I've grown to love my class like one loves a dysfunctional family. Even the self-appointed class clown who doesn't know when to stop talking—who actually recognizes that he should shut it, says "please somebody stop me," and then keeps talking anyway until all of our faces are buried in our hands and our entire bodies are cringing—even he has carved himself a space in my improvisational heart.

And to think, I knew none of these people a year ago.

Another bonus of being 75 percent through? After months of being the initiator, invitations now come my way, too. I'd been waiting for the tide to turn, for my friendships to become universally reciprocal, and in the past few months the shift has become obvious. I have a barrage of text messages to prove it.

What I still don't have, what might not even be possible in one short year, is the type of intimate friendship on par with any of my close friends around the country. I could probably text someone for brunch, but do I know the strengths and values and insecurities at the core of any of my new companions? Do I understand the history and intricate relationships that make them who they are? No.

I recently came across an essay in which author Ann Patchett beautifully sums up the crux of what I hope will emerge in the final months of this search. "[Here's] my idea of real intimacy," she writes. "It's not the person who calls to say, 'I'm having an affair'; it's the friend who calls to say, 'Why do I have four jars of pickles in my refrigerator?'" I want someone with whom I can talk about the deep stuff—hopes and dreams and expectations and disappointments—and also the minutiae. Sometimes it takes talking about everything to get to the place where we can talk about nothing.

In the time since my six-month assessment, friendships have evolved. I might call Natalie for a ride to the airport, or Hannah or Rachel or Jillian for a shoulder to cry on after a fight with Matt. I'd bounce health questions—is that a freckle? Or a mole?—off of Lynn, Kari, Ashley, or Joan. But the four-jars-of-pickles analysis? We're not quite there yet.

CHAPTER **12**

I've given in to paying for friendships. If eHarmony can charge two hundred forty dollars a year, then coughing up five dollars per month for GirlFriendCircles or thirty dollars for the personal attention of Meet Joe or fifteen dollars for speed-friending isn't so bad. Considering that studies show people value time with friends more than time with their romantic partners, these sites might be a bargain.

There's a difference, though, between subscribing to a service that will connect you with potential friends and straight up paying someone to hang out with you.

Enter RentAFriend.com.

The website is exactly what it sounds like. Unless it sounds like an escort service. Because the company promises in **BIG BOLD LETTERS** on its homepage (which looks like it was designed for my 1987 Apple IIe computer) that solicitation is prohibited and the site is for "friendship purposes only." It bears noting, however, that plenty of the friends-for-hire post pictures that I'd qualify as more suggestive than friendly—

hello, cleavage—and the majority of customers rent friends of the opposite sex.

While I can peruse the site (narrowing my potential pals first by zip code and then by gender) for free, I'll need to hand over some cash—$24.95 per month or $69.95 for the full year—in order to contact anyone. And if I find someone I want to hang out with? I'll need to pay her directly on top of my monthly fee. "Friends" charge anywhere from ten to one hundred fifty dollars per hour, though twenty to fifty dollars is the norm.

Kari told me about RentAFriend in May after she saw it on a local news segment. In June my aunt emailed me an article about the service. A month later a blog reader sent the link my way. Sure it may be a prostitution ring, but who better to give it a test drive, they said. I can handle shady and inappropriate advances if need be. I'm tough.

RentAFriend is modeled after similar successful sites in Asia and boasts more than three hundred thousand friends for rent. People hire friends for anything from a business trip dinner date to a weekly companion for their elderly mother. According to an MSNBC profile of the company, two college kids once rented friends to pose as parents after they were caught drinking on campus.

Um, those are not friends. Those are called actors.

If I sound skeptical, it's because I am. Isn't the very nature of friendship reciprocal? If I have to pay someone for her company, it's not exactly a partnership of equals.

But I've come this far, so it's only logical that I should rent a friend. At least see what it's about. I'll find the one Chicago-based woman on the site who gives off no I'll-pleasure-you-for-money vibes and invite her on an outing. In a public place. In broad daylight.

Maybe my cynicism is misguided. The friends-for-hire might be regular Janes, looking for new pals and some extra cash. Come January I'll be a pro at girl-dates. Perhaps I could lease myself out.

This afternoon, while sitting in Starbucks, I type my zip code into the site's search field. I narrow the results to female only. Of the women within six years of my age, only three aren't ogling the camera. (Four if you count the girl who I'm pretty sure is flashing the Bloods gang sign. I don't.) Two of those three, Sascha and Christine, are my age.

Sascha's profile reads: "I just want to have a good time, whether it's drinking coffee while figuring out which destinations should be on the short list or dancing on the beach with our smuggled cocktails (umbrella usually not optional, even if it's an Old Style tall boy) or getting dressed up for a nice night out. Gals, I know how to meet boys. Guys, hard to find a better wingwoman. I've been lucky enough to meet a whole gaggle of incredible people over the last year, and always love meeting more." In one of Sascha's profile pictures she's in the stands of a football game, her arm around a middle-aged shirtless guy wearing a cowboy hat and what appears to be a Wyoming Football barrel around his waist, held up by suspenders.

Candidate number two, Christine, has a much shorter profile. "I am very outgoing and love connecting with people! I love living in Chicago and exploring different neighborhoods. I can strike up a conversation with anyone and put people at ease. Let's hang out!"

I'm leaning toward Sascha—she sounds like a party animal!—until I come to my senses. She sounds like a party animal. Every now and then I have a momentary memory lapse and forget I'm not in college anymore. I don't want to smuggle cocktails on the beach. I hate the beach! Taking pictures with beer-soaked locals in crazy costumes doesn't crack me up, it makes me uncomfortable. Christine seems more like the me I *actually* am, as opposed to the me I sometimes pretend I am.

I send Christine an email explaining that I am new(ish) to Chicago and am always looking for different ways to meet people. And though I've never used RentAFriend before, it seemed an interesting concept. Would she be up for meeting?

Within a few hours I have a response.

"Hey Rachel—

I got your info from RentAFriend and wanted to connect! I am new to this site and basically wanted to find ways to supplement my part-time job with some income. I decided to charge $20 an hour, and would love to get together. Let me know."

After we exchange some more emails and I explain my background (i.e., I am not a creep trying to solicit sex), I suggest a trip to the farmers' market next week. She ups the ante to lunch and the farmers' market and the museum. At twenty dollars an hour.

It's a date. Likely a pricey one.

■ ■ ■

Of all the various organizations and classes I've joined since starting this search, I was most leery of LEADS, the young Jewish group that Pam, the *JUF News* editor, told me about earlier this year. For whatever reason, I've always avoided religiously oriented events. Maybe it's because I don't usually click with those who frequent Purim Parades and Matzo Balls, the Christmas Eve party for Jewish singles. (I've never been, but I hear some of the antics that take place are, shall we say, not kosher.) Or perhaps Matt's objection to organized religion has influenced my own take on temple. (I can't remember the last time I entered one for anything other than a wedding or funeral.) I know it sounds silly, given that so many of my friends are Jewish, but very few of them are religious. Forget orthodox, conservative, and reformed. To me, Judaism has two sects: Those who equate Jewish geography with a map of Israel, and those who play by asking if you know the Rosenbergs of Scarsdale. My Jewish friends have always been the latter.

I worried that signing up for LEADS (which stands for Leadership Education and Development Series) would be akin to a lie. Wouldn't I be declaring that Judaism was deeply important to me just by enrolling in the eight-week course? Didn't it imply that I'd lit the Shabbat candles more recently than twenty years ago?

Jewish organizations host programs like LEADS in order to recruit young Jews like me and to invite outsiders into the community, so I decided the false pretenses argument didn't hold water. It's not like I'm Catholic, showing up to a Jewish mixer wearing a tallis.

At the inaugural session we spent most of the evening playing Fun-Fact Bingo. Another icebreaker game! My specialty! (My fact: I coached a third-grade girls Catholic Youth Organization basketball team to win the New York State Archdiocesan Championship. It seemed apropos.) Group introductions came next. As we went around the room explaining why we joined LEADS, I noticed a recurring theme: "I'm the only Jew in my group of friends, so I figured this would be a good way to expand my Jewish network." Probably two-thirds of our group gave a variation of that explanation. A few said their friends had tried LEADS and loved it, so they were jealous. And one girl, with a thick southern accent, said "Hey, y'all! I just moved here from Alabama and I don't know anyone here or have any friends. So if you need friends, I do, too!"

Bless her heart. There were some nervous giggles in response to her impromptu speech, but I applauded this girl's candor. The ladies who announced they joined LEADS to meet their future husband got laughs, but they were laughs of recognition, not pity. Most everyone nodded in agreement (I'm one of only three married people in my group, and the other two are married to each other). When the southern belle declared she needed new friends, the look on the guy sitting next to me seemed to say, "Oh, this poor girl just admitted she was a loser."

Much has changed during this year of friending, but one thing has not. In the eyes of 20- and 30-somethings, a proclamation of friendlessness still equals loneliness, while admitting you want a lover just makes you a modern woman.

I admired her. Maybe if I'd been so bold when I first moved to Chicago I could have saved myself two years of frustration.

Then came my turn. "I'm always looking to meet new people, and someone suggested I try LEADS, so here I am."

We all joined for the same basic reason—to meet new people. No one said, "I'm here because I am super-religious and was hoping to deepen my understanding of the Israelites." Sure, there are varying degrees of observance in the room— from me, the borderline nonpracticer, to Miriam, the conservative Jew who leads our meetings' infrequent prayers—but the organization is focused on building a community rather than pushing a religious viewpoint.

I hit it off pretty quickly with Meredith, a pharmaceutical sales rep who is from Rhode Island but has lived in Chicago for five years.

"I need to meet some Jews!" Meredith told me when I asked why she signed up. "Seriously, I want to date Jewish guys and I don't know how to meet them in this city. Although, considering I was one of, like, ten Jews in Rhode Island, I've never had an easy time of it."

Last Friday was our LEADS Shabbat dinner. If I had any residual worries that this program might be too pious for me, the sausage and pepperoni pizza entrée took care of them. The festivities kicked off with an übercompetitive game of charades (to be fair, I might have contributed to the cutthroat nature of the game. What can I say? I like to win, and I can act out "Jesus Take the Wheel" like nobody's business. Just part your hair in the middle and stand there like the Crucifixion. Duh.) and continued on to some serious beer pong.

I was partnered with Rob, our LEADS leader and my first straight male potential friend to come out of this search, while Meredith was teamed up with Steve. Given the amount of unnecessary hugging and touching going down on their team, I had a hunch where their evening was headed. So when Meredith said "Please stay!" after I started to pack up my things, I could see the pleading in her eyes and dropped my purse. There's no fast track to BFFship like being someone's wingwoman.

FRIEND-DATE 40. On Monday, I'm hungry for some good girl talk. When I left the party on Friday it was 1 A.M. and the rest of the group was heading to a neighborhood bar. I, being the old married lady that I am, couldn't fathom going out that late.

"Okay, tell me everything," I say to Meredith when we meet at our mutual yoga place for our first official girl-date. "Did you guys make out?"

"We did," she says sheepishly. "He's really sweet, isn't he?"

"Totally! I think he's great."

"He's only twenty-five though. I'm twenty-eight."

"And? Three years is nothing," I say. "So what happened? Fill me in!" I sound like a fiending crack addict who's fallen off the wagon. I didn't know how much I've missed talking about boys until this moment. Most of my friends have paired off by now, and as for the ones that haven't, it's harder to get worked up into high-school-gossip mode when you're hundreds of miles away and don't know the guy in question. It's been a while since I've gone to a party and witnessed the first bats of an eyelash, so I feel like a part of the action for the first time in too long.

Getting the details from Meredith—he kissed her good night, she didn't invite him up but definitely wants to see him again, he asked her out the next day—makes me realize just how much I've missed gossiping. Not chatting—swapping stories about our jobs or husbands or stance on Letterman vs. Leno—but truly gossiping. As in, comparing notes about other people and revealing details that might not be public information.

Before you cast me off as the next Blair Waldorf, hear this: Plenty of studies have confirmed that gossip can be good for you. It can promote trust, forge connections, and provide an informal method for learning unwritten social norms. Positive gossip—the kind where you shower an unknowing third party in compliments about how great her outfit looked or how cute her baby is—can raise self-esteem and reduce negative emotions. Office gossip, which my workday is drowning in, can create employee camaraderie. I'll never forget, at my first job out of college, the day my entire department inadvertently discovered how much a long-distance consultant was getting paid. (Note to office managers: Never leave a freelance employee's invoice on the printer all day.) As far as we could tell, his only job requirement was to call in to a department meeting each morning. Everyone felt equally underpaid, outraged, and slightly amused. What better way to bond a group of women—from intern to senior staff member—than to collectively calculate how much our British adviser made each time he said "Cheerio!"

The flip side of that coin is that negative gossip—the kind that's more common and, let's face it, usually more fun—has the opposite effect, and is a much more powerful influence. Nice gossip only gives a 3 percent positivity boost, while trash-talking makes us feel 34 percent worse.

I'm not necessarily looking for someone to share a bitchfest with. I just want to say "She said what?!?!" and "Give me every detail about your date," and this has been my first opportunity as of late.

"He is so adorable," I say when she tells me Steve has offered to take her on a music-themed first date. "I can't wait to hear what happens next."

■ ■ ■

As I add notches to my girl-dating belt, I've started reflecting on my strengths and weaknesses as a friend. I like to think I'm a pretty good one. I pride myself on my willingness to drop what I'm doing for a BFF in need. When I got a text from Callie one Friday night this summer—"Can you call me??"—I immediately ducked into the bathroom of the party I was attending to check in. There were some wedding woes, and I was happy to do my best to calm her down. Even if it meant locking myself in the host's bathroom for twenty minutes.

When friends have birthday parties or performances, I rejigger my schedule to make sure I'm there. I've been lucky to have friends who are healthy and happy, but I'd be by their side if one day they weren't.

Still, I'm hardly perfect and lately I've become increasingly aware of my shortcomings in the friendship department. When you spend some five nights a week with friends—whether they're potential or established—you notice patterns in your own behavior, even when they are less than flattering.

To start, I am an interrupter. I'll think I'm listening, but just as my friend is wrapping up a thought, as she's presenting the big conclusion, I'll jump in with my two cents. As I've become cognizant of this tendency I hear myself apologizing a lot—"Sorry! I interrupted. Continue"—and recoiling, but after twenty-eight years of cutting people off it's as natural as blinking. I can't stop myself. I'm trying, but so far my success rate is pitiful.

It would be one thing if I were interrupting with helpful insights—"It sounds like that was really hard on you"—or prodding questions—"And how did that make you feel?"—or even with requests for clarification—"Now, where did this happen again?" But no. I interrupt with stories. About myself.

If I'm talking to a friend about her relationship woes, I might offer a story about Matt and me. My side of conversations often sound like this: "Oh my God, you got mugged? Let me tell you about my friend who got carjacked." Or "You love *Sex and the City*? I once saw Sarah Jessica Parker on the street!"

It's obnoxious, I know, and now that I've realized I do this, I'm horrified. My improv teacher recently told a story about his neighbor, who is constantly only half listening.

"He's one of those guys who, as you're talking, it's like you can see him scrolling through his mental Rolodex, looking for the perfect story that is related enough for him to bring up, but it's better because, you know, it stars him."

Ew. That's me.

It's not that I'm trying to one-up anyone—if you tell me you ran the marathon, I'll counter that I once trained for the half—it's just my backward way of empathizing. I communicate that I hear you and I understand by saying "You'll never believe what happened to me," when what I should be saying is "I hear you and I understand."

There was a brief period in high school when I wanted to be a psychologist one day. I think we can all agree it's best that never came to pass.

My other friendship flaw dawned on me last night. It was my friend Lindsey's birthday party. Lindsey was the only new friend I'd made in Chicago before this year started. For her big night, she invited a few girls out for drinks. I arrived a little late because Matt and I had been bowling with Gretchen, my new friend from the Mac 'n Cheese Minglers adventure, and her boyfriend. When I showed up at Benchmark, the new sportsbar-meets-nightclub in Old Town, there was already a line to get in. So I waited. Solo.

"Thank you so much for coming!" Lindsey said when she saw me.

"Oh, of course, I wouldn't miss it," I said. "I can't believe there's a line here already. I just had to wait alone for ten minutes in a mass of miniskirts to get in. I felt so lame in my normal-person clothes, but I haven't even had a chance to go home yet."

See that? What I did there? I passive aggressively said "Look at me! I am such a good friend, I would never bail on your birthday party. But let's just recognize all the amazing things

I did for you like waiting in line alone and coming out even though it's been such a long day."

Sometimes I hate myself.

Why do I say these things? Do I think I deserve a medal for fulfilling the obligations of a good friend? It's like I'm saying "Please, you don't have to thank me! That's what friends do," and in the same breath trying to prove how good a friend I am for showing up when there were a few annoyances on the way. The best kind of friend shows up, period. No mention of how she fought through hell and high water to get there.

I've probably known for a while, at least subconsciously, that I do these things. But it's only now that I'm majoring in friendship analysis that my faults are wriggling their way to the forefront of my consciousness. If recognizing the problem is the first step to recovery, then I'm on my way.

FRIEND-DATE 41. I arrive at the El track at 12:45, the appointed meeting time for my RentAFriend date. Christine and I made plans to grab lunch and visit the museum. It has turned out to be too cold for the farmers' market, and I've never been to the Museum of Contemporary Art.

"Christine?"

"Hi! How are you?"

My friend-for-hire is wearing jeans, a black sweater, and a blue puffy North Face jacket. Nothing about her outfit suggests that she moonlights as an escort. Good news.

As we ride downtown, Christine tells me she grew up in the northern suburbs and went to the University of Wisconsin. She's a social worker at a nearby hospital four days a week, and lives with three roommates in Lakeview, a few blocks north of my apartment. We talk about her upcoming high school reunion, our plans for Halloween (she'll be dressing as a dinosaur, I'll be hiding out at home. Costumes aren't my thing), and how she is "single and ready to mingle." Basically, we discuss everything except the giant elephant on the El—the fact that I leased her on the Internet.

I finally bring it up at lunch.

"So how long have you been on RentAFriend?"

"A few months maybe. Not that long. I read an article about it earlier this year, and I figured it would be a good way to make some extra money since the hospital only has the budget to pay me for part-time. It seemed shady at first, but since I have total control over who I meet I figured it would be okay."

"Have you met anyone else through the site yet?"

"Nope, you're my first. I've heard from a few men, but they all seemed totally creepy or their English was so bad I didn't see how we'd communicate. So I told them it probably wasn't a good idea."

"Yeah, this is my first time, too," I tell her. "But it sounded sort of intriguing, and I've been looking into new ways of making friends, so I figured I'd give it a try."

Christine seems like a nice, normal girl, so I want to make clear I'm looking for real friendship. The free kind.

"My friends all think I'm crazy," she says. "Even today, after I told them I was meeting a girl my age, my roommates were all 'Make sure you bring your mace!'"

"That's exactly what my family said!"

There's something amiss about a get-together in which both parties are encouraged to carry pepper spray.

The strangest thing about this lunch is that it isn't particularly strange. Our date is quite . . . usual. Almost as if we are actually friends.

Until it comes time to pay for lunch. Though we haven't discussed it explicitly, I figure picking up the tab is part of the gig. But then, when the check arrives, Christine does the fake wallet reach. Ladies, you know what I'm talking about. It's classic first-date behavior. You don't actually intend to pay, but it would be rude if you didn't at least *pretend* to offer, right? Um, yeah, I know that move. I've used that move.

"Don't worry, I've got this," I say.

"Are you sure?" Christine has already stuffed her wallet back in her purse, so this is all just courtesy.

"Yup, it's part of the deal."

After lunch we wander around the MCA—the first floor is closed for an auction so it doesn't take long—and prepare to part. On an otherwise solicitation-free corner of Michigan Avenue, I look at my watch. It's almost 3 P.M. I dig sixty dollars out of my purse.

"I feel weird taking money from you," she says.

"Oh, you know," I mutter as I awkwardly shove a wad of bills into her hands. "If you ever want to hang out again—like, for real—you know where to reach me."

Yeah, this doesn't feel like an escort situation at all.

As we head our separate ways, I take another glance at the time. Wait. If we met at 12:45, and it's ten to 3, then I only owed Christine forty dollars. I gave her one twenty too many.

I tipped my rented friend! Kill me.

I guess she didn't feel *that* weird taking my money.

■ ■ ■

Tonight is Mia's 35th birthday party. It's at a bar in our neighborhood and the ladies from our cooking club were all invited. Only three of us make it. Jackie and Brynn are settled at the bar when I arrive. Brynn even brought her husband, Jesse, which makes me wish Matt wasn't out of town for work so I could have dragged him along. A good majority of my new friends still haven't met my husband and I'm pretty sure they think I made him up.

After about twenty minutes, Mia, who has been working the room in sexy over-the-knee boots that scream birthday girl, makes her way to our end of the bar.

"You came!" Her higher-than-normal pitch makes clear she's already a bit tipsy, but it's her birthday. She's entitled.

"Of course! I wouldn't miss it." (I don't mention that to get here I had to trek from downtown, where I skipped out early on a cousin's birthday dinner. Progress.)

Mia drapes her arms around Jackie and Brynn and leans her head toward me so we're standing in a football huddle.

"You guys, I'm so glad we met. You're all so great. I love our cooking club." Mia's making a drunk profession of love and I'm eating it up. When I get some extra alcohol in me, you'll never catch me dancing on the bar or falling over myself. No, I'm the girl telling everyone just how great she is and how lucky I am to have met her. I don't confess deep dark secrets. I confess girl-crushes.

"I'm glad, too," I say. Jackie and Brynn smile and nod. We're too sober to reciprocate the lovey-doveyness, but I know we all feel similarly. I'm grateful for this moment. Once in a while it's nice to be on the receiving end of the friend-love declaration. And it's comforting to hear that my quest has affected my new friends. Not that Mia was lacking in the social department, it turns out. When she wrote me after reading my essay, I figured she was in the same boat. Judging by the size of this crowd, it's clear she was in my shoes once, but not anymore.

"This is quite a crowd you've got here," I tell her. "You're so popular."

"You know what's amazing? I didn't know a single person at this party when I moved to Chicago five years ago."

"Really? What a testament to the life you've built," I say.

"I know. It makes me never want to leave."

As I look around the room I'm impressed and encouraged by this detail about Mia's guest list. I didn't host any festivities for my birthday this year, partly because 28 is a boring age but also because, at the time, so many of the people I'd met fell into the more-than-an-acquaintance-but-not-yet-a-friend category. I didn't want anyone to feel obligated.

I'll be celebrating my 30th birthday around the same time as the five-year anniversary of my Chicago relocation. If I have a party, there will definitely be guests there—family, old Northwestern classmates—who I knew when I arrived. But if the friendships I'm building stay on track, I should be able to boast mostly new additions.

Two days later, Brynn and I are at Mia's house for an afternoon of pumpkin carving. I haven't carved a pumpkin since I was 10 years old, but Mia has stencils and actual carving tools. Bring on the jack-o'-lanterns.

"It was nice to hang out with Jesse the other night," I tell Brynn. "He was a trouper to come along."

"He had fun. He'd had a long day so was exhausted by the end of the night, that's why we left early." Brynn didn't actually leave earlier than the rest of us, but she and Jesse led the charge out of the bar at about 12:30.

"Well, I was impressed. He didn't even seem put off by all the girl talk. It's too bad Matt wasn't there to discuss sports and Camp Cobbossee with him." (Brynn and I recently discovered that our husbands went to the same summer camp, though they had the same reaction when we shared this revelation. "Oh, yeah, I think I remember that kid.")

"Where is he again?"

"New Orleans. It's his annual work retreat."

"Sure it is," she jokes. "Are you sure he really exists? He's like Snuffleupagus."

(Interesting factoid: Big Bird's BFF was an imaginary friend from 1971 to 1985. Only Big Bird and the kids at home could see him. The writers only made him visible to the *Sesame Street* adults after a number of child abuse cases made headlines. They worried if young viewers saw the adults accusing Big Bird of lying about Snuffleupagus, they might be scared no one would believe them if they reported abuse happening behind closed doors. But I digress.)

I get what Brynn is saying. I've definitely felt like I'm straddling two worlds this year. Rachel the friend and Rachel the wife are still two separate but equally important people. (To quote the great Mr. Costanza: "A George, divided against itself, cannot stand!")

Back in January I was keen on making this search only about me and my lack of local friendships. I wasn't looking to make couple friends, though I knew some might emerge. I wanted women I could count on and vent to and call for brunch. None of those things involved Matt.

Friends who passed muster would meet my husband eventually, I thought.

Except most of them haven't.

I've done a decent job of balancing my friend self with my wife self this year—consciously scheduling husband-date nights amid all this friending—but a pretty bad job of integrating them. If I made Matt join each time there was a boys-allowed friend event, he might divorce me. That much estrogen once in a while is fine. Once a week might be a bit much.

Now that I've forged some legitimate friendships, it's time.

I want these people to know the most important player in my life. They hear about Matt a lot, so it would be nice for them to see him live and in person. To know, once and for all, that I don't sleep next to a blow-up doll.

When I pick Matt up from the airport I tell him what Brynn said.

"What does she mean, Snuffleupagus?" he asks.

"He was Big Bird's imaginary friend at the beginning. Whenever adults were supposed to meet him he disappeared."

"Really? This changes everything I ever thought about *Sesame Street*."

Not exactly the "I better meet your new friends and fast" that I hoped for.

FRIEND-DATE 42. My friend Chloe—the effortlessly stylish one whose visit earlier this year prompted a blowup with Matt—was supposed to be in Chicago this weekend. Her best friend from business school moved here in August, so she was coming to town to see us both. Jordan and I haven't yet had occasion to meet—I think Chloe was waiting to set us up until she could introduce us in person—but considering Chloe's other best friend is Sara, *my* Sara, I'm guessing she's my type.

Yesterday, Chloe canceled her trip. Clients needed her in the office at the last minute. "That's the life of a consultant, I guess," she wrote in her email to Jordan and me.

We had planned to all go to a Cardio Hip Hop class on Saturday morning. When Chloe warned us she might have to bail, Jordan and I decided to go regardless.

I haven't been to All About Dance, my favorite dance studio, in a while, so the fact that Jordan goes every Saturday is encouraging. A workout buddy is just what I need.

While friends giveth pounds, friends can taketh away. Research has shown that the average female will lose more than ten pounds when she has a diet-and-training buddy, and one study found that while 61 percent of women say they struggle to get moving alone, the same percentage say they love working out when they can do it with friends. Plus, women push themselves harder under a partner's watchful eye.

Jordan and her dancing shoes couldn't have come at a better time.

After class we head to Nookies, my regular brunch spot. Jordan, I can tell, is a keeper.

First of all, she writes an idiom newsletter.

"What does that even mean?" I ask.

"Well, my parents are from Syria and not native English speakers, so I wasn't raised hearing many idioms. I hardly know any! Now, when I come across a new one I write it down and research its meaning and where it came from. In the newsletter, I explain where I heard it, what it means—sometimes they have multiple definitions—and the origin."

"For example?"

"The most recent one was about 'golden handcuffs.' All the monetary incentives that you get at a job that would keep you tied to the position. Like salary, stock options, great benefits, bonuses."

Jordan tells me the phrase originally came from John Steinbeck, who once called the city of San Francisco "a golden handcuff with the key thrown away."

The newsletter, which has only had three issues thus far, is called "Making Heads or Tails of Idioms." It's so nerdy that I can't believe I didn't think of it first. I immediately subscribe.

Jordan has as much enthusiasm for her newsletter as she does for her upcoming Halloween costume (she's going as *The*

Girl with the Dragon Tattoo's Lisbeth Salander, and has bought the wig and body art to pull it off) and the night of partying that will ensue. She's 29, single, and loves to go out.

During brunch I keep thinking about Rom Brafman and his take on the power of storytelling. Jordan is a storyteller. She doesn't say, "I'm from Michigan and went to U of M and work as a consultant." Instead she regales me with stories about her trips to Peru (I particularly enjoy her sitcom-worthy misunderstanding when a local told her to visit Saqsaywaman) and Guatemala (she and Chloe went together and made a pact to lose their newly discovered "third and fourth legs," their pet name for love handles).

After a long lunch and some shopping—which I really shouldn't be allowed to do while I'm still sweaty from dance—we plan to meet at the studio again next Saturday. Time to lose *my* third and fourth legs.

I'm still a sweaty mess when my mom buzzes my apartment.

"I want you to meet my new friend," she told me on the phone when she invited herself over.

Janie lives in Boston but recently bought an apartment in my mother's building because her sons both live in Chicago. "When my boys called and told me they found a perfect place for me, I couldn't resist," she says.

My mom's neighbors are mostly in their thirties, so finding another 50-something widow was fate. Now they get together whenever Janie is in town.

"Do you come out this way a lot?" I ask her.

"Well, now that I have a new friend I'm going to come even more!" She gives my mom a friendly tap on the arm and they giggle like schoolgirls.

I want to hug her.

■ ■ ■

Cooking clubber Jackie and I are on our way to a Seven for all Mankind warehouse sale. Considering how much I hate shopping for jeans—it often ends with me fighting back tears at how hard it is to find a flattering pair—the simple fact that I'm okay with her witnessing my spiral into crazytown means I must like her a lot. During the drive I ask Jackie about her wedding planning.

"The big stuff is done. I got the dress, the DJ, the location. The rest is just details that I don't have the energy to think about right now," she says.

"Understandable."

"Oh, that reminds me. What's your address?"

A friendship milestone! This is my first wedding invitation to come from this search. There haven't been many tangible measures of success this year, but a formal invitation? To a wedding? Everything is going according to my grand master plan. Cue evil laugh.

■ ■ ■

I'm wrapping up a friend-filled weekend at dinner with someone I haven't seen—haven't even spoken to—in about seven years. Nick and I worked together during the summer of 2002. I was an intern at *The Westchester Wag,* a small socialite magazine in my native New York suburb, and Nick worked for some science journals that we shared office space with. I was 20, just finishing up my sophomore year at Northwestern, and he was 18, getting ready to head off to Franklin & Marshall. We were work buddies—we made each other mix CDs and did the *New York Times* crossword together (though I could never get past Wednesday). We hung out a lot that summer, but it was a seasonal thing. When school started in September we mostly lost touch, communicating every now and then over instant message.

The following summer we met up for pizza one night, playing catch-up and gossiping about old coworkers—Nick was back at the same office, I was interning at *Field & Stream*.

We hadn't been in direct contact since that night in 2003, but we quickly became "friends" when Facebook came on the scene. There was no true reconnection (the social networking definition of "friend" is a pretty loose one) but occasional status updates and newsfeed alerts told me that Nick graduated college, that he moved to San Jose, that he was in a relationship, and then, that he wasn't.

Earlier this week I received an unexpected Facebook message.

Hey Rachel,

Long time no see. I'm going to be in Chicago on Sunday and Monday nights and thought I'd drop you a note to see if you're interested in getting a drink and reliving the summer of many moons ago. Let me know.

—Nick

Facebook is an interesting beast. It's old news that it has completely changed the way people socialize, enabling us to post our thoughts, whereabouts, and photos for all our friends (one hundred thirty of them, on average) to see at a moment's notice. We can keep up with one another's lives as they're happening, no sixty-minute catch-up phone call required. Relationships that would have otherwise fizzled out—like my friendship with Nick—are given new life. But for all its mastery of relationship maintenance—Facebook is the reason I've seen pictures of an elementary school classmate's baby or discovered a friend of a friend of a friend's blog—it's not especially helpful for making entirely new connections. In fact, research shows that online networks neither expand the number of people to whom we feel close nor do they deepen our already-tight friendships.

Personally, I have not made one new friend via Facebook. I wouldn't even know where to start. I guess I could blindly message Chicagoans who also "like" *Keeping the Faith* and *School of Rock,* but that seems a stretch. Even for the new I'll-talk-to-anyone-anywhere version of me.

The world's most popular social networking site was never intended to help foster new connections. In a 2007 interview with *Time* magazine (three years before he was named the magazine's Person of the Year), Mark Zuckerberg explained that Facebook is about making communication more efficient between existing friends, not creating new ones, and that's what makes it work. "Our whole theory is that people have real connections in the world," he said. "People communicate most naturally and effectively with their friends and the people around them. . . . That's a really big difference between Facebook and a lot of other sites. We're not thinking about ourselves as a community—we're not trying to build a community—we're not trying to make new connections."

And so it seems I have used Facebook for its intended purpose. To look at Matt's ex-girlfriend's wedding photos, to be reminded of friends' birthdays I might have otherwise forgotten, to get a where-are-they-now update of my childhood neighbors. And to reconnect with an old coworker—someone who, without Facebook, I would not be dining with tonight.

Nick and I meet outside a bar near my apartment. It becomes clear pretty quickly that I would have been perfectly happy had Facebook not brought us back together. The quirks I thought were annoying but excusable when he was 18—the cockiness, the condescension (I chalked it up to him having a lot to learn)—are just plain rude at 26.

Like when we first start catching up. I'm giving the Cliffs Notes of my life over the past seven years, talking easily as if we're old friends. Which we are.

Nick interrupts me mid-sentence.

"I don't recall you being so amped up," he says. "I remember you more reserved."

Sorry to disappoint?

"Reserved is not a word I've ever heard describe me," I say. I'm laughing it off but he's studying me as if he just realized he reached out to the wrong person.

Later, when I mention that I've never been to New Orleans, he looks shocked.

"That's so weird. I thought you were well-traveled."

These mini-jabs aren't so bad individually, but as Nick tallies all the reasons I'm not who he remembers, I want to explain that he's exactly who I remember, and that it's less charming on an adult.

The average friendship doesn't last a lifetime. In her book *Best Friends Forever: Surviving a Breakup with Your Best Friend*, psychologist Irene Levine writes, "A friendship, like a romantic relationship, is founded on two different personalities, both of whom grow and change, for better or for worse, over the course of time. There is no guarantee that two individuals, however close they once were, will grow in the same direction or remain compatible. Even when friendship is built on a solid foundation, the odds are overwhelmingly high that it will eventually fracture for one reason or another . . . Most friendships, even best or close ones, are fragile rather than permanent." Nick and I fall under this fragile category. It seems ours was a situational friendship, born from a need—on both sides—to have someone our own age to talk to during those long summer workdays. It served a purpose, but that need is no longer.

The evening makes me think Facebook is a blessing and a curse. Sure, it helps us keep track of people with whom we otherwise would have fallen out of touch. But sometimes relationships fade for a reason. They're better left a memory.

FALL:

"COME HERE OFTEN?": THE ART OF THE PICKUP

CHAPTER **13**

Lately I've been trying to meet a friend at the local Starbucks or neighborhood bookstore. They seem like natural places for me to find a kindred spirit. In my imagination the encounter goes something like this:

I'm camped out at the Paperback Favorites table, striking up conversations with women as they check out titles I love. "Oh, that's a great one," I'll say.

"Really? I've always wanted to read it," potential BFF says.

"You've got to. It's smart but not too heavy, and it'll make you laugh/cry/[insert verb here]."

"That sounds perfect."

"Here's my number, let's chat once you've finished."

Starbucks would be a similar situation. I'd spot a seemingly friendly 20- or 30-something sitting at the table next to me, another writer tapping away at her keyboard on a Sunday morning. Maybe we'd chat about our respective projects, or knowingly joke about the regulars in line—a cast of characters themselves. We'd make another writing date, eventually meeting weekly to work side by side, becoming regulars ourselves.

So far it hasn't gone that way.

Weekend bookstore shoppers aren't there to linger and debate the merits of Jonathan Franzen or Dave Eggers. They have a laundry list of errands and want to get in, buy Oprah's Book Club selection, and get out. I've stood at that Paperback Favorites table, waiting for my would-be friend to show up, and all that came of it was the store security guy eyeing me funny. I guess shoplifters linger, too.

Thinking that customers with more time on their hands might settle in with a cup of coffee, I've tried hanging out in the bookstore café. Two problems with this plan: One, I couldn't tell if the readers buried in books were open to approach. I want to be friendly but not annoying, and it can be a thin line. Two, there were no outlets. My half-juiced computer didn't have much life left, so I had to abandon ship pretty quickly.

There was one promising encounter at Starbucks a few weeks ago. I had set up my computer, phone, and entire home office when I noticed a girl at the next table over. She was around my age, looked friendly enough, and had on a red-and-white plaid scarf that reminded me of a hoedown. In a good way. We made eye contact and exchanged a friendly smile.

A few minutes later she caught me checking her out again. Another smile.

Eventually, she approached.

"Would you mind watching my stuff while I run to the bathroom?"

This was a good sign. She must have thought I looked honest and trustworthy, two prime attributes in a friend.

"Not at all," I said. "Also, that's a great scarf."

Things slowed down after that. The sun glare through the

window washed out my computer screen, so I switched seats. Now my back was to my new friend, which meant whenever I wanted to make my move I had to crane my neck to see her.

In *The 40-Year-Old Virgin*, Steve Carell's friend emphasizes the importance of using your "peripherals." It's one of Matt's favorite movie quotes and comes up often since I'm a gawker. I'd hardly been nonchalant in my staring at scarf-girl before, and now I had to swing my whole body around to get a good look. Even I knew there was nothing discreet about my behavior. Plus, every time I turned around, ready to strike up conversation, she was on the phone. Probably saying, "Some crazy girl keeps making eyes at me."

I found Callie on Gchat and asked for advice. She's always been good at talking to random strangers. "Go the scarf route," she said. "Ask her where she got it. That can lead to 'Oh, I know that store,' and then suddenly you're talking. I've started so many conversations with strangers over shopping."

It's not a bad idea. My inclination was to be more direct, to actually use a variation of "Come here often?" I was going to tell scarf-girl that I worked in Starbucks a lot and would love a study buddy. But I've been at this quest for so long now that I tend to bypass the art of friendly banter—conversation foreplay—and go in for the kill way too soon. I've gone from unnecessarily shy around potential friends to entirely too direct. Callie's scarf approach seems more appropriate than "Hi. Nice to meet you. How often are you here and can you be my best friend and hang out with me every Sunday morning?"

I prepped my opening line—"I hate to bother you, but can I ask where you got that scarf? I love it"—but I never got a chance to try it out. Scarf-girl was on the phone for the duration of her visit, and then she left. Just like that.

My Starbucks trips since then have been even less exciting. If I'm trying to give off an open-for-friendship vibe, everyone else in the coffee shop is doing the opposite.

Today I have the day off from work and am giving the bookstore-and-coffee-shop thing one last shot. I get to my local bookstore at 10 A.M. It's filled with young moms—and one dad—awaiting storytime with their kids. I hadn't antici-pated this. It's not ideal for friending, but I'll work with what I'm given. Since everyone is gathered in the children's section, I do a walk-through myself. Though I adore children's books, I don't stay longer than two minutes. Considering I'm the only adult here not accompanied by someone under the age of 7, I'm terrified of being mistaken for a child predator.

I move on to the Starbucks across the street, a different one than where I met scarf-girl. Like any major city, Chicago has an outpost of the coffee chain every couple of blocks. You're never more than five minutes from a Caramel Macchiato, or in my case, a hot apple cider.

The only available outlet near my seat is underneath the table next to me, where a good-looking guy is typing away.

"Can I share your outlet?" I ask.

"Umm, I don't know, it's pretty valuable." He's joking, and flashes a smile that kind of makes me love him.

"You've got a hot ticket there," I say.

"Don't I know it. Hand me your plug."

We chat a bit more about nothing much—the weather, the day of work ahead—and turn our attention back to our com-puters.

I've had no luck striking up conversations with women on these outings, but the first time I speak to a guy I've got a pal within minutes. One might argue that men are friendlier to women because they always have sex on the brain and every female is a possible partner, but that's got to be oversimplifying it. I do think, however, that both genders have been trained in friendly flirting with the opposite sex since youth. It's harmless, easy banter.

Talking to women, specifically ones we don't know, can be tougher. We fear being judged or laughed at, subject to mean girls who have become mean women. I've been lucky this year. Pretty much all the ladies I've met have been receptive to new friendships. Even if we weren't the perfect fit, they've given me a fair shot. I truly believe that women are more open to making new pals than the haters give us credit for. As I've said, I expected to get the stink-eye from some of the women I tried to befriend, but that hasn't happened. At least not yet.

Still, it cannot be denied that women are hard on each other. In her book *The Twisted Sisterhood,* author Kelly Valen presents the results from a survey she conducted about female friendship. Seventy-four percent of respondents said they'd been "stung by other women's criticisms and judgments" and 60 percent said they feel "uncomfortable, anxious, wary, awkward, cautious, intimidated, or even distrustful of other females."

Valen describes the moment when two women meet—whether it be in line at Starbucks or at a Mommy-and-Me group—like this: "Pay attention and you're bound to see a curious, almost primitive ritual playing out whenever girls and women come together. Female checks out female, sizes her up, compares self. Hmmm, she may be thinking. Prettier? Smarter? Better pedigree? Better job? Better house? Better figure? More charming? More attractive-successful-attentive boyfriend, girlfriend, husband, kids? Better accessories? Better vacation? Better life? Find a flaw and you can exhale—luxuriate in your superiority."

Obviously, if we're just meeting near the Paperback Favorites table, a woman can't size up my career or my relationship with my husband. But Valen's assessment has some validity when it comes to blindly picking up a friend I know nothing about. There's no question that I'm nervous. Female judgment is scary. We all do it, but no one wants to be subjected to it.

The women who responded to Valen's survey weren't happy about their take on female relationships—96 percent said they want something better for women and "lamented what they see as a growing insincerity to our interactions, a more guarded and unwelcoming vibe, and a very real challenge to make genuine reliable friendships."

My luck with women has probably been because I've found most of my new friends in situations where I knew we'd be on the same page. You don't sign up for a class or a meet-and-greet if you aren't willing to at least consider new friends. You don't agree to be set up, or respond to a want ad, if you're too busy for a relationship. Meeting women in their natural habitat will be significantly more difficult. No one on the coffee line asked for more friends. I'm just foisting myself on them.

The rest of the day is productive on the work front, if not the friending one. There's a table of women in their seventies who appear to meet here weekly, and it's a nice reminder of why I launched this search in the first place. Even if I don't meet a new friend at Starbucks today, I could be meeting old ones here soon enough.

* * *

FRIEND-DATES 43 AND 44. Kelly and Julie are both writers. I met Kelly at a reading for her new novel. I hadn't read
it yet, but I decided to go to the event anyway because a) her
book, *The Lost Summer of Louisa May Alcott,* is a fictional story
of the *Little Women* author, right up my alley, and b) despite
my recent misfires, I still thought a book event would be perfect for picking up a compadre. Amanda—the new friend who
blogged about me back in the day and is now in my cooking
club—came with me. She was the perfect partner in crime.
She loves making new friends and I knew she wouldn't be offended if I made a move on someone else during our date.
Also, she's the type who's good at approaching total strangers,
so she could inspire confidence.

I didn't end up finding a new friend in the crowd of book
buyers that day, but when I realized that Kelly lived nearby, I
took the plunge and asked her out as she signed my new copy
of her novel.

"I'm a writer, too, and I'd love to pick your brain about the
business," I said. "I was wondering if you would be up for getting a drink sometime?"

"Of course! We writers need to stick together," she said.

I followed up by email the next day. A week later we were
eating sushi and trading war stories from our New York City
publishing days. After dinner, we had a beer at the bar next
door while Kelly graciously fielded my barrage of publishing
questions and prepped me on what to expect if I pursued the
life of a full-time writer. We parted with plans to get dinner
with our husbands.

Julie is a freelance magazine writer. She's working on her
first book—the story of her ten-year friendship with an online pen pal she's never met—and came across my blog during
her research. When her email address appeared in my in-box I

couldn't figure out why it looked so familiar. Until I searched my old mail and realized we'd exchanged messages three years earlier, when I'd just moved to Chicago and she was editing a local fashion magazine. My networking has come full circle.

Swap the sushi and beer for tea and cookies and my date with Julie wasn't much different than the one with Kelly. Publishing stories, advice, repeat. But I'd been craving the writerly camaraderie, so I could have talked shop all day. Julie says she may leave Chicago for her home state of Michigan soon, but until then I plan on making her my Starbucks buddy.

Writing can be a lonely endeavor. Kelly was exactly right when she said writers need to stick together, not only because it's such a solitary pursuit but because there aren't many of us in the Midwest. If I still lived in New York City—or, even better, Brooklyn—I'd probably meet an author or journalist at every turn. In L.A. I could maybe carve myself a niche in the screenwriters' circle. But in Chicago we are few and far between. It's a culturally rich city for sure, yet finding someone who can pass along editor contact information or tell you what to expect from the publishing process, someone who gets what you do, isn't easy.

Expanding my social circle this year has helped me widen my professional network, too. I have no fear anymore when it comes to contacting an author I admire or requesting a meeting with a local writer who might be good to know.

I've sent very little fan mail in my life. My brief love affair with writing to celebrities came when I was in fifth grade and got one of those books filled with the addresses of where you could contact the stars. It even told me which of them would write back. I sent a note off to Whoopi Goldberg and shared a bedroom with the signed 8x10 photo I got in return (I'd framed it of course) until I graduated high school. But, until this search started, I'd never sent a note to say "great article!" or tried to make any professional connections with writers I didn't know. *What's the point?* I thought. *It's not going to make any difference. It won't even get read.* And maybe that would have been true in a pre-email world. But when I wrote my essay about feeling locally friendless, I was ecstatic to get messages from people who could relate. And sure, I'm not exactly a famous journalist, but I figured the same might hold true for more established writers. If they share their email address on their website, I choose to believe they want to hear from me.

Recently I wrote to two authors, both New York–based, to tell them I admired their work and that they've inspired me. It's a lesson my parents taught me ages ago, but one I've seen realized repeatedly this year: You never know what kind of opportunity a new connection might bring. And who doesn't like to be told they're brilliant? You really can't go wrong.

I heard back from both writers within a week and each sent thoughtful, funny, and personal notes in response. One even offered to mention my blog on her popular website.

Professional networking is very similar to personal friending. You have to believe that people will be open to your advances. We psych ourselves out of approaching a potential BFF or emailing a role model because it seems far-fetched that they'd want to be friends or network with us in return. But, as has always been the case this year, people are happy to make new connections. More often than not only good can come of it and, at least in the case of networking, writing an email doesn't take much time or energy.

My girl-dates with Kelly and Julie were a refreshing change

of pace. I could talk about the specifics of my career goals and failures without having to do the kind of explaining I might when chatting with a lawyer or a consultant. They're not only potential friends but potential colleagues, and each gave me great insight into local opportunities for writers. It's not only what you know but who you know, and I've made some serious progress on the latter.

■ ■ ■

As much energy as I've dedicated to new friends this year, I've spent a fair amount of time with old ones as well. This weekend, Jenny, one of my old college roommates, is in town with her boyfriend. They live in Manhattan but Eric was in Chicago for business, so Jenny came at the tail end of his trip to show him our alma mater. The three of us spent all day in Evanston—walking by the lakefront, showing Eric where we lived senior year (and where the homeless man made his home on our front porch), and eating lunch at Jenny's favorite café. Tonight we're dining, with Matt, at a restaurant around the corner from our apartment.

"Would it be possible to get some bread, please?" Matt asks our waitress. "For the mussel broth?"

"Our chef doesn't want to serve bread," she says. "I've recommended it to him before—people are always asking—but he feels pretty strongly. And I'm kind of intimidated by him, so I was just like, 'Whatever you say.'" She puts her hand up in a "don't shoot" gesture and laughs.

I like this girl. She's friendly and chatty. She seems easygoing and funny, and reminds me of my friends.

"Maybe she could be my BFF," I joke as she walks away. "She's all cute and spunky."

"You should ask her out," Matt says.

"How? That would be so embarrassing!"

But now the idea's in my head, and the question of how to make my move nags at me the entire meal, like that feeling you can't shake when you forget what you're going to say. I try to let it go but I can't focus on anything else.

This is my chance! It might be awkward, I might be rejected, but I've wanted to blindly ask a girl out all year. I need to just do it.

Problem is, there are people watching. As uncomfortable as I would be if it were just me and the waitress, it'll be ten times weirder in front of Matt and my friends. The pressure will be serious.

"Thank you guys so much for dining with us," the waitress says with a slightly southern twang as she hands us the check. "Have a really great night."

"You've got to do it," Matt tells me. "This is what you've been working toward."

"I know, I know." I'm wringing my hands, unsure of my next move. Jenny and Eric are, understandably, laughing at me. Not with. At.

"Write her a note," Matt says. "Then if you get rejected it won't be to your face."

"Yes! Perfect. But I have horrible handwriting. And what if she sees me writing it, never responds, and then she's our waitress the next time we eat here? This is our favorite restaurant, I don't want to ruin it for us."

I decide to have Jenny write the note. Her handwriting is legible, and if the waitress sees her writing it and decides we're freaks, at least Matt and I can show our faces here again. Jenny has nothing to lose, while I stand to sacrifice the best scallops in Chicago.

The finished product is written in perfect script on the back of our check:

Hi,

I'm new(ish) in town and live around the corner with my husband. You seem cool and like we could be friends. Would you be interested in having lunch sometime? Hope to hear from you.

—Rachel

After my name, Jenny adds my phone number and email address per my direction.

"That's lame, just put your number," Matt says. "Email address is a cop-out."

Matt's a big believer in live phone conversations. He just recently, and reluctantly, jumped on the texting bandwagon. "Email makes it easier for her," I say. "Gives me a better chance of seeing her again."

If you're trying to make a new friend, you need to make it as simple as possible for her to get on board. The less work she has to do, the better chance you have of hearing back.

See, I've learned a few tricks this year.

We've now been lingering with the check for a good fifteen minutes.

"She's looking at us," Matt says. "She's definitely wondering why we're still here." Jenny and I can't stop laughing.

"Okay, go! Go!" I'm like a police officer sending out the SWAT team. I'm nervous to be there when our waitress— whose name I don't even know—sees the note. Yes, I've gotten braver this year, I've gotten better at going outside my comfort zone, but I'm not made of steel. And this leaving a note thing is new territory for me. I'm anxious and excited all at once.

"I probably won't hear from her," I tell Matt later that night. "What if she doesn't turn over the check? Then she won't even see what we wrote."

"She'll see it. You're right, she probably won't call, but you never know. At least you can say you tried."

The next morning I wake up with the slight headache of someone who drank just enough wine to think it was a good idea to ask out a potential friend on the back of a restaurant check. Does that even happen in real life? I've definitely only seen it in the movies.

"At least I made Jenny write the note," I tell Matt as we're lying in bed. "We can go back there anytime with no weirdness."

I check my email while I'm eating my morning oatmeal. And there, the only thing in my in-box, is a note. From her. The waitress. Maritza.

Hey Rachel,

I got your note. I guess I didn't really get a chance to talk to you guys that much but y'all seemed very nice as well. I just moved here from Texas myself in November. Funny that you're "newish," too. Let's do lunch for sure! When is good for you? I'm off Sunday, Monday, and Tuesday so if those days work, let me know. I look forward to seeing you again.

—Maritza

She wrote the email at 2:40 A.M. She must have sent it as soon as she got home from her shift. I immediately forward her email to Matt, Jenny, and Eric with a note of my own: "She didn't get a chance to talk to us? I thought we were best friends!"

Jenny tells me I probably found the one waitress out of a hundred that would actually respond, but I don't know. A year ago, maybe even last night, I would have agreed. But it's hard to believe I could have struck gold on the first try. And haven't I found, over and over this year, that people are flattered when someone extends a hand of friendship?

I write Maritza back that afternoon. (I'm succumbing to game-playing—a Shasta Nelson no-no—but I wait a few hours to respond. After writing the note, I don't want to come off as desperate. Or, any *more* desperate.) I thank her for not thinking I'm crazy and we make a date for next Sunday.

Buoyed by my success with Maritza, I head to the clothing boutique on my corner. Celia, the store manager, and I have become friendly since I've moved to Chicago. When I wanted an outsider's opinion on my would-be wedding dress, I showed her the pictures on my iPhone. She said I looked like a ballerina. Considering I've always said I was a ballet dancer in a former life, she pretty much won my heart with that single observation.

Since we first met, I've learned Celia has an older sister who is her best friend and that she's dating a guy in the finance world. I've wanted to befriend her since I first started this project, and not only because she knows what clothes work for my body and could possibly hook me up with a discount. I put off asking her out for a while because I hadn't built up the nerve. Starting the year with friend setups was my way of wading into the friendship waters. This direct pickup approach? It's the friendship plunge.

I made my first attempts a few months ago. I went to the boutique ready to make a move, but each time I tried Celia was either not working or was there with another salesgirl. It seemed wrong to ask her on a friend-date while another perfectly nice, friendable person stood watching. I didn't want to leave anyone out.

But today I'm feeling lucky, high off my earlier triumph, and when I walk in the door I quickly see that Celia's the only employee on duty. Can I just cut to the chase? Shouldn't I at least pretend to be shopping? I mean, there *is* a sale going on. And I could certainly use a new dress. It only seems right to try on a few options.

"I'm looking for something to wear to a rehearsal dinner," I tell Celia. "Nothing too fancy, but with sleeves for winter."

She offers a few options and I settle on a black number with short sleeves and a ruffle down the side.

As I hand over my credit card, it's time. "I've been meaning to ask you for while, would you maybe want to get lunch one day?"

"I'd love to! I really would." Celia sounds genuinely excited by my invitation. "You know, I meet great people here all the time, but it's so hard to ask anyone to hang out."

"Yeah, believe me, I know what you mean."

"Especially since I work here. I don't want customers being like 'Why is the salesgirl asking me to lunch?' It would be unprofessional."

In all the time I've thought about asking Celia out, it never occurred to me that maybe she wanted to be my friend, too, that perhaps something was holding her back. Celia's approximately seven feet tall and impossibly thin and pretty. Almost intimidatingly so. And she has an impeccable fashion sense. For whatever reason, this combo told me she was probably pretty well-stocked in the friends department.

I never would have thought of it on my own, but Celia's hesitancy to personally befriend customers makes perfect sense. Of course she can't risk potential business by asking customers to drinks. What if she asked me and I got weirded out and never returned? Or worse, I complained to her boss?

It's another reminder of why, when I meet someone who could make a great best friend, I should just go for it. I'll never know the other person's story. She could be a store manager anxious for new friends but reluctant to look unprofessional. Or she could be a waitress even newer in town than I.

In the last twenty-four hours I've successfully tried to befriend two women, and the takeaway? You'll never know what she's thinking until you ask.

Well, that and a little black dress.

FRIEND-DATE 45. Jordan's friend Hallie joins us for dance class almost every Saturday. Today the three of us go for our usual post-cardio brunch, but Jordan, still hurting in the aftermath of a late Friday night, bails mid-meal. Hallie and I finish lunch—including Jordan's leftover hash browns—and decide to do some early holiday shopping. It's our first time hanging out just the two of us. This is my favorite kind of friend-date—the impromptu, we're-just-gals-doing-our-thing-on-a-Saturday-afternoon outing. It's exactly what I was missing at this time last year, the void that inspired me to start this search in the first place. There's a quiet feeling of victory surrounding this date.

My brother and Jaime are hosting our family for a welcome-to-the-neighborhood dinner party tonight. Alex has finally settled into his Chicago life—a new job, some furniture, a working knowledge of the city's grid layout—and we've spent a Saturday or two sitting around in his apartment, watching TV and not-talking like only siblings can. Witnessing his new beginning has been a bit like peering into Dumbledore's Pensieve, giving me an opportunity to look back in time at my own Chicago start from a third-person perspective.

Alex is me three years ago. He has plenty of family in Chicago, and is acquainted enough with Jaime's friends and their significant others, but he doesn't have many—or, maybe, any—of his own local friends. Yet. He left a tight-knit group of buddies behind in New York, moved here for love, and is currently too busy enjoying the spoils of sharing a hometown with his girlfriend to be upset about a lack of male bonding time. And when Sunday football rolls around he watches with Matt. He's taken care of.

For now, Alex is totally satisfied. He's happy and fulfilled, and if you ask him about his friends—or lack thereof—he'll say, "I'm fine with it. I'm doing great." And he means it.

My brother might change his mind one day and launch a (more low-key, less obsessive) BFF search of his own. Or he won't. At the moment, I feel worse about his social circumstances than he does—due in equal parts to my new hypersensitivity to relationships and the fact that I'm a girl—so I'm keeping my mouth shut.

Taking stock of Alex's situation has shed light on how far I've come. On quiet Friday nights I'll get a text from him that says "What are you up to tonight?" and I'll almost always have plans, usually with a friend I've made this year. I feel guilty that I can't be there for him the way I wish someone had been there for me, but I know he's happy for me. Not too long ago I was the one on the couch figuring out who I could call. Now I've got the packed social calendar.

"How's the quest going?" Jaime asks me over dinner.

"Really well," I say. "I've definitely made some new friends, if not a very best one." I'm excited to tell her about my recent conquests and my dates on the books with Maritza and Celia.

"It's amazing the way you find these people," she says. "The new friends I've made in Chicago have always been through my existing friends. I'll go to one girl's bachelorette party, where I'll meet some of her other friends, and then we'll exchange numbers and start hanging out on our own."

"That's a pretty ideal way to meet people," I say. "The problem for me was that when I moved here I didn't have that base level to get the ball rolling. I couldn't meet friends of friends because I didn't have enough friends in the first place."

If I haven't found one single best friend forever this year, maybe I've done one better. I've planted the seeds for a future in Chicago. I've built a life here, and established the first layer of connections that Jaime is talking about—the people through which, in time, I will make even more friends. Jaime's method of meeting people is probably the most organic—her BFFs "just happened," as everyone thinks friend-making should—but it's impossible without some first-degree companions to kick-start the process.

This project started in January, and now, in early November, I finally have enough new friends to meet people the way Jaime has, the way we all want to. I found Alexis through Hannah, Hallie through Jordan.

The "just happening" is finally happening, it simply took a year of work to get there.

FRIEND-DATE 46. Maritza waves at me from a table in the corner. Considering she commented on how little we talked at dinner, I wasn't sure she'd recognize me.

"I had to Facebook you to figure out who the note was from," she says. "You know what's so funny? I actually got two notes that night, and they were both from girls."

"*Two* notes? Does that happen a lot? I thought I was so crazy." The big stink I made about leaving my little message seems a tad melodramatic now.

"It's not so uncommon, but they're usually from guys. The night you were there I served a big group of girls at another table and they left a note saying 'When will we see you again?' I must have been really on my game."

I thought I'd noticed something under the surface with Maritza, a spark that spoke to me as her BFF-to-be, but apparently she's just charming. Still, two notes in one night? Both from friend wannabes? What are the chances?

"I think you were my server last time," Maritza tells our waitress when we start to order.

"Yeah, I probably was. I basically live here."

They get into a long conversation about the restaurant business. Our waitress is in fashion school and debating a move to New York to follow her dream.

"She's from New York!" Maritza says about me.

"It's true," I say.

"Oh really? I'll totally need to pick your brain. How do you guys know each other?"

"She picked me up when I was her server," Maritza tells her. "Watch out, we might recruit you."

I can see now why Maritza would get two notes in a night. She's clever, friendly, funny. She's magnetic. The kind of girl that everyone wants to be friends with.

Over the next hour I learn that Maritza is from Austin, she was once an aspiring actress though now she likes working in the restaurant biz, she's a big-time indie music lover, and she found the *Flashdance*-esque T-shirt she's wearing—with a picture of Madonna on the front—at a local thrift shop.

Oh, and she was on *Road Rules*.

"Like on MTV?" I ask.

"Yup. I was almost cast for *Real World Las Vegas*, but I was only 19 at the time. Really dodged a bullet with that one." She wipes her brow in mock relief. You might remember Vegas as the season that kicked off the whole *Real-World*-as-soft-porn thing.

I didn't watch her *Road Rules* season, but this news solidifies what I've been starting to realize about my current girl-date: She's totally too cool for me.

"What do you mean too cool?" Jenny's laughing as I recap my lunch date over the phone.

"For starters, she basically travels the country going to music festivals. Very cool. She was on *Road Rules*, which I know is a bit suspect, but mostly makes her pretty badass. And she says that at 26 she's too old for MTV and rejects all requests to go back for any Challenges. Meaning, she's smart. Also her boyfriend is a server at Topolobampo, Rick Bayless's restaurant, and his sister lives on Bayless's property. So cool! And also so delicious. I've got to get in on that." (Rick Bayless is one of Chicago's most famous chefs. His Mexican feast earned him the inaugural *Top Chef Masters* title.)

"But you're cool," Jenny says.

"Jenny, I'm as cool as the next guy, I guess. I can talk pop culture and play beer pong. She's like, actually, legitimately, cool. So obviously I adored her and have a total girl-crush. And I think she liked me—she kind of made me nervous, but she laughed a lot at my one-liners and texted me as soon as she got in a cab to say she wanted to invite Matt and me to a dinner party. So we'll see."

"I wish you could hear yourself. You're hysterical."

I am a bit over the moon about this one. I've got friendship butterflies.

■ ■ ■

The StoryStudio is a Chicago writing center that Kelly the author told me about over dinner, and tonight I'm checking it out for the first time. I signed up for The Write-In, a writing marathon and pizza party in honor of National Novel Writing Month. I'm not actually writing a novel, but I figure no one will check the text on my computer as long as I look busy. I'm not actually here to write, anyway. I mean, I *could* write, if I have to, but I'm here to—what else?—pick up some women.

Writing may be a solitary enterprise but pizza party sounded social enough to me. Not so much. There's pizza and soda, but party there is not. Just a handful of people spread out in the studio lobby, typing away on their would-be masterpieces. I try to make eye contact with a few fellow writers, maybe flash them a smile, but no matter how intensely I stare I can't get anyone to lift her head or glance in my direction.

That's okay. This feels like being in a library and is certainly a more calming environment than my home—with washing machines humming and football announcers yelling in the background—so I plug in my laptop and get to work.

Nothing changes as the night progresses. I trade some pleasantries with the studio owner but that's about it. I don't mind, though. I'm enjoying the quiet.

As I explore the studio, I'm reminded of all the activities I've tried out by myself this year. A flyer with next month's schedule has me wondering if I should sign up for a class. And then I have an epiphany. This year hasn't just made me more social, it's made me more independent. I'm at once better at making friends and better at being alone. And not merely because I have less time to myself and thus appreciate the time I do have more, though that's certainly part of it. It's because in order to meet new friends I've had no choice but to go on some solo adventures—meetups and volunteer outings and religious groups, oh my. A year ago I would have thought, "That write-in sounds cool, I wish I had a friend to go with me." But my internal dialogue has shifted. Now I think, "That write-in sounds cool, maybe I'll meet a friend there."

FRIEND-DATE 47. I've been trying to meet up with Bridget for two months now. We met in September, on the flight back from Callie's wedding. She was sitting next to me. I spent the first hour—while we were sitting on the tarmac, not moving and getting increasingly frustrated—trying to figure out how I knew her. She looked so familiar. For a while I thought she might be Stephanie LaGrossa, the three-time *Survivor* contestant. The voice in my head kept saying, "Talk to her. This is your in. You've been wanting to pick someone up on a plane." But she seemed really engrossed in her book, and there's noth-

ing more off-putting than being interrupted while reading. Instead I kept checking her out, racking my brain for what our
connection might be.

When she put the book away and stared into the distance
with the glazed expression of a disgruntled airline passenger, I
struck up conversation.

"Do you live in Chicago?" I asked.

Her eyes focused in on me.

"Sorry," I said. "It's just that you look so familiar."

"Really? I was thinking the same thing about you."

We figured out we both went to Northwestern, but were
different years, different majors, and in different sororities.
When we exchanged names, nothing rang a bell for either of
us. We've never worked together. The only thing we can think
of is that we used to see each other around campus, as we have
some common friends.

By the time we finally took off, Bridget and I were old pals,
gabbing about Northwestern weddings (she married her college sweetheart, too), and European travel (she was leaving for
a birthday trip to Paris in a few days). Eventually she went back
to her book and I to mine. When we landed, I didn't know
how to ask for her number or email address without sounding
presumptuous, so instead I took out my business card. I sat
there holding that 3.5-by-2-inch piece of cardstock for fifteen
minutes, waiting for the exact right moment to give it to her.
(Insert another internal pep talk here. Like I said, picking up
friends is getting easi*er*, not easy.)

I don't know if it was the perfect time, or just the last chance,
but as we were gathering our bags I handed Bridget my card
and said, "Here's my info, I'd love to get together sometime."

"For sure! Let's make a date after I get back from Paris."

There was no time for her to give me a card or phone number, so I could only cross my fingers and hope.

This would be a better story if Bridget had in fact emailed me for that date. She didn't. One lesson that's been continually hammered into me this year? If I want a friendship to happen, especially in the early stages, I have to do the work. I can't count on others to reach out to me. Maybe they will—certainly a number of people have—but I can't rely on it. I've learned, though, that if I carry the load, people will come along for the ride.

In October I found Bridget on Facebook and sent her a message asking about her trip and inviting her for a drink. She got back to me two weeks later. I wrote her back immediately, she took another two weeks to respond. If this were a romantic pursuit I'd tell myself to get a life, but this is friending, and I'm on a mission. I don't think Bridget is giving me the brush off, anyway. I think she's just busy.

We meet for coffee at 8:30 on the Tuesday morning before Thanksgiving. Bridget—quite the world traveler—is leaving tomorrow for a Hawaiian holiday. I really like her. She's talkative, intelligent, and generally pleasant. We catch up as if we've known each other forever, but I can already tell that she's someone who means well but isn't great with follow-up. She's one of those would-be companions who, every time you see them, say "We should really get together more often!" or "Can we please keep in better touch this time around? Seriously?" And even while the words are coming out of her mouth, you can tell it's an empty promise. Not a lie exactly, because I think she really means it in the moment, but an intention that will fall through the cracks in favor of already-established friends and work responsibilities and a husband.

I don't hold it against her. Bridget never asked for a new

friend. She was just sitting on an airplane minding her own business when I picked her up. Perhaps she's already at her one-hundred-fifty-friend capacity.

In case I'm wrong, I send Bridget an email two weeks later wishing her a happy holiday season and inquiring about her trip to Hawaii. She doesn't write back.

■ ■ ■

This Thanksgiving, Matt and I are celebrating at my brother-in-law's in New York, twenty minutes from where I grew up. Because we usually visit my family at Christmastime—my dad and all three of his siblings converted from Protestant to become two Jews, a Catholic, and a Buddhist nun (we're way modern) but we still gather and sing "Jingle Bells" every December—Matt's side always gets Turkey Day. Usually we go to his mother's house in Cape Cod, but the plans have changed this year.

A bonus to this holiday relocation is that I get to visit my dad's grave. He's buried in a cemetery less than five minutes from my childhood home, but now that Alex and my mom both live in Chicago I don't get out there much. .

I'm not sure exactly why—I think it's a combination of not wanting to take Matt away from his mom during the holiday, my own need for time away from the in-laws, and, mostly, my desire to stay at the cemetery longer than usual—but I decide to visit the gravesite alone for the first time ever. In the past I've always been with my mother or Matt. We stand at the top of the hill, underneath the birch tree (a fitting tribute), and admire the headstone for five minutes or so. Per Jewish custom, we place small stones on top of the grave. Per Bertsche custom, we take a picture of it with our camera phones and send the photo to the others with notes like "Looking good" or "Dad says hi." It's our strange, twenty-first-century way of feeling close to him. We virtually visit so that we can be there more than the two times a year we make it out to Westchester.

Holidays are usually the hardest for me and seeing other dads in action—our Thanksgiving dinner was filled with great ones—always hurts the most, so I want some alone time to process the pain. I wish I didn't get jealous, that I didn't immediately think of all that I've lost when I see happy families. Maybe one day, when Matt is the great dad wowing me at my own family table, I won't. But today I'm feeling a giant void and I want to try and close it up, or at least start filling it, if only for a few minutes. Maybe I'll use the opportunity to talk to my dad. Or, more likely, I'll just sit on the ground next to the stone. I feel closer to him on that patch of grass than I do anywhere on earth, and today I want some father-daughter time.

As I pull into the gates, a man standing at the entrance looks annoyed. "We close in five minutes," he barks.

"Seriously?"

"Four P.M. every day," he says. I want to scream that I don't live here, how am I supposed to know the cemetery hours? But instead I nod and book it up the hill.

I place a stone, take a photo, and sit on the ground. I cry. And then, four minutes later, I leave.

On the drive home I want to call Callie or Sara. Or maybe Brooke, my New York City roommate who lived with me when my dad died and in the grief-filled aftermath. I want to talk to someone who knew my father, who can picture the man who helped raise me as I rage about the cemetery's closing time.

I need an old friend.

I don't pick up the phone at all because I'm already crying and I only sort of know the way home and I'm driving my mother-in-law's car. I hardly need the added (and illegal) distraction of a cellphone. Instead I think about my lifelong friends, the people who knew me long before I could find my way around a cemetery, and my new ones. I've been searching for a BFF like I had in my childhood, another Callie or Sara who will understand me implicitly. But I'm not sure that's possible anymore. No one I met this year will have known me before my father died or before I met Matt. Who I was then is so important to who I am now that it's hard to imagine anyone can ever know me as completely as my lifers do.

In *The Girls from Ames,* Jeffrey Zaslow's book about the lifelong friendship of eleven women, one of the "girls" explains her relationship with the others: "We root each other to the core of who we are, rather than what defines us as adults—by careers or spouses or kids. There's a young girl in each of us who is still full of life. When we're together, I try to remember that."

No matter how hard I try, I can never recapture my 16-year-old self with someone who wasn't around to meet her.

When I get home I send an email to a journalist friend who's been following my quest from afar. I tell her I'm worried that I'll never find what I'm looking for.

That afternoon she writes me back and explains that in the wake of her ten-year high school reunion she too has been reflecting on friendship.

"Sometimes when I see people from high school I feel trapped in the persona I maintained then," she says. "Ten years have gone by, and I've changed a tremendous amount—both emotionally and in circumstance. So while my oldest relationships are incredibly dear, and it's true that they know me so intimately, it can be freeing to have relationships built on exactly who you are at this moment. As you ease into these new friendships, you start working backward and putting the pieces together from the former lives you both had. If it's a good match, you'll find that it wasn't actually necessary for you to have shared all those experiences. Some of the friendships I've found as an adult are far more rewarding than those forged out of the convenience of adolescence."

She's seriously wise.

I think back to my own high school reunion, specifically to the insecurities and jealousies that bubbled up as if I'd traveled back in time, and realize my friend is right. There's a place for both kinds of friendships. I'm only 28. There are years—decades!—still ahead, and one day in the not-too-far future my new friends will be new old friends. They'll be the ones who knew me before I had kids. Before my kids had kids.

They'll be lifers.

CHAPTER **14**

It's crunch time. There are only five weeks left of the year and the same number of dates. I've had a surprisingly easy time finding potential BFFs thus far—between setups and mixers and my essay, I've been able to schedule some weeks ahead—but now, just as I'm nearing the end, I've tapped out all my resources. The next two get-togethers are on the calendar (Celia the boutique manager and Joanna, an ex–Tripp Lake Camper who recently moved to town) but then I'm at a loss. Part of me feels like, enough already. Once I have forty-nine dates to show for this search, do I really need to scrape up three more just to make the number prettier? But I'm not one to give up, and what if girl-date 52 is The One? It could happen.

The holiday season, for all its good tidings and comfort and joy, is sucky for friend-making. Schedules don't allow for girl-dates. They're too packed full of holiday parties and vacations and family time and old friends. Potential friends are not top priority.

Like everything in this world, friending has seasons. This particular calendar mirrors the academic year. In September, people want to start fresh and welcome new pals into their lives. You can friend like crazy for about three months. Then, the holidays. Potential BFFs retreat to the comfort of old friends and family and too much eggnog. Come January, attitudes turn around in the wake of our second fresh start. As winter turns to spring it only gets better—warm weather! walks along the lake!—until summer hits. Suddenly weddings and vacations take precedence over fledgling connections. And then the cycle starts anew.

Unfortunately, my project ends smack in the middle of the holiday rut. My would-be pals have no extra time for themselves, much less for me. The phrase "let's get together after the new year" gets thrown around a lot. That, however, doesn't work with my plan.

I ask everyone I know for advice. "Where should I try to meet someone? I've exhausted my options."

"How about a religious event?"

"Already did it."

"A meetup group?"

"Same."

"Have you tried getting fixed up, or—oh, I know!—how about an airplane?"

"Done and done."

"Something will come up," my mom tells me over the phone. I'm on my way to pick up the final ingredients for tonight's chicken curry dinner. "You're the best friender there is."

Awww, Mom.

It's November, it's cold, and while the walk to the grocery store is short, it's still outdoors. I'd been cooking in my comfy around-the-house clothes when I realized I was short an onion and some green curry, so I threw on my pink-and-orange-striped pom-pom hat, an old winter coat, and my slippers. I'm wearing an extra-large white V-neck T-shirt that says "Team Bill"—it's the family uniform when we do the Leukemia and Lymphoma Society's Light the Night walk in honor of my dad—and gray sweatpants. Not cute, fitted Lululemon ones that make my butt look great. Ratty, stained, old sweats that I probably should have thrown out years ago. I look homeless.

Next to the cheese section, I do a double take.

"I think I just passed my neighbor," I whisper, still on the phone with Mom. I put my head down and plow past the dairy. "I hope she doesn't see me. I'm not fit for public consumption."

"You're ridiculous."

"Wait, I should probably talk to her. Maybe she'd go out with me. I've been wanting to socialize with a neighbor."

No matter how much friendlier I've become this year, when I'm dressed like a bum and running an errand, it will always be my first instinct to run in the other direction when I see a semi-familiar face. But I can't pass up this opportunity.

I hang up with my mom and turn back to where I came from. "You're Irene, right?"

"Huh?"

"I'm Rachel. I live in your building? We've worked out in the gym together."

"Oh right! How are you?"

"I'm good, thanks. I just wanted to officially introduce myself, I don't really know many of the neighbors."

Irene is chatty, and starts asking me about our apartment. What's the layout like? Do we own or rent? She's in her mid-to-late thirties, I'd guess, and from what I can tell is single with no kids.

"We should get lunch sometime," I tell her. "I've always wanted a neighbor friend. It would nice to have someone to borrow a cup of sugar from." It's an old-fashioned idea, the neighborly drop-by. One that has been largely replaced by the "good fences make good neighbors" mind-set. According to recent research, 28 percent of Americans know none of their neighbors by name, and this has a lot to do with why Americans are more isolated than ever. I'd love for Irene to keep a copy of my keys or pick up my packages while I'm away. And I'll do the same for her.

I grew up on a small street with neighborhood block parties and garage sales. It's not quite the same when you live in an apartment building, but it could be.

She laughs. "For sure! Let me give you my card."

"Great, I'll use it," I say. "I'm a good follow-upper." It's important to give people this warning. Oftentimes I'll exchange email addresses with someone, tell them I'll be in touch, and they're still shocked to hear from me. People expect it's all lip service.

"Fantastic! I'm not."

I appreciate her honesty.

FRIEND-DATE 48. There's a lot riding on this date. Celia the clothing store manager has been a hot prospect since the beginning. I really want it to work out. So much so, in fact, that I revisited *Click* for advice: Be vulnerable, sit close, call attention to all our similarities no matter how seemingly insignificant, and casually touch her shoulder or elbow when possible. I know, it sounds weird. But according to the Brafman brothers we associate physical contact with closeness. "Being touched, even for a second, makes us far more attracted to the person touching us," they write. "It makes us more prone to form a connection. A similar pattern emerges with casual eye contact."

We'll see. I'm a big believer in personal space. Women who touch my arm too much in conversation generally turn me off. But maybe touching isn't strange. Maybe I am.

I also need to keep in mind the importance of storytelling. I know enough about Celia, the basic who-what-where of her life, to jump right into funny stories and skip the small talk.

I get to the restaurant a few minutes early. When Celia arrives, wearing a cashmere wrap sweater that I would die to have in my closet and her down-to-there hair pulled half-up with a barrette, we greet each other with a strange wave. The worst. It's like we know each other too well to shake hands, but we're not at a hugging place yet. I've been working on honing my is-she-a-hugger radar (you learn the importance of such a skill after the tenth bumbling embrace) and Celia doesn't have a warm and fuzzy aura. So much for touching.

As soon as we sit down I can feel the tension. I wonder if I ruined our chances by placing the stakes too high. It's like when I finally forced Matt to watch an episode of *Friday Night Lights* after continually telling him it was the best show on television. Of course it was that weird one where Julie was looking at colleges and half the episode was filmed in Boston. Hello? Where was Texas? It did not represent the show's brilliance one bit. So frustrating.

I built Celia up too much.

There's nothing wrong with our dinner, per se. It's perfectly friendly, civil. Celia's really nice. But it's not easy, the way conversation is with Jillian or Hannah or Hilary. After four dozen dates the difference is obvious. Here, I'm constantly trying to decide what I should say next because I can see the long pauses coming down the pike.

"I don't know why, but I have a tendency to befriend women who are all older," Celia says. She's 27, but tells me that most of her friends are in their mid-to-late thirties. "I'm just a homebody. I don't like going out, and maybe that's what the girls my age want to do."

I'm a homebody. I don't go clubbing. I'm pretty sure her low-keyness isn't what's making this tough. Celia's just . . . serious. I can't picture her cracking up or letting loose. I'm the opposite. I like to make fun of myself, be silly, laugh uncontrollably.

At least the date didn't go *badly*. There was no conflict or hostility. I can still go to Celia's store without it being uncomfortable, thank God. Losing a potential friend *and* potential outfits would be a real tragedy.

Considering how much I wanted this to work out, I may even follow up. Perhaps we need a second date. But for the moment I've curbed my expectations for BFFdom. Reluctantly.

Maritza, the other recent pickup, isn't looking good in the follow-up department either. It was only two weeks ago so I'm not discounting her, but she already canceled our first follow-up date. When she suggested we reschedule and I sent over some dates that worked for me, I got radio silence. I'll try again soon, but this is not a good sign.

■ ■ ■

"It's December first. One month to go."

"You're so close," Matt says.

"I know it. For the next thirty days I'm going all out. And I'm dragging you with me."

It's time for Matt to meet my friends. Yes, he's met Margot and Hannah, and he works with Natalie. But he's been out of the picture for the last few months. Holiday parties seem like a good venue for jumping back in. I've already gotten five invitations from people I didn't know last year, plus I'm doing gift exchanges with my coworkers and my book club.

Not to toot my own horn, but I'm feeling pretty satisfied with my efforts.

"Okay. For this month, I'm game," he says.

"Great. I've already RSVP'd us for a Chanukah party on Friday—my friend Meredith from LEADS is hosting—and on Saturday we have dinner plans with Rachel from improv."

"Can't wait."

I thought about hosting a holiday party of my own. What better way to see the fruits of my labor than to gather all my new friends in one living room? But the calendar is already so full that I'm not sure where I'd fit my soiree in. Not to mention that a rager of some fifty-one women and one gay guy might make for an odd Friday night.

At Meredith's house, I look around the room. It's all women. Matt is parking the car and I'm pretty sure he's going to want to kill me when he sees this.

"So, are any guys coming?" I ask. Her brief romance with Steve from LEADS has fizzled, so I don't anticipate seeing him.

"They were supposed to but three just canceled. One's sick, one's studying for the GMAT, and I don't know what's going on with the last one," Meredith says.

"What about Rob?" Meredith and I have both become friends with the leader of our LEADS group.

"Oh yeah! He's coming with a friend in about an hour."

The buzzer rings. It's Matt. I intercept him at the door.

"So, I really appreciate you coming with me. Thank you," I say. Always good to build them up before you knock them down.

Matt nods, aware there's more to this conversation.

"And I just want to warn you before you go in that it's all girls."

Matt's eyes are wide. He's not legitimately mad, I know, but he'd rather be anywhere but here. "Are you serious?" He says it with a laugh, a distinct you-owe-me-one tone.

"Rob's coming, though. With a friend," I say. "I've told you about Rob right? And in the meantime, talk me up. I still need two more dates."

It's a pretty uneventful dinner. Meredith tries to explain the story of Chanukah to her non-Jewish guests who want to understand the prayers and the food and what Meredith and I do at LEADS. We eat latkes and chicken soup and light candles. Eventually Rob and his friend come, and Matt has some testosterone to back him up.

At about 11 P.M. Matt ducks out to meet some friends at a bar. I'm having fun and I think there's a potential girl-date in Samantha, Meredith's friend who keeps saying we should do yoga together, so I stay put.

Like I said, it's pretty uneventful. Until Rob asks Meredith to show off her strength. I hadn't noticed until now, but Meredith has a pull-up bar hanging in the doorway to her living room. Rob's not so sure she can execute.

Of course, child that I am, I want in on the action. "I wanna try!"

I have no idea if I can do a pull-up, but I've got decent upper-body strength. I can do push-ups, and not the on-your-knees kind. Naturally, my first go should be in front of a roomful of people.

Meredith's up first. She jumps for the bar, and suddenly it comes crashing down. On my head.

"Ow!" My hand flies to my forehead. It feels like a minor headache. Nothing major but definite pain. And then: "Oh my god there's blood. Lots of blood."

According to the bathroom mirror, there's just a small cut. I can't quite figure out how all that blood—it's covering my hands, and my shirt, and Meredith's floor—could have come from such a tiny scratch. Meredith gives me a Band-Aid and when I glance back in the mirror, maybe three seconds later, my small cut has become a goiter. There's an egg protruding from my forehead.

My first battle wound! I've been in the trenches for almost a year and today I've been injured in the line of duty.

I think poor Meredith is more upset than I am. A little ice will make the wound go down, no stitches are necessary, and now my new friend and I have a great story. Clobbering someone on the head with a big metal bar is a pretty direct route to shared memories.

In fifty years we'll be drinking iced tea in our nursing home reminiscing about the time I almost bled out on her floor.

Seriously, it's the stuff that dreams are made of.

FRIEND-DATES 49, 50, 51. Joanna, Irene, Meg. All fine. I knew Joanna from my summer camp days and recently bumped into her at a neighborhood restaurant. Meg and I went to college together. When I saw her at a holiday party, I invited her out for drinks. I was friendly with both of them in my former camp-and-college lives, but not friends with them, and I anticipate this is how things will stay. Not because the dates were bad—they weren't particularly—but they weren't great, either. And I finally have the luxury of holding out for great.

But was the just-okay-ness my fault? Have I resorted to merely going through the motions to reach my goal of fifty-two?

I don't think so. I mean, I wanted to amp up the date with Meg to a full dinner. She opted instead for a quick drink. And I was sure Joanna and I would be a perfect fit. We both left New York magazine jobs for Chicago, we're both writers and bloggers, and we know plenty of people in common. She was more formal than friendly, as if we didn't perform in summer gymnastics shows together when we were kids. I got the sense she wasn't interested.

Taking a second stab at friendship sometimes works and sometimes doesn't. This time, it didn't.

I met Irene, my neighbor, at a diner near our apartment. Considering her admission that she's terribly busy and bad at follow-through, I don't have high hopes. She doesn't seem anxious to expand her social network. At least not in the female department. But we shared a perfectly pleasant meal. Irene's a talker, and told me all about her family, her job, and her take on Rahm Emanuel. We don't seem destined for BFFship, but there is real value in even a casual friendship here. In fact, just this week a Christmas present I ordered went missing from our lobby. I sent an email to my neighbors asking if anyone had mistakenly scooped up my package in their travels, and Irene was the one who wrote back with the suggestion that I scour the hallways.

"Maybe it was delivered to someone's door who's out of town?"

It wasn't, but still. She probably wouldn't have reached out if we hadn't had the lunch date.

As we left the diner, Irene told me that we should definitely grab lunch again. "Don't forget I'm bad at initiating, but I'll definitely respond if you email me."

Those aren't the words of someone who wants to be bosom buddies, but I'd certainly invite her over for drinks or ask her for that cup of sugar.

███

If this whole year was an experiment in extreme friending, this last month is like the X Games. And not just because I bashed my head in. In an effort to find my final dates, I did a wellness cleanse at my yoga studio, a flash mob with my dance school, and sent three invitations to women on GirlfriendSocial .com, another online friending site. The cleanse and flash mob were semi-successful. I met Georgia and Judy, both of whom seemed like ideal friend material. And both seemed eager to hang out . . . after the holidays. The same was true of Samantha, the new yoga buddy I met at Meredith's Chanukah party. My January is already packed.

GirlfriendSocial.com, where you can read women's profiles and email them through the site, was a bust. I heard back from none of my prospects.

Like Mom said, something will come up. I'm confident. Until it does, I'm using this time not to scavenge for dates but to let the effects of this year soak in.

Take two weeks ago. It was a Friday night and my nerves were working overtime. Why? Because I was about to get on-stage, in front of strangers, and perform.

I'd just finished my third level of improv class, and graduation from level three involved a show. (Or a "demonstration," as my teacher said to ease my anxiety.) I'd never planned on progressing that far, but when registration came around a third time I couldn't bear the thought of dropping out. Having this group of people to come back to every week, friends with whom I played silly games and who encouraged me to act childish and crazy, became a necessary comfort. I was part of something. I felt loyal to my classmates. When they asked me to keep going, how could I say no?

And so this friend-search led me to the Second City stage. Matt was in the audience, with my mom, Alex, and Jaime. I was so nervous about performing that I didn't invite any of my new friends. I can only make an ass of my myself in front of so many people at a time.

I ended up in a skit with a male classmate. Thanks to an audience suggestion, we were beekeepers, and I'd been stung.

My costar grabbed me by the shoulders.

"You need to wear your official beekeeping gloves!"

"I know, but I hate them," I said. "They make me look fat."

It got a hearty audience laugh. I could see Matt in the audience, beaming with pride, and I could see the question on his face was the same one in my head.

Where did this girl come from?

My quest for friendship hasn't just made me more independent, it's made me more adventurous. Relationships are solidified in these vulnerable, step-outside-the-box, how-did-I-get-here moments. And if they're not, you still have something to show for your time. Dancing in a flash mob on the cold and rainy streets of Chicago was embarrassing. Certainly. I wasn't especially good and I forgot the moves a few times. And since we danced to the eighties track "Weird Science," I had to wear glasses that I guess were supposed to resemble a mad scientist's but looked more like Edna Mode of *The Incredibles*. So yeah, it was a bit mortifying. But mostly it was fun. Hopefully I'll go out with Judy one day, but even if I don't, at least I can say I did it. I used to watch flash mob videos—the Grand Central Station or Trafalgar Square viral hits—and get jealous because it looked like so much fun. Now I've been there.

Rachel and I celebrated our big stage debut at dinner with our families. Our moms sat next to each other, talking quilts, while we debriefed the show. After two margaritas and too much guacamole, we met our classmates at a nearby bar. It was a treat to finally introduce Matt to my fellow improvisers. Hearing Eddie tell me my husband was supersexy? The cherry on top.

As promised, Matt has been a real sport this month. Aside from the Chanukah party and improv outing, he hung out with the book club girls at Hannah's 30th birthday party, ate dinner with Jordan, and joined me for dinner dates with Kelly and her husband, Bob, Jillian and the kids, and Margot and Daniel. Some of these encounters were a hit—Matt thought Jordan was hysterical, and really got along with Bob and Daniel—and will hopefully be repeated down the road. Others, like girl talk with the book club, were cut short because he wanted to go to bed early and forcing him to stay and talk books was more trouble than it was worth. Matt doesn't read much fiction, so it's useless to drag him into the conversation just because I feel like he's supposed to be there.

The only friends he hasn't met yet are the cooking club girls, the very same ladies who think he's Snuffleupagus. One day . . .

Tonight is the holiday party and gift exchange with my co-workers. The plan is to go to Kari's house for dinner, drinks, and Glee Karaoke Revolution. I'm excited to celebrate this year with my work BFFs. When I started my search I said these ladies were probably my closest friends in Chicago. A year later this is still true. Given the amount of time we spend together during the week, it's no surprise.

If there's one single factor that can turn a potential BFF into a real one, it's consistency.

But still, we rarely see one another on weekends and, while we're close, I know some of them have deeper local friendships than ours. Who knows what will happen when we change jobs and don't have work gossip to dish or get to see one another every weekday? It would certainly eliminate one of our most popular conversation topics. This is what frightens me most about the idea of ever giving up the office life.

Just last week I left a particularly stressful day of work and all I could think about was going home and feasting. I've watched enough *Biggest Loser* to know that's called eating your feelings, so I made the executive decision that instead of devouring my stress that night, I'd drink it. Not at alcoholic levels, just a glass of wine—or two—after work. Drinks would better help curb the stress than shoving my face full of cheese, and Dr. Oz says one glass of red a night does the body good, right?

The moment I got home I was struck with an overwhelming urge to run this stream of consciousness by my coworkers. If I'd been at work I would have IM'd Ashley immediately— "I've decided to drink my stress instead of eat it, thoughts?"— and she would have said "great decision" and that would be that. I've come to rely on them as a sounding board for my every minor musing, whether it be, "Should I read *The Hunger Games*?" or "Do you support my decision to buy Birkenstocks?" (The answers were "Definitely" and "Absolutely not" respectively.) I talk to them about the big stuff, too—my career goals and family issues—but I don't *need* them for that. I have Matt or Callie or Sara or Alex or my mom or any of my close friends across the country for the serious issues. It's the trivialities that I crave my coworkers for. They have become my four-jars-of-pickle people.

We get to Kari's house at 7 P.M. Our host was in Australia for the last two weeks, so there's a lot of catching up to do. After we inhale two homemade pizzas and plenty of appetizers, Kari makes an announcement.

"I got you guys a little something while I was away," she says. "They're nothing huge, but were made by the Aboriginals."

We dig our hands into her gift bag and each grab a different colored beaded bracelet.

"They're like grown-up friendship bracelets," Kari says.

Wowser. I don't believe in The Secret, but if I did I would swear I manifested this moment. My bracelet is white, gold, and yellow, and fits my wrist perfectly.

Our gift exchange is similarly successful. We know each other so well that each present is tailor-made for the recipient. I got Kari a Young Adult book I'd recommended for her trip— she passed because it was still in hardcover—and the debut album from Mark Salling (aka Puck from *Glee*).

Joan gave me three books she knew I'd love, and a pinecone ball—a nod to a project we worked on together during which I got enraged that children would actually give pinecone balls (not pinecone ornaments, mind you, just balls for an end table) to their teachers for Christmas. Perhaps it's a question for another day, but seriously, why would someone want a ball made out of pinecone for Christmas? It's like getting coal! Coal that sheds pinecone needles all over your living room floor!

"Why is it so much more fun exchanging gifts with friends than with family?" Kari asks.

"Because friends actually know you," Joan says.

Amen.

"It's amazing that you found people so much like you," my mom says when I tell her that I sang the *Glee* soundtrack at the top of my lungs all night.

"I know, I lucked out."

But it's not just my coworkers. The book club I'm in with Hannah and Jillian had a gift exchange, and one of the members got me a T-shirt with my favorite *Modern Family* quote. ("WTF? Why the face?") Natalie constantly forwards me articles about our favorite branch of yoga or *Harry Potter.* Hilary consistently invites me out to meet more of her friends, since she knows I'm on the hunt. And at our last dance class, Jordan brought me a mix of her favorite studying music to help me cope with my mounting workload. It's these moments that make me think, "It worked. I have real local friends."

Deep relationships are made of more than gifts and emails, of course. Looking back, part of my loneliness last year came from having so much friendly energy to give and nowhere to direct it. Now I get a rush from being the great pal I set out in search of. Like last weekend. Cooking club Jackie had surgery on her deviated septum Friday night, so on Saturday I brought her a Snuggie and read in her living room while she slept. Or a few Tuesdays ago, when I told the guy working the Second City front desk that Rachel thought he was cute and slipped him her number.

They went out the following week.

The night after my coworker gathering is my final holiday party of the season. It's the eve of Christmas Eve and the theme is Ugly Christmas Sweaters. I'm wearing a red turtleneck and black cardigan with puffy-painted holly designs that I bought at a thrift store. Not the best wardrobe for picking up new friends, but it'll have to do. I'm still one date short of the finish line, and while I met a freelance writer at Hannah's birthday party who might be a match, I'd like to meet someone tonight too. It's good to have reserves.

"Rachel, this is my friend Taylor." Riki, a girl with whom I went to college but hardly know, gives a thin brunette wearing a light purple shirt and a silver scarf—no reindeer sweater for her—a friendly shove in my direction. "She just moved here from New York, where she worked in publishing. I thought you guys might have a lot to talk about."

Taylor relocated to Chicago in September. She was a children's book editor in Manhattan, but after four years in the Big Apple she was ready to come home. Now she's living with her parents in the suburbs while she looks for a job.

"What kind of work are you interested in?" I ask.

"Anything editorial. I'm doing some freelance copywriting at the moment, but would love a more steady gig."

"There might be an opening in my office. This is our copy editor's last week and I don't think we've hired a new one."

Taylor looks interested but skeptical. When you're job searching, most potential leads amount to nothing.

We chat a bit more about the editorial scene in Chicago, and, later, as Matt and I say our goodbyes, Taylor asks me to let her know about the job.

"Sure thing." The problem is that I don't have Taylor's contact information, or even her last name. If she's serious about wanting a job, isn't that something she should have provided?

Yes, I could have asked for it. Maybe I *should* have asked for it. But I didn't realize the mistake until I was in a cab home.

On the Monday after Christmas, my final girl-date prospect—the one I met at Hannah's—tells me she's in Florida and asks if we can get together after the new year. I'm slamming my head against the wall—what's a girl gotta do to get a date around here?—when I remember Taylor.

Anna, our current copy editor, sits in the cubicle across from me. "Has your position been filled yet?" I ask.

"No. We can't find anyone good."

"I think I might have the perfect fit." I do some Facebook handiwork, finding Taylor through Riki's page, and send off a message telling her the job is still available. Is she interested? Is she so interested that she wants to go to dinner with me and talk publishing?

By the end of the day, I've placed Taylor's résumé in the right hands. On Tuesday, my boss schedules her interview. Wednesday night we meet for dinner.

FRIEND-DATE 52. "Tell me everything I need to know," Taylor says over my last sushi plate of the year.

"You'll be great. A lot of the job is just about being good with people and handling deadline pressure. Nothing you haven't dealt with before."

There are zero moments of silence during this meal. I give Taylor interview tips and a general lay of the office land. She gives me insight into the book publishing world from someone who worked on the editorial side.

An email comes in twenty-four hours later.

"I got the job! See you tomorrow!"

Taylor has gone from total stranger to coworker in the span of a week. Tomorrow, she will join the ranks of those I see almost every day. We'll sit next to each other, chatting across the aisle about weekend plans and upcoming movies and, every once in a while, actual work.

Date 52. Last but not least. I think this is the beginning of a beautiful friendship.

◼ ◼ ◼

I can't believe it's over.

I've gone on fifty-two friend-dates in the past year. I've met closer to one hundred people if you count everyone in my improv class and LEADS group and book clubs and mixers. Maybe even more. I've gone out with some people who became great friends and some who I never saw again. A good handful of potential friendships fizzled after the second date. In some cases, I tried to follow up with ladies only to never hear back. In others, my new friends moved out of state. A lot can happen in a year.

Let's tally, shall we?

In fifty-two first friend-dates, I went out with . . .

- 59 people
- 24 women I never saw again
- 7 women on second dates that were also the last date
- 3 women (Kim, Stacey, Bridget) with whom I tried to pursue friendships but got no response. Whether it was because they were at friend capac-

ity, too busy, skeptical of my blog, or just not that into me I'll never know.

- 4 women who moved by the end of the year (Sally, Rebecca, Alison, Julie)
- 22 people who I consider legitimate friends (and still live in Chicago). Of that 22, I met: 4 at work, 2 in improv class, 5 through friends of friends, 5 via my online essay, 1 at my wedding dress appointment, 1 on an online message board, 1 at her author reading, 1 through Matt's office, 1 at LEADS, and 1 at Northwestern back in the day.

Remember the Dunbar number? At the beginning of this year I did the math and found I had twenty openings for friendship. Twelve months later, I have twenty-two new pals. Whoa. Science is creepy.

Some status reports of note:

- I haven't gone out with Maritza the waitress again. We have texted back and forth, but every time we try to make plans, they fall through. I ran into her at the restaurant the other night and she brought Matt and me free glasses of wine. We promised to get drinks soon.
- Stacey, my Meet Joe match, disappeared. We made tentative plans to go to a film festival but she had to cancel when she went out of town for work. I tried to reschedule by email but she never wrote back.
- Alexis, the friend of Hannah's who called me

out for ogling her arm, went on her trip to Italy shortly after our second date. She just got back to the states after three months away. We saw each other at Hannah's birthday party and plan to pick up where we left off. After the holidays.

- I heard from the speed-friending women one more time. They planned a pizza outing that I couldn't attend because of my Tuesday night improv class. After that declined invitation, our communication petered out. I like to think that they're still friends with each other, though.

- I wrote Celia the boutique manager telling her I'd love to get together again sometime, for lunch or maybe a pedicure. She never responded. I bought a great pair of fleece-lined tights from her, though, and our stellar in-store relationship is still intact. No harm done.

- Jillian's husband is still waiting on word regarding his nursing school applications. If he gets into his first choice, they'll be moving to Philadelphia in a year. I would never wish him rejection, but . . .

- My mom's mini-search is faring well. She has a solid group of quilting friends—they recently had an overnight retreat at one guild member's house—and when I called her the other day she ushered me off the phone with a "Well, my friend Francine's here, so if you don't need anything . . ." I know she still gets lonely sometimes, but this is a good start.

Have I found a best friend forever? The One who is my other half? It's too soon to tell. But even if none of these relationships rise to the BFF level, I might have something better: A bouquet of friends, people I can call for any occasion or activity, from an all-day *Friends* marathon (enter Mia or Ashley) to a night out on the town (Jordan, please). If I want to go to the Muppets Exhibit at the Museum of Science and Industry, I'll call Jillian or Natalie or Kari or Joan. For a keen eye on a shopping trip? Margot or Hilary or Lynn. An easy Sunday brunch? Hallie.

And for something deeper? A shoulder to cry on? An ear for advice? It seems too good to be true, but I'd trust them all. I used to think someone needed to be my best friend before I'd burden her with my problems or my tears. Now I think those interactions—the sobfest or therapy session—are the encounters that earn someone BFF status.

A year ago I defined what I was looking for as someone that I could call and say, "What are we doing today?" or "Let's meet for brunch in an hour." I wanted a best friend like I had when I was 6 or 10 or 15. Twelve months later, I'm struck by how naïve that was. I don't know that I believe in the idea of the attached-at-the-hip BFF anymore. At least not in adulthood. Sure, I've met some people I can call and invite to lunch at the last minute, but the chances that they could actually come are pretty slim. Everyone is stretched thin. We have jobs and families and significant others and friends and errands and dance classes and book clubs to attend to. Sara and Callie became my best friends not because they were always available or I saw them every day, but because they made me laugh and dropped everything when I needed them and understood me in ways no one else could.

Down the line, some of my new friends could very well join those ranks. Our friendships are still young. They haven't had to survive much in the way of hard times. But relationships are constantly growing and evolving, and in time my new friends and I might have fights or lose loved ones or face life changes—babies, marriage, divorce—that challenge the relationship. Either we'll make it or we won't.

∎∎∎

When I leave the house these days, I'm constantly on the lookout for familiar faces. The chances that I'll run into someone I know seem pretty high. It feels like I've conquered the town.

But I haven't. In a city of 2.8 million, meeting one-hundred-ish people doesn't even make a dent. There are plenty more potential best friends out there. And sure, I won't be signing up for any more meet-and-greets or speed-friending in order to find them. I'll avoid getting-to-know-you games and name tags for a while. I've certainly rented my last friend. Still, I'll always be open to meeting new people. There's no off switch for the changes that have taken place within me this year, and even if there were I'd hide it under duct tape so it always stayed on.

And it's not just me. The search is starting to rub off on people. Just last week, a girl in my book club told me about an encounter with a new-in-towner. "I normally would have just smiled and moved on, but I thought of you and gave her my number. What if she needs a friend?!?"

Jaime, my brother's girlfriend, went on her first blind girl-date recently, while Alex watched football with a man-friend setup. I'm not saying it's a movement, but if weight gain and loneliness and smoking are contagious, it's nice to know that friendliness is, too.

I'm still the same person. To a Callie or a Sara, I'd be perfectly recognizable. But I'm a happier, nicer version of myself. I talk to strangers instead of avoiding them. I do the work to bring people together, personally or professionally. When I'm invited somewhere, I say yes and show up. I try not to interrupt, especially with stories about myself, and I don't point it out whenever I go out of my way for a friend. I get a kick out of new people instead of just acting awkward around them. I get phone numbers, and I use them.

In short, I'm a better friend.

◼︎◼︎◼︎

Matt and I are spending New Year's Eve at my former roommate Brooke's wedding. I'm not in the bridal party, so I was surprised and honored when Brooke's sister asked me to speak during the rehearsal dinner. Telling an old friend how much she means to me seems a fitting way to close out the year.

Before the speeches start, one of the guests tells me she reads my blog.

"A ton of my friends have gotten married recently, and they won't leave their husbands even for a night," she says. "I have no choice but to go out and make new ones."

I nod in recognition. Plenty of the women I met this year had the same story.

"So?" she asks. "What's your advice?"

Hmmm. What *is* my advice? From this vantage point my journey feels circuitous. It's hard to pinpoint exactly what made it effective.

"It takes a lot of work," I say. "You've got to say yes to all the invitations that come your way. The more you say yes, the more invites you'll get. You have to follow up with all those meetings where you say 'We should totally get together!' instead of just saying it to sound nice. And signing up for things helps. Oh, and asking for setups. You know, basically all the things you do when you're dating."

"Sounds exhausting," she says.

I want to tell her to just go for it. That I was nervous when this year began. Very nervous. I was scared that women would think I was hitting on them or that I was a pathetic loser not worth their time. I thought they would find me annoying or burdensome or strange. But as it turns out, everyone likes friends. Not everyone is willing—or motivated—to do the work it takes to make them, but they're not put off by your desire to hang out. They're flattered.

But she'll figure that out for herself.

"It is," I say. "But it's worth it."

■ ■ ■

The countdown clock reads 20 seconds until the New Year. 19. 18 . . . Matt is wearing a festive lei, I'm rocking a 2011 headband. Our marriage has survived the search. In fact, it has thrived. Matt's taking me out to dinner tomorrow—a surprise he only told me about this morning.

"It's to celebrate the end of the quest, but also to toast its success," he said.

We've come a long way since the day I told him our move may have been a mistake.

11. 10. 9 . . . Next Tuesday the fourth level of improv starts. I have cooking club on Wednesday and Thursday is my

girl-date with the writer from Hannah's birthday. While the official search may be over, my new life is not.

But right now I'm focused on my husband.

5. 4. 3. 2 . . . Matt and I ring in the New Year together. The two of us, surrounded by friends.

It bodes well for our future.

ACKNOWLEDGMENTS

Before anyone else, I should thank all the women—and one man!—who agreed to friend-date me this year. Whether I never saw you again or we had brunch just yesterday, I am forever grateful. It follows that I should also thank my wonderful pre-existing friends—Sara, Callie, the girls of 1113 and Fieldston, and Brooke, my post-college roomie—for setting my friendship standards so high.

I'm eternally indebted to my agent, Alison Schwartz at ICM, who believed in this book from *the very day* I sent her the proposal.

If Jennifer Smith weren't my editor, I would try to friend-date her, too. I am so thankful for her editorial insight, support, and for answering my every last question—and always with a friendly exclamation point, no less!

Also at Ballantine, thanks to Jane von Mehren, Melissa Possick, Leigh Marchant, Susan Corcoran, Ashley Gratz-Collier, Hannah Elnan, and everyone else who supported this book from its inception.

Brooke Kosofsky Glassberg has set the bar for friendship

in my eyes. Aside from being my perpetual cheerleader and confidante, she is a brilliant editor who read this book chapter by chapter and gave me invaluable notes. This memoir would have been much worse without her. In that category of friendly (and volunteer) readers, thank you also to Lauren McBrayer Miller.

Thanks to John Cacioppo, Shasta Nelson, and Rom Brafman for sharing their friendship expertise.

Thanks to Stephanie Snipes, who supported this book from the get-go and allowed me to pursue this dream job while keeping my day job.

To the readers of my blog—who cheer me on whenever I hit a friending milestone and who always weigh in on every relationship conundrum—thank you. Your virtual friendship has been inspiring.

A very special thanks to my family—the entire Bertsche-Epstein-Levine clan—for their unbridled support and enthusiasm for this book, especially my mother-in-law, Jane Levine, for being one of my biggest fans.

I could write my second book on the wonders that are my mother, Harriet Bertsche, and brother, Alex Bertsche. But I won't. I am especially grateful to them for—on top of, you know, raising me, and, in Alex's case, sometimes harassing me—reading every sentence of this book five times over, weighing in on every minor detail, and for genuinely being as excited for this project as I am.

Finally, I can't thank my husband, Matt, enough. For sharing our first year of marriage with all my new potential BFFs, for forcing me to go on another friend-date when I wanted to stay on the couch, and for always, always believing in me. He may not be my BFF but he is certainly the love of my life.

FRIEND-DATES: THE INDEX

ABBY: Met at a Meetup.com Chicago Cooking Chicks event, which she attended with a college friend. Recent Indiana University graduate.

ALEXIS: Met through Hannah. An aspiring food personality who wanted blogging advice.

ALISON: Part of the Jen-Alison duo, both of whom I met when we were students at Northwestern. Best friends with Matt's ex-girlfriend.

AMANDA: Met after she responded to my online essay. Cursed a lot and referenced "John Ritter's balls." Wrote about being nervous for our first date on her blog.

ASHLEY: Part of my group of coworker friends.

BECCA: Met through a mutual friend. Seemed more interested in romantic-dates than friend-dates.

BRIDGET: Met on an airplane, where we were seated next to each other. Gave her my card after the flight.

BRYNN: Met after she responded to my online essay. Recently relocated from Boston to Chicago with her husband.

CELIA: Manager of the clothing boutique on my corner.

CHRISTINE: Met through RentAFriend.com, the friend-for-hire website.

CLAIRE: Accompanied Hilary to our first meeting.

DANA: Met after she responded to my online essay. Recent New York City transplant. Doesn't seem to love Chicago and misses living in Manhattan.

DIANNE: New coworker who introduced me to Grubwithus, the social dining company.

EDDIE: Met in improv class. Hoped he could be my gay BFF.

ELLEN: Met after she read my online essay. A consultant, she says that work travel prevents her from taking surface friendships to the next level.

ERIN: Met at speed-friending. Does lighting for a local dance company and loves to travel.

GRETCHEN: Met at Mac 'n Cheese Minglers. Wore a "Mr. Darcy" name tag in our icebreaker game. Was appalled when guests didn't know of Ira Glass.

HALLIE: Met through Jordan. Part of our Saturday morning dance-and-brunch trio.

HANNAH: Met through my longtime BFF Sara. Invited me to join her Chicago book club.

HEIDI: Met as children at summer camp, reconnected on an airplane last year. Invited her best friend and another former camper, Michelle, on our dinner date.

HILARY: Met through a mutual friend. Serious runner hoping to qualify for the Olympic trials.

IRENE: Lives in my apartment building. Met at the grocery store, though we had crossed paths in our building's workout room.

JACKIE: Met when she responded to my online essay. Recently moved to Chicago with her fiancé.

JEN: Part of the Jen-Alison duo, both of whom I met when we were students at Northwestern. Best friends with Matt's ex-girlfriend.

JILLIAN: Met when she saw my online essay on a mutual friend's Facebook status. Mother of 2-year-old twin boys. Fellow *Harry Potter* and pop-culture lover.

JOAN: Part of my group of coworker friends.

JOANNA: Met as kids at summer camp. Recently moved from New York, where she was a magazine editor, to Chicago, where she is a writer and blogger.

JODIE: Met after she responded to my online essay. A mother of two in her mid-forties. Moved to Chicago from Los Angeles after her ex-husband got a job in Indiana and she wanted to keep the kids close to both parents.

JORDAN: Met through my old friend Chloe, her best friend at business school. Writes an idiom newsletter. Part of our Saturday morning dance-and-brunch trio.

JULIE: Met when she reached out after reading my blog. A freelance magazine writer working on her first book.

KAITLIN: Met after she responded to my online essay. Said most of her best friends have married or moved away. Graphic designer who could make a good "let's do artistic things together" friend.

KARI: Part of my group of coworker friends.

KELLY: Met at the reading for her debut novel, *The Lost Summer of Louisa May Alcott*. Gave me advice on pursuing the life of a writer during our sushi dinner date.

KIM: Met in a cooking class last year, before this friend-search started.

LACEY: Met after she responded to my online essay. Moved to Chicago from Kansas City for work and love, but says her girlfriend already has her own friends.

LAUREN: Met when she did my wedding makeup.

LOGAN: Met through GirlFriendCircles.com, an online friending site. A 4'11" spitfire with endless energy.

LYNN: Part of my group of coworker friends. The first coworker I tried to befriend outside of the office, before the start of my official BFF search.

MAGGIE: Blogger. Commented on my blog that she was also in Chicago, so we made a date.

MARGARITA: Met through the no-commitment volunteer organization, One Brick, where she was a group leader.

MARGOT: Sold me my wedding dress. Pastor's daughter, was home-schooled and has seven siblings.

MARITZA: Was my waitress at a neighborhood restaurant. Responded to my note asking her out.

MEG: Met in college, reconnected at a holiday party.

MEREDITH: Met at LEADS, a group for young Jews in Chicago.

MIA: Met after she responded to my online essay. Lives around the corner from me. Loves travel and would make a great activity partner.

MICHELLE: Met as children at summer camp. Invited to the girl-date by her best friend (and another former camper) Heidi.

MORGAN: Met after she responded to my online essay. Was a child actress who appeared on *Sisters, Roseanne,* and *Buffy the Vampire Slayer.*

MUFFY: Met through my longtime BFF Callie. From Arkansas, moved to Chicago with her husband. Went to Yale. Worked at Burberry in London and now serves on a number of Chicago auxiliary boards.

NATALIE: Colleague of Matt's. Invited me to join a book club and brought me to her friend's cookie party.

NICOLE: Met at speed-friending. Works in finance and is an amateur photographer.

PAM: Met after she wrote an article recruiting a new best friend in the Jewish United Federation newspaper.

RACHEL: Met in improv class. Twenty-two-year-old recent University of Iowa graduate. Goofy in a self-deprecating and endearing way. Our moms are in a quilting group together.

REBECCA: Former office intern and senior at Northwestern University. Has been called a "mini-me" by the coworkers who know us both.

SALLY: Met through a mutual friend. Recently moved to Chicago from Manhattan to be with her boyfriend. On second date, went to her boyfriend's sister's apartment, where there was much talk of going shooting.

SONIA: Met at a dinner hosted by Grubwithus, the social dining company. Nurse practitioner.

STACEY: Set up through Meet Joe, the friend matchmaker. Works in marketing. A wine connoisseur.

TAYLOR: Met at a holiday party. Recently moved from New York, where she was a children's book editor, to Chicago.

VERONICA: Met through the comments section of Jezebel.com. Recently moved to Chicago from North Carolina.

WENDY: Met after she read my online essay. Does not speak in contractions.

RECOMMENDED READING

The books about friendship are many. Here are just a few that informed my search—whether by enlightening me to new research, inspiring me with tales of devoted relationships, or frustrating me with the brilliant authors' lack of Chicago residency, thereby making it impossible for them to be my new BFF.

RESEARCH ON FRIENDSHIP AND FRIENDLESSNESS

Brafman, Ori and Rom Brafman. *Click: The Magic of Instant Connections*. New York: Broadway, 2010.

Cacioppo, John T. and William Patrick. *Loneliness: Human Nature and the Need for Social Connection*. New York: W. W. Norton & Company, 2008.

Christakis, Nicholas A. and James H. Fowler. *Connected: The Surprising Power of Our Social Networks and How They Shape Our Lives*. New York: Little Brown, 2009.

Dobransky, Paul with L. A. Stamford. *The Power of Female Friendship: How Your Circle of Friends Shapes Your Life*. New York: Plume, 2008.

Epstein, Joseph. *Friendship: An Exposé*. New York: Mariner, 2006.

Gladwell, Malcolm. *The Tipping Point: How Little Things Can Make a Big Difference*. New York: Back Bay, 2002.

Levine, Irene S. *Best Friends Forever: Surviving a Breakup with Your Best Friend*. New York: Overlook, 2009.

Olds, Jacqueline and Richard S. Schwartz. *The Lonely American: Drifting Apart in the Twenty-first Century*. Boston: Beacon Press, 2009.

Pahl, Ray. *On Friendship*. Cambridge, England: Polity Press, 2000.

Putnam, Robert D. *Bowling Alone*. New York: Simon & Schuster, 2000.

Rath, Tom. *Vital Friends: The People You Can't Afford to Live Without*. New York: Gallup Press, 2006.

Valen, Kelly. *The Twisted Sisterhood: Unraveling the Dark Legacy of Female Friendships*. New York: Ballantine Books, 2010.

Vernon, Mark. *The Meaning of Friendship*. Hampshire: Palgrave Macmillan, 2010.

Yager, Jan. *Friendshifts: The Power of Friendship and How It Shapes Our Lives*. Stamford, CT: Hannacroix Creek, 1999.

TRUE STORIES OF UNFORGETTABLE FRIENDSHIPS

Caldwell, Gail. *Let's Take the Long Way Home: A Memoir of Friendship*. New York: Random House, 2010.

Jarvis, Cheryl. *The Necklace: Thirteen Women and the Experiment That Transformed Their Lives*. New York: Ballantine Books, 2008.

Offill, Jenny and Elissa Schappel. *The Friend Who Got Away: Twenty Women's True-Life Tales of Friendships That Blew Up, Burned Out, or Faded Away*. New York: Doubleday, 2005.

Patchett, Ann. *Truth & Beauty: A Friendship*. New York: HarperCollins, 2004.

Zaslow, Jeffrey. *The Girls from Ames: A Story of Women & a Forty-Year Friendship*. New York: Gotham, 2009.

ADULT AND YOUNG ADULT NOVELS ABOUT FRIENDSHIP

Blume, Judy. *Just as Long as We're Together*. New York: Delacorte, 1987.

Brashares, Ann. *The Last Summer (of You & Me)*. New York: Riverhead, 2007.

Dart, Iris Rainer. *Beaches*. New York: Bantam, 1985.

Martin, Ann M. *The Baby-Sitters Club* series. New York: Scholastic.

Sullivan, J. Courtney. *Commencement*. New York: Vintage, 2009.

Weiner, Jennifer. *Best Friends Forever*. New York: Atria, 2009.

BOOKS WHOSE AUTHORS I WANT AS MY BEST FRIENDS

Crosley, Sloane. *I Was Told There'd Be Cake*. New York: Riverhead, 2008.

Fey, Tina. *Bossypants*. New York: Reagan Arthur, 2011.

Jacobs, A.J. *The Year of Living Biblically: One Man's Humble Quest to Follow the Bible as Literally as Possible*. New York: Simon & Schuster, 2008.

Kaling, Mindy. *Is Everyone Hanging Out Without Me?* New York: Crown Archetype, 2011.

Rubin, Gretchen. *The Happiness Project: Or, Why I Spent a Year Trying to Sing in the Morning, Clean My Closets, Fight Right, Read Aristotle, and Generally Have More Fun*. New York: Harper, 2009.

RACHEL BERTSCHE is a journalist in Chicago, where she lives with her husband. Her work has appeared in *Marie Claire, More, Teen Vogue, Every Day with Rachael Ray, Fitness, Women's Health,* CNN.com, and more. Before leaving New York (and all her friends) for the Midwest, Bertsche was an editor at *O: The Oprah Magazine*.

mwfseekingbff.com